CREATING THE
HIGH-FUNCTIONING
LIBRARY SPACE

CREATING THE HIGH-FUNCTIONING LIBRARY SPACE

EXPERT ADVICE FROM LIBRARIANS, ARCHITECTS, AND DESIGNERS

Marta Mestrovic Deyrup, Editor

LIBRARIES UNLIMITED™

An Imprint of ABC-CLIO, LLC

Santa Barbara, California • Denver, Colorado

Library of Congress Cataloging-in-Publication Data

Names: Deyrup, Marta Mestrovic, editor.
Title: Creating the high-functioning library space : expert advice from librarians, architects, and designers / Marta Deyrup, editor.
Description: Santa Barbara, California : Libraries Unlimited, an imprint of ABC-CLIO, LLC, [2017] | Includes bibliographical references and index.
Identifiers: LCCN 2016029361 (print) | LCCN 2016048852 (ebook) | ISBN 9781440840586 (paperback : acid-free paper) | ISBN 9781440840593 (ebook)
Subjects: LCSH: Library buildings—United States—Design and construction. | Library buildings—Remodeling—United States. | Library architecture—United States | Libraries—Space utilization—United States.
Classification: LCC Z679.2.U54 C74 2017 (print) | LCC Z679.2.U54 (ebook) | DDC 022/.3—dc23
LC record available at https://lccn.loc.gov/2016029361

ISBN: 978-1-4408-4058-6
EISBN: 978-1-4408-4059-3

21 20 19 18 17   1 2 3 4 5

This book is also available as an eBook.

Libraries Unlimited
An Imprint of ABC-CLIO, LLC

ABC-CLIO, LLC
130 Cremona Drive, P.O. Box 1911
Santa Barbara, California 93116-1911
www.abc-clio.com

This book is printed on acid-free paper ∞

Manufactured in the United States of America

To my mother, Jane Esmay Mestrovic

Contents

Preface

Marta Mestrovic Deyrup

The contents of this book grew out of a series of discussions at the American Library Association's Annual Conference that Barbara Ittner and I had with architects, interior designers, and librarians at academic and public institutions who have a great deal of experience with library-building projects. All of us saw the need for a book that focused on providing practical information for library administrators and planning committees who have been put in charge of a building project—often for the first and only time in their careers.

The idea behind *Creating the High-Functioning Library Space* was to create a book in which contributors could speak from their particular area of expertise and serve as even-handed, unbiased consultants to you, the reader. Although the chapters stand on their own and can be read separately, the book is organized around core themes related to an expansion or renovation project: understanding the principles of good design and the current thinking about the best usage of library space; how to explain your vision to your administration and constituencies; working with your design and building teams; and handling technical issues specific to libraries, such as special collections security, lighting, and wiring for computers and other devices.

Some of the chapters are geared to academic librarians, some to public librarians, and some to both; however, the intended audience for this book is the library community. Because many of the contributors represent some of the top architectural firms involved in library projects today, it is hoped that the market also will include interested members of the design trades.

Retrofitting or expanding a building is one of the most costly and lasting decisions a library can make. We hope this book proves useful as you launch your building project. Smooth sailing!

Introduction

Henry Myerberg

"Form follows function"—first coined by the famed American architect, Louis Sullivan, in 1896—was the twentieth-century battle cry for modern design.[1] In order to create high-functioning spaces in the 21st century, we need to add an "s" after "function." Spaces are more functional if they have more than one purpose. A high-functioning space works and feels great. "People want experiences that make them feel good," says Sandra Treadway, director of the Library of Virginia.[2]

SMALL IS BIG

Creating a library space that performs well is a big project, no matter how small the space. Plan small changes to have big impacts. Moving chairs into a circle rather than a line can invite collaboration amongst strangers. If you are reading this book, you probably love libraries and are in the act of reconfiguring a library space. It is sometimes better to start with a small project to get people excited about something big later.

EVOLVE TO SURVIVE

Libraries are evolving in order to survive and thrive. As library staff and services adapt to a changing technological, cultural, and economic environment, so must library spaces and their functions. Not just a place for books, libraries are adapting to the needs of people who want spaces to work, be online, learn new software, write a report, meet friends, hear a lecture, edit a film, start a business, do 3D printing, eat and drink, apply for a job, rest, receive social services, buy a gift, get free advice, and feel welcomed and safe. Almost any social and educational activity has the opportunity to take place in a library. The old-time library, once a warehouse for books, has turned into a department store for learning and an agency for career and social services. The first step is to identify and prioritize the activities your community needs. Successful evolution is a response to local conditions.

LESS BOOKS, MORE PEOPLE

Lively exchange of ideas is a goal of libraries. Those ideas, however, do not come from books sitting on shelves alone. Ideas are more likely to flow in spaces that stimulate conversation both between users and between staff and users. Today's libraries are less about housing collections of books and more about housing collections of people. As Maxine Bleiweis, former director of the Westport Library, observed, "People have become the new books."[3]

Outside of asking a question at the circulation or reference desk, people generally kept to themselves in the traditional library. Today, libraries are social and collaborative places. Knowledge can easily be shared with other people in spaces that are conducive to conversation. Teens help seniors on the computers. Parents exchange tips at children's programs. Interactions are opportunities to learn about a user's expertise and share it with others. Overheard conversations can lead to business collaborations and potential job opportunities. The librarian is at the hub of all these conversations and can orchestrate collaborations.

Libraries were often perceived as quiet and reclusive. Now libraries can also be places for people to be seen and heard. Libraries once personified as introverts are now poised as extroverts.

STAID TO DYNAMIC

Traditional libraries were generally staid places where printed information was stored and retrieved. The digital revolution liberated libraries to become dynamic places where any form of information can be exchanged and created. Modern libraries can foster multimedia creations. 3D printers teach design and demonstrate manufacturing in the library alongside roaming robots that teach and demonstrate computer programming. Information technology has not hindered the relevance of libraries. Instead, technology has enabled libraries to offer more useful services for more people through free Internet access and all kinds of computer software systems that might not be available at home.

THE LEGACY OF THE PAST PREDICTS THE FUTURE

The idea of the library as the cornerstone of civilization and an oasis of learning is as old as the scrolls once stored in the ancient Library of Alexandria. Andrew Carnegie recognized the possibility of the library to improve anyone's life and enabled the construction of public libraries in the 19th and 20th centuries across America. More recently the Gates Foundation has enabled public libraries to provide free Internet access to spur equal opportunity and economic development across the world. The legacy of libraries is their impact on improving people's lives.

SPACE IS AN ASSET

Physical space has always been and always will be an essential asset of the library. As books, periodicals, and reference collections become available online, those shelf spaces formerly filled with these items can now become spaces for people to meet and work. Space will remain an effective multisensory, emotional, and interactive tool for socializing and learning. At the primal level, a well-designed library space provides warmth on a cold day. It offers light when it's dark and provides shade from the sun. Functionally, the space is inviting and can simultaneously fulfill needs and surprise users. Space is virtuous and its value should be articulated.

USE SPACE WISELY

Compared to the large costs for servicing, staffing, and reconfiguring real space, virtual space is relatively cheap, mobile, and always available. Screen space is versatile, customizable, efficient, and often in your pocket. Increasingly expensive real space has to prove its worth by offering more with less square footage and less energy. Space for stacks of popular fiction, science journals, and government documents is very costly compared to the available online services for the same content. The future viability of libraries depends on their ability to leverage space for better social and learning outcomes. Virtual space is infinite and inexpensive. Real space is precious and costly, so use it wisely. For this reason, libraries have a responsibility to leverage their existing spaces before expanding.

LIBRARIANS LEAD THE WAY

The library's role as a cultural and community center is led by librarians. No library board of trustees, no university president, no city mayor, and certainly no architect is better positioned to affect the evolution of the library and the accompanying reconfiguration of library space. The reconfiguration of library space parallels the reconfiguring of librarian roles. Instead of processing books behind closed doors and tall desks, librarians need opportunities and places to interact directly with library users. Within library spaces, librarians need to be integrated into and not separated from public spaces. Tear down office walls whenever possible.

LIBRARIANS JUST DO IT

Librarians are in a unique position to perform in the current service and information economy. Their roles range from community activist to IT specialist, social worker, museum curator, retail merchandiser, foreign ambassador, program director, interdisciplinary teacher, fund-raiser, hotel concierge, TED talk presenter, and stand-up comic. As author Neil Gaiman says, "Google can bring you back 100,000 answers, a librarian can bring you back the right one."[4]

Susan Perry, former academic library director and senior adviser to the Mellon Foundation, advises librarians, "It's important to make places that generate curiosity. You need to create attractive spaces where people will want to work." The role of librarians is "to build . . . community" while being "helpful but not intrusive."[5] Librarians are poised to make functional as well as emotional connections to people who need and love their libraries.

PROCESS, PROCESS, PROCESS

The three most important elements of a keeping a project on track are process, process, and process. An impactful reconfiguration of library space requires a good collaborative process to envision, program, plan, price, and execute. A successful process that is invariably time-consuming and challenging will lead to success with the right team. The expression "measure twice, cut once" is a wise guide for those about to expend capital funds. The money and time spent in planning is a fraction of what is expended in construction and execution. A dollar spent in planning can save ten dollars in construction.

INGREDIENTS FOR SUCCESS

A successful reconfiguration of space, no matter how many people it serves, generally needs the following mix of ingredients to launch and complete a successful project:

- *Vision.* Make a compelling case to knit together the needs of the community using the space. Vision is not about following trends but about the future needs of your constituents that they may not yet be able to articulate.
- *Ownership.* Make the process inclusive of stakeholders and funders while soliciting diverse points of view. The completed reconfiguration should not be handed off to stakeholders. Instead, throughout all phases of the process, include stakeholders and users, who will ultimately feel a sense of ownership of the space. Shared ownership promotes comfort, goodwill, and a feeling of responsibility for the reconfigured space.
- *Leadership.* Have a leader who can articulate the vision, build a team, command attention, drive excellence, collaborate with consultants and related experts, welcome diverse points of view, include stakeholders, overcome naysayers, and attract funding.
- *Urgency.* Identify urgent needs, not amenities. If a proposed reconfiguration is not urgent, it is less likely to get funded and built.
- *Money.* Identify the source and path to financial resources. Funding is not necessarily about spending what is available. It is about sourcing the funding that is necessary to make an identifiable impact that embodies the vision.
- *Empowerment.* Empower the stakeholders in the process. The key stakeholders are the librarians leading the process along with trustees, funders, and community participants.

The acronym of these ingredients is VOLUME. Make sure the volume is at the right level for your project.

SPACE PLANNING FOR SUCCESS

Over the years, I have learned that high-functioning spaces that support multiple uses and feel great tend to have three interrelated qualities: visibility, flexibility, and density.

- *Visibility* means the space is highly visible to people. Such visibility can be achieved by direct sight lines from one open space to another. Glass can address acoustic, climatic, and security concerns. What is the value of visibility? Seeing an activity from the other side of a building can arouse a curiosity to learn what's going on, to engage, and to participate. We live in an era of "participatory culture" enabled by smart phones and social media where conventional boundaries of producer and consumer appear to be happily erased. How do we translate participatory culture into functioning space? Part of the answer is visibility. What would Facebook and Instagram look and feel like in a library space?
- *Flexibility* means a space can be adapted to multiple uses for different groups at various times. Many libraries have designated multipurpose rooms. What if every space in the library was multiuse? Part of a wide hallway at different times can be a study lounge, a café seating area, an exhibition gallery, or a computer lab. Furniture on wheels is an invitation to customize space for the needs of different users and different functions. Flexibility empowers people to take control of a space.
- *Density* refers to the compactness of people within spaces. The density of cities like New York creates energy and blurs the boundaries of spaces seemingly into an infectious choreographed dance. There is a sweet spot feeling of comfort that comes from being with more people in less space. A crowded restaurant or café is more welcoming than an empty one. As William Whyte, the noted urban anthropologist, noted, "What attracts people most, it would appear, is other

people."[6] Density also conserves energy and costs. Consuming fewer square feet helps to optimize energy consumption and construction costs. Look for opportunities in your library spaces to overlap and blur the boundaries between uses without disrupting activities. Avoid corridors where possible. Minimize the back of the house by bringing services out from behind closed doors.

CONCLUSION

Libraries are a strong species in a Darwinian world of scarcer financial resources. In 1998, Google was launched and soon thereafter the support for many libraries was in the crosshairs in trustee rooms and governmental chambers around the country. Since then, libraries have evolved to prove their worth. Technology was ultimately a gift to the future of libraries by connecting more resources to more people.

Library spaces should be improved from a position of strength and confidence that turns solving a functional need into a social or community cause. Librarians and their leadership team need to assert their role and the future viability of libraries in their local political, cultural, and economic arenas. The timeless value of people coming together to discover, exchange, and create ideas is the enduring goal of all libraries.

NOTES

1. Louis H. Sullivan, "The Tall Office Building Artistically Considered," *Lippincott's Magazine,* March (1896): 403–409.
2. Sandra Treadway, interview with author, April 10, 2015.
3. Maxine Bleiweis, interview with author, June 19, 2015.
4. Neil Gaiman, interview with J. Barnes, Indianapolis Public Library's 33rd Annual McFadden Memorial Lecture, April 16, 2010.
5. Susan Perry, interview with author, August 2, 2015.
6. William H. Whyte, *The Social Life of Small Urban Spaces* (Washington, DC: Conservation Foundation, 1980).

1

A Brief History of American Library Design

Cynthia Sorrell, Uche Enwesi, and Patricia Kosco Cossard

Different buildings by their layout, by their structure, and by the manner in which they are decorated ought to tell the spectator their purpose.
—Germain G. Boffrand, "Livre d'Architecture," 1745

How to best configure and furnish a library has been the subject of interest since librarian and architectural practice were professionalized in the years following the Civil War (Breisch, 1982). This period saw the expansion of educational opportunity for a growing urban population. Contemporaneously, professional librarians were actively developing planning standards in order to help architects meet their needs as practitioners (Van Slyck, 1991).

In the second half of the nineteenth century, American library architecture evolved into three main types: the alcoved book hall or the *library as sacred space*, the departmental/seminar book room or the *library as laboratory* type, and the book stack or the *library as stage* (Oehlerts, 1975, pp. 36–58). In the post–World War II period, a change in shelving technology and materials allowed a fourth type to arise, that is, the modular library or *library as functional box*. All of them, however, use the same basic abstract concept, architecturally known as the *parti* (Bermudez, 2013). Often referred to as the *big idea,* it is the chief organizing concept of a design.

These four types have served as models for new academic and public library buildings until very recently. The advent of digital publication has caused print collections to contract rather than expand with implications for library building and expansion projects. Recent trends have been to build additions or to renovate rather than build new structures, especially as green initiatives and sustainable design have been promoted by institutions of higher education as well as federal, state, and local governments.

In the prosperous years following the Civil War, significantly larger library collections and rising levels of literacy gave birth to the need for more and larger libraries. Design and construction were financed by private munificence (Breisch, 1997). Self-made millionaires, such as George Peabody, Walter L. Newberry, and Charles Bower Winn, financed library buildings in the second half of the nineteenth century and employed professional architects, who used aspects of high culture in their designs (Van Slyck, 1991). These donors wanted monuments that exhibited universal and historic forms expressed by the most durable materials for their construction.

American architects, many of whom had studied at the Ecole des Beaux-Arts in Paris, were adept at presenting *parti* that would meet donors' requirements. Their designs would include all building furnishings including materials, furniture, and decoration, which would give form to the benefactor's aristocratic aspirations.

The first of the four main library types, the grand hall of books, the *Saalbibliothek*, draws from renaissance monastic library architecture (Thompson, 2011). These halls were monumental, being up to 100 feet long and 80 feet wide. They were at least two stories high, lit by roof skylights, and their clerestories or windows were placed high in heavy masonry walls. All or most of the book collection was shelved along the walls. These halls had tables in the center for readers, but a librarian always mediated and guarded the collection (Figure 1.1).

The book hall also draws from ecclesiastical architecture. Henry Hobson Richardson, using the compositional principles of the Ecole des Beaux-Arts, almost single-handedly created this American library building type. In his Winn Public Library (1879) in Woburn, Massachusetts, Richardson articulated each of the building's functions separately. The orientation and scale of assigned rooms and their furnishings correspond to the relative importance of each function, that is, architects and patrons placed primary importance on the storage and display of cultural artifacts (including books). Public reading rooms were added, but seen as of secondary importance (Al Shihabi, 2013). Ecclesiastical precedent is evident in the plan of the Winn Library (Figure 1.2). The design is made up of six fixed functions: book hall, reading rooms, delivery desk (and de facto librarian offices), gallery, museum, and vestibule (Randall, 1962, p. 361). In this design, the library corresponds to a nave and the museum and the gallery to an apse and choir, respectively, and the reading rooms form the transept. The book collection, unlike the gallery and museum, is only to be seen, not browsed.

While Richardson's designs may have suited the trustees, his and others' designs were criticized by librarians for their lack of practicality, for example, the Boston Public Library (1894), which was designed by McKim, Mead & White, without librarian input or consultation. Ladders were required to reach the top bookshelves, and the poor light in the alcove, due to narrow windows in the walls and circular reading rooms, made reading taxing. The presence of interior load-bearing walls made

Figure 1.1 Example of a book hall–type library. The South Hall on the second floor of the Astor Library building.

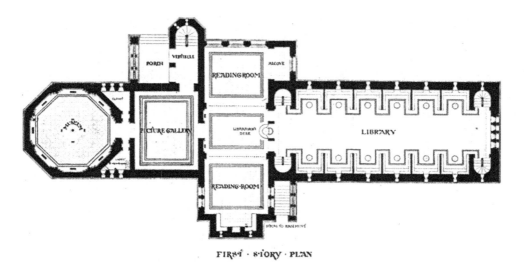

FIRST · STORY · PLAN

Figure 1.2   Winn Memorial Library (Woburn, MA)—first story plan.

the rearrangement of furniture impossible, and it is nearly impossible to extend the building to accommodate ever-growing collections (Oehlerts, 1975).

The second library type, the book stack, began to emerge partly in response to this criticism and, in equal part, due to advances in shelving technology. It is described as tripartite because the collections were centralized into one mass, completely separate from the patrons seated in a reading room, with workrooms for staff and librarians, and located in different parts of the building. The style is based upon Henri Labrouste's design of the Bibliotheque Sainte-Genevieve (Figure 1.3). The stacks themselves were a compact iron structure housed within the library envelope. The advantage was that the stack structure was expandable. The stacking allowed the design of enormous reading rooms.

The Enoch Pratt Free Library (1882) is perhaps the most important public library built in the nineteenth century. Enoch Pratt was a Baltimore businessman committed to philanthropy. Not only was his gift large enough to build a central library, but it also included an $800,000 endowment, which was given on the condition that the city government continue an annual appropriation to fund four branch libraries. Pratt set a precedent with his design for a library system that included a central research library in the business district and local branches in residential areas. The Carnegie Library Building Program later expanded upon this idea. The original central library plan included workrooms for staff, a large reading room, and a reference room (Oehlerts, 1975, pp. 46–47).

The New York Public Library (1911) is one of the most famous examples of a book hall-type library. The New York Public Library avoided the critical mistakes of the Boston Public Library by appointing as head librarian Dr. John Shaw Billings, who subsequently collaborated with William Ware and Bernard Green, library consultants. Dr. Billings designed a huge reading room that sat on top of seven floors of book stacks. Billings sought the advice of other librarians and published his vision in the *Library Journal* (Oehlerts, 1975, pp. 97–99).

Figure 1.3 Henri Labrouste's Bibliotheque Sainte-Genevieve.

Contemporaneously, librarians were organizing under the direction of Melville Dewey, Justin Winsor, and William F. Poole, to develop library planning and furnishing standards. William Frederick Poole (1821–1894), an American librarian and bibliographer, whose works include the creation and publication of the *Index to Periodical Literature*, was also a founder of the American Library Association (ALA) in 1876 as well as the American Historical Association (AHA). By 1879, members of ALA began to discuss how the practical considerations of library administration should inform design. William F. Poole, Alfred M. Githens, Normand S. Patton, Edward L. Tilton, and Joseph L. Wheeler articulated professional librarian practice and became the recognized experts in the field of library planning. Librarians and architects debated library design and its relationship to professional practice in the *Library Journal, American Architect*, and *Architectural Review* (Breisch, 1982, pp. 140–159).

Poole held posts at the Brothers in Unity Library (Yale), Boston Athenaeum, Boston Mercantile Library, Cincinnati Public Library, Chicago Public Library, and ultimately at the Newberry Library, where he developed the third type of library, the departmental/ seminar book room (Williamson, 1963). His vision of library practice was informed by a library's collections. Collections were organized according to their subject matter in direct opposition to the book stack type, which centralized each collection into silos. Unknowingly anticipating the next library type, architect Henry I. Cobb modeled his design for the Newberry on Richardson's Marshal Field's Warehouse (Wetherold, 1962, p. 19).

Poole's ideas were informed and supported by his association and friendship with Herbert Baxter Adams, a professor and librarian at Johns Hopkins University. Adams changed American graduate study by introducing the seminar model that he had experienced at the University of Heidelberg (Cunningham, 1986). Seminar libraries were essential to this type of pedagogy. The seminar library was a working library, similar to a scientific laboratory or medical clinic (Morey, 1932).

While library architecture in this period developed prior to a recognized canon of theoretical writing, certain principles emerged. Print collections were central to librarians' professional practice. Accommodating collection growth, in terms of both space and organization, was essential in any library design. The secondary activities of reference and book circulation emerged with the provision for a reading room and a delivery room. Emphasis was placed upon securing the collection from human and natural damage rather than readers' needs. The library building was to be centrally located, either in the heart of business districts, if a public library, or in the campus center, if an institution of higher education.

Librarians advocated for longer hours, flexible space, planned expansion, and consultation in the design process (Atkins, 1991). They viewed library buildings as embodiments of their applied practice. Thus emerged two types of libraries: those that had closed stack compact storage located away from reader access and those that had open stack subject collections that brought together collections, readers, and librarians in intimate settings.

Any chapter on American library building history would be incomplete without covering the Carnegie Library building program. Between 1890 and 1920s, nearly 1,700 public and university libraries were built with funding from Andrew Carnegie. Although perhaps not producing the most original architectural designs, there were two elements of the building program that continue to influence libraries today: the government funding of annual operating funds and attention to the choice of site. In the early part of the program, Carnegie favored large central library buildings in urban areas, but in the end, he privileged the growth of branches (Oehlerts, 1975, pp. 100–109).

Public libraries in the interwar period (1920–1940) saw the rise of large central buildings that began adopting open stack book shelving and developing services to specific populations. The second Enoch Pratt central library building (1933) is the best example from the period, being the result of excellent planning by the skilled chief librarian and experienced library architects. In 1925, the first professionally trained head librarian, Joseph Wheeler, was hired. He immediately set himself to the task of formulating a plan for a new building. He engaged Edward L. Tilton and Alfred Githens as architectural consultants (Oehlerts, 1975, pp. 117–127). A number of specialized reading rooms were distributed on the first and second floors, and a children's library was placed in the basement with its own entrance. The building accommodated 1,400 readers, 1,600,000 volumes, and a large professional librarian staff (Wheeler and McCauley, 1933, pp. 386–393). Significantly, design elements were taken from retail buildings, for example, placing the ground floor at sidewalk level, creating display windows for exhibits, and placing adult services and open-stack subject collections on this level in an open plan (Githens, 1933, p. 384). Wheeler, Tilton, and Githens influenced both public and academic libraries from the late 1930s onward.

In the second half of the twentieth century, the design, structure, and style of libraries radically changed. Githens's work with Angus Snead McDonald made open plan, open stack, and subject department organization the standard fare. Immediately after World War II, a new stack technology was made available by manufacturer Angus Snead Macdonald and popularized by the Cooperative Committee on Library Building Plans, whose members consisted of both librarians and architects (Kaser, 1997, p. 113). The modular stack system was the essential technology that was needed to create the easily expandable and configurable library that library planners like Poole had advocated 75 years earlier

(Breisch, 1982). The influx of federal and state money that became widely available in this period enabled architects and librarians to focus on the functional aspect of practice.

Moving from a traditional fixed-function building to a modular building had implications for the whole of library administration (Burchard, 1946). Stacks could be easily reconfigured, meaning that over time open-stack orientations could easily accommodate patron needs and ever-expanding collections. Beginning with Hardin-Simmons College in 1947, the modular library was designed with spacious open areas that were easily furnished with a variety of standardized reading/study equipment and furniture adjacent to collections. The impact on librarian practice was to free the researcher from librarian mediation and free the librarian to provide more individual research support via intimate reading spaces, carrels, and study rooms.

Opened in 1972, designed by the Seattle architectural firm of Kirk, Wallace, McKinley and Associates, the Odegaard Undergraduate Library at the University of Washington was among the many modular libraries at this time that featured an expansive atrium and a monumental central staircase as a device to break up the boxlike shape of the building. Problems soon became evident with this design. The open atrium allowed vertically transmitted noise and the staircase created 6,000 square feet of unused (read wasted) space (Kaser, 1997, pp. 139–145).

In 2014, the Odegaard Library received the American Institute of Architecture's Honor Award for Interior Architecture for the renovation by the Miller Hull Partnership (Figure 1.4). The renovation and reuse of the building was hailed as an example of sustainable design. The atrium was reconfigured by adding a large skylight, and the staircase was replaced with a more efficient design recouping usable study and social space. Moreover, in keeping with sustainable design principles, the original oak stair railings were adaptively reused throughout the atrium space (American Institute of Architects, 2014).

Figure 1.4   Interior, Odegaard Undergraduate Library, University of Washington.

In his book *The Evolution of the American Academic Library Building*, David Kaser coined the phrase "the rise of the Anti-Building" to describe the current phase of library planning and building. In the era of the anti-building, new building construction has been replaced by additions and renovations. Access over ownership has been the prevailing methodology especially since the advent of electronic formats (Kaser, 1997, pp. 155–164). The increasing reliance on digital delivery by society as a whole has fundamentally changed the functions of librarian practice. A great example of the anti-building is the Lawrence Public Library, Kansas, winner of *Library Journal's* 2015 New Landmark Libraries. Instead of tearing down or adding a new wing, the entire building was encapsulated in glass (Barbakoff, 2015).

Built in 2013, designed by Snohetta, the Hunt Library at North Carolina State University, Raleigh, expresses the *library as lab parti*. Its five-story bent rectangular structure, enveloping 220,000 square feet, is technologically hierarchical; that is, as students climb levels, the more rarified the functions and the more intense the technology. It functions as a laboratory for students in engineering, textiles, and other disciplines that need equipment that crosses departments and occurs at the intersection of big data and the tools to make sense of it. Its vision is to immerse students in multimedia creation, large-scale visualization, and interactive computing (Schwartz, 2013).

A primary feature of Hunt is not books, but the bookBot. On Robot Alley, visitors can follow the bookBot as it pages items from closed stack compact storage (Madsen, 2013). Entering the Hunt, visitors will not see a book, a staff member, or even library furniture. To replicate the serendipity of browsing, a large research collection Virtual Browse is available through a large touch screen. The bookBot delivers volumes within five minutes of receiving a request (Schwartz, 2013).

Hunt Library houses a Maker space, a GameLab, and other various technology labs used by designer and engineers alike. But it wasn't just built with the best cutting-edge technology; this library also fosters creativity and design through its collection of more than 60 types of designer furnishings for public use (Madsen, 2013). The library comes with both a black box creativity studio that allows students to explore digital projected environments and a white box visualization lab that comes with a green screen, motion capture, and theater lighting.

Opening fabrication labs in areas where bookshelves have been removed, or would have traditionally been, is one example of how librarians are expanding their mission as technology centers (Agresta, 2015). Maker spaces make technology, tools, and material available for hands-on learning, enabling the development of skills that cannot be practiced virtually. An emerging type is the materials library. Librarians are agents in bringing together designers, industrial engineers, material scientists, and commercial enterprises in the field of materials and design, and potentially find cross-applications for contemporary and future materials.

A similar *parti* was used by the Denver Public Libraries in its 2014 renovation of the Rodolfo "Corky" Gonzales Branch Library. Designed by studiotrope Design Collective, the planners used a *parti* of *library as greenhouse*. In the sense that the library is an incubator for growth, it is similar to the academic example of the Hunt Library. Placed in the center of a diverse neighborhood, the library serves as a place to cross-pollinate and grow, strengthening the human ecology of community.

Donald Beagle (1999) was on target when he forecasted that "the information common creates a synergy between the user support skills of the computer staff, the information skills of the reference staff and production skills of media staff." Commons spaces can be seen as an evolution of mass reading rooms, where passive reading is replaced by dynamic engagement. Commons are meant to offer one-stop service, combining access to both information and technology in one site in order to facilitate academic task completion in a socially inviting space. The emergence of the information or learning commons can be deconstructed as space reinventions and retrofitting to provide access to multiple technologies simultaneously.

The earliest example of an information commons, or *library as classroom*, is found at the University of Iowa. Beginning in 1990, the University of Iowa Libraries, the Office of Information Technology, and instructional faculty collaborated to initiate what would be known as the Information Arcade. Officially opened in 1992, it is considered the seminal model for information commons in higher education. Its purpose was to provide new information technology and facilitate its application to the teaching and research process by uniting the legacy library collection with online resources (Bennett, 2015).

With approximately 6,000 square feet dedicated to the Information Arcade educational facility, users found a place for consultations with library and university staffers, group instructional session space, and computer workstations with how-to sessions for available electronic resources (Lowry, 1993). In 2005, as in 1992, the Roy J. Carver Charitable Trust of Muscatine financially assisted renovations in the amount of $236,000 toward the $1.36 million project that would update technology along with constructing a second "electronic classroom." The Information Arcade continues to improve its infrastructure and services to what is considered the original information commons model for today's educators and learners in a rich educational environment (Snee, 2005).

A more recent iteration of the information commons is the Perkins Library Renovation Project at Duke University. The renovation and expansion by Shepley, Bulfinch, Richardson, and Abbott added three new facilities: the five-story Bostock Library, the von der Heyden Pavilion Café, and the Perkins Tower. The new facilities added a total of 122,275 square feet to the original building. While the older Perkins was a traditional librarian mediated space, with the 1928/1948 building being multitiered stacks, the additions embodied the *parti* of *library as commons* (Lombardi and Wall, 2006).

The first floor houses a student writing center, a technology support desk, a number of technology-infused group study rooms, and project development space. The Duke librarians practice ubiquitous service as opposed to a location-based traditional model. Augmented with wireless connectivity, white boards, and comfortable seating, the new commons space has taken on new purpose and meaning. Removing shelving capacity has cleared space for human interaction. The result has been a rediscovery of *library as place*. Duke's information commons model recognizes that space design influences human behavior.

Coffee shops are now a common part of the libraries' landscape (Watson, 2014, p. 121). This small change, the *library as kitchen parti*, has improved building gate counts. Clients prefer to combine the joy of a snack with study and collaboration—a more relaxing way to get studies and research accomplished in proximity to needed library services and resources.

Delaware State University's William C. Jason Library, completed in 2009, is an example of how sharing a *parti*, such as *library as student center*, with another entity on campus can be a wise funding strategy. After decades of disrepair and dwindling use by campus constituents, the library secured the needed funds by partnering with the university's athletic department. An amount of $1.2 million was needed for the renovation. The library's extraordinary partnership with athletics allowed an expansion of space from 60,000 to 98,000 square feet throughout the library's six floors, a major upgrade of the IT infrastructure, and five new smart classrooms. Known as the Athletics for Academic Excellence Centre, it provides athletes, whose physical stature is larger than the average student, more than adequate space to comfortably use the center's resources. Moreover, to enhance the partnership, the assistant athletic directors' offices were also housed in the center (Watson, 2014, pp. 29–30).

The newly constructed smart classrooms varied in size and were built to be used for multiple purposes, including Rosetta Stone Language Laboratory, as well as space for the Delaware Online Education Library instructional office. Other enhancements included two traditional classrooms, compact storage, and a bistro. The multipurpose space was completed by an exquisite art exhibit area in the library's lobby and a historic Steinway piano, which regularly features both local and national artists (Watson, 2014, p. 30).

Often minor changes and retrofits can have big impacts. Consider the *parti* of *library as bar*. In 2014, the University of Maryland, College Park (UMCP) Libraries' IT department initiated a project with the research services department to convert the former reference desk into a "Laptop Bar." Research Services was consolidating the reference desk and the circulation desk into one service site in order to more efficiently utilize staff resources. The original plan was to demolish the desk. Instead, IT allied professionals recommended that the counters be adaptively reused for student use. All that was needed was seating and power for students to have an additional space to use their personal laptops in the library. This space is now heavily used and really liked by students for its proximity to the main entrance of the library. Many students just pop in between classes to check their schedules and e-mail.

As opposed to the hard wooden seating of traditional libraries, collaborative spaces with upholstered soft seating have become common. The *library as living room parti* has given rise to the ubiquity of Wi-Fi; new devices such as iPads and smart phones demand robust wireless networks. Wi-Fi offerings benefit both library staff and clients since they can each do their work in any library area of their choice (Graham, 2002). For example, library staff can perform their collection duties in the stacks while clients can perform digital research comfortably seated on the newly installed furniture. Clients are able to collaborate more easily because they are not tied to a specific location or they can use smart tables provided in designed collaboration spaces.

The Sante Fe Springs Public Library, renovated in 2010, is another example of the *library as living room parti*. The original 1960s' building was designed by William Pereira paying homage to Wright's textile block and Hollyhock House, with a neo-Aztec frieze wrapping around the fascia. Perhaps because the majority of the city council had gone to the library as children and teens, approval for a new building was not forthcoming. The need to "weave the new with the familiar" was necessary. Without adding any additional internal square footage, the design team, LPA, Inc., addressed the functional needs in a beautiful way, as well as brought visual excitement using contrasting colored free form elements that announce the library's functions inside with similar forms at the outside reading gardens. In addition to lighter, expanded spaces and a chic, fresh look, the renovation included expanded literacy offices, access to daylight, and multifunctional spaces. There is a café and working fireplaces. The exterior Cesar Chavez reading garden expands the library's programmable space. The green space provides a residential feel in the middle of an urban environment (Case Study, 2010).

With the increasing use of technology comes the high demand for access to the electrical grid and power supply. Eighty percent of the Rollins College library's main floor was renovated in 2012. In response to the ethnographic study done prior to the renovation, more electric outlets were installed. By 2013, a follow-up survey indicated that still more outlets were desired (Montgomery, 2014). At Nelson Poynter Memorial Library, at the University of South Florida, St. Petersburg, a focus group was conducted to find out students' needs for library use after renovation. This study also found that students were demanding more electrical outlets (van Beynen et al., 2010). These examples demonstrate how important it is to assess the electric supply capability before retrofitting space cleared by relocating collections. Various studies of space use confirm that electricity is a key concern (Applegate, 2009).

CONCLUSION

This chapter has provided a theoretical and historical overview of how and why library buildings have developed the way they have by identifying their individual most basic abstract concept, architecturally known as the *parti*. Identifying the *parti* for a library building is the initial step in planning. It is also an excellent way for librarians to articulate their vision to their design partners, architects.

American library architecture can be categorized into four main types: the alcoved book hall or the *library as sacred space*, the book stack or the *library as stage*, the departmental/ seminar book room or the *library as laboratory*, and the modular library or *library as functional box*, each with its own structural limitations.

The seminar and the modular library were designed for open stack access. The design of the Newberry Library, the first example of the seminar style, utilized a Marshal Field's Warehouse plan. The second Enoch Pratt central library building also employed retail details and introduced open plan design through Tilton and Githens's collaboration with librarians. Again, it was the collaborative relationship among Githens, MacDonald, and librarians (Cooperative Committee on Library Building Plans) that gave birth to the essential technology, that is, the modular stack system, enabling the flexibly configurable library that Poole had advocated 75 years earlier.

The multitiered book stack structures present particular complications because building load is borne on itself as it sits within the building envelope. Rearrangement is nearly impossible without intervention. For instance, in the final stage of the Perkins Renovation Project at Duke, the 1928/1948 building had the entire stack core removed and replaced by a new independent flooring structure with independent footing supporting high-density compact shelving ("Rubenstein Library Renovation in Pictures," 2014).

Traditionally, print collections were central to librarians' professional practice. Accommodating collection growth was the professional's essential concern. Librarians viewed library buildings as applied practice embodied. In the 2010s, design, structure, and style are radically changing, driven by technology and, in the case of higher education, pedagogical change. While librarian practice is coevolving with technology, libraries remain a space where social infrastructure and knowledge creation meet (Mattern, 2014).

Library building programming traditionally have *parti* such as *library as museum, library as sacred space, library as aristocratic monument*, or *library as functional box*. This chapter has provided examples of *parti* of the *library as classroom, as lab, as clinic, as infrastructure, as platform* or, even, *as kitchen*. Since the 1990s, a widespread *parti* is *library as commons* where commons is defined as a specific interior public service space where library-owned computers and equipment are provided to access resources and manipulate them. Generally available 24 hours and located near main entrances, they drive the public's perception of the library. More recent commons have expanded to include different instructional spaces, media labs, food service areas, group studies, and tutoring offices. The examples presented in this chapter have taken used different *parti* to distinguish themselves. Such are *library as . . . place, kitchen, student center, bar* and *living room*.

This chapter has broadened our understanding of why libraries are constructed the way they are. As functions and practice change, so do library building forms. By understanding the historical development of libraries, it is the authors' hope that you will be able to understand the response you have to particular kinds of library space. By understanding past and current trends, you will be able to do better planning for the future.

BIBLIOGRAPHY

Agresta, M. "What Will Become of the Library? How It Will Evolve as the World Goes Digital," *Slate Magazine*, April 30, 2014. Accessed 6/15/2015. http://www.slate.com/articles/life/design/2014/04/the_future_of_the_library_how_they_ll_evolve_for_the_digital_age.html.

Al Shihabi, D. V. "Capitol Furniture Types of *Beaux-Arts* Architect: Design Hierarchy Reveals Meaning." *Journal of Interior Design* 38, no. 1 (2013): 33–48.

American Institute of Architects. "2014 Recipient | Institute Honor Awards for Interior Architecture." AIA Awards. Accessed October 26, 2015. http://www.aia.org/practicing/awards/2014/interior-archi tecture/odegaard-library/.

Anderson, R. "5 Million Public Domain Ebooks in HathiTrust: What Does This Mean?" *Scholarly Kitchen*, posted April 7, 2015. Accessed 6/15/2015. http://scholarlykitchen.sspnet.org/2015/04/07/5-mil lion-public-domain-ebooks-in-hathitrust-what-does-this-mean/.

Applegate, R. "The Library Is for Studying: Student Preferences for Study Space," *Journal of Academic Librarianship* 35, no. 4 (2009): 341–346. Accessed 9/11/2015. doi: 10.1016/j.acalib.2009.04.004.

Atkins, S. *The Academic Library in the American University.* Chicago: American Library Association, 1991.

Barbakoff, Audrey. "Wrapping Up the Old," *Library Journal* (2015). Accessed January 22, 2016. http://lj.libraryjournal.com/2015/09/buildings/lbd/lawrence-public-library-new-landmark-librar ies-2015-winner/.

Baumann, Charles H. *The Influence of Angus Snead MacDonald and the Snead Bookstack on Library Architecture.* Metuchen, NJ: Scarecrow Press, 1972.

Beagle, D. "Conceptualizing an Information Commons," *Journal of Academic Librarianship* 25, no. 2 (1999): 82–89. Accessed September 11, 2015. doi: 10.1016/S0099–1333(99)80003–2.

Bennett, S. "Putting Learning into Library Planning," *portal: Libraries and the Academy* 15, no. 2 (2015): 215–232.

Bermudez, Juan. *On the Architectural Design Parti.* www.academia.edu. 2013. Accessed September 23, 2015. http://www.academia.edu/4020964/On_the_Architectural_Design_Parti.

Breisch, K. A. "Small Public Libraries in America 1850–1890: The Invention and Evolution of a Building Type." PhD diss., University of Michigan, 1982.

Breisch, K. A. *Henry Hobson Richardson and the Small Public Library in America.* Cambridge: MIT Press, 1997.

Burchard, J. E. "Buildings and Architecture," *College & Research Libraries* 7 (January 1946): 78–79.

Case Study: A Sustainable Renovation: The Santa Fe Springs Library. whymasonry.org, 2010. Accessed February 1, 2016. http://whymasonry.org/wp-content/uploads/2010/06/WHY_MASONRY_CASE_STUDIES_SFS_LIBRARY.pdf.

Courant, Paul, and Matthew Nielsen. "On the Cost of Keeping a Book," in *The Idea of Order: Transforming Research Collections for 21st Century Scholarship* by the Council on Library and Information Resources. Washington, DC: CLIR, 2010, 81–105. Accessed June 1, 2015. http://www.clir.org/pubs/reports/pub147/pub147.pdf.

Cunningham, R. "Historian among the Librarians: Herbert Baxter Adams and Modern Librarianship." *Journal of Library History* 21, no. 4 (1986): 704–722.

Drew, Wilfred Bill. "Wireless Networks: New Meaning to Ubiquitous Computing." *Journal of Academic Librarianship* 29, no. 2 (2003): 102–106. Accessed September 11, 2015. doi: 10.1016/S0099–1333 (02)00420–2.

Gaytons, J.T. "Academic Libraries: 'Social' or 'Communal'?" The Nature and Future of Academic Libraries." *Journal of Academic Librarianship* 34, no. 1 (2008): 60–66. Accessed September 11, 2015. doi: 10.1016/j.acalib.2007.11.011.

Githens, A. "The Complete Development of the Open Plan in the Enoch Pratt Library at Baltimore," *Library Journal*, 58 (May 1, 1933): 384.

Graham, R. "Wireless Use in Libraries." *Library Hi Tech* 20, no. 2 (2002): 237–240.

Holland, B. "21st-Century Libraries: The Learning Commons." *Edutopia*, January 14, 2015. Accessed September 11, 2015. http://www.edutopia.org/blog/21st-century-libraries-learning-commons-beth-holland.

Hughes, C. " 'Facework': A New Role for the Next Generation of Library-Based Information Technology Centers." *Library Hi Tech* 16, no. 3–4 (1998): 27–35.

Kaser, David. *The Evolution of the American Academic Library Building*. Lanham, MD: Scarecrow Press, 1997.

Leighton, Philip D., and David C. Weber. *Planning Academic and Research Library Buildings*, 3rd ed. Chicago: American Library Association, 2000.

Lewis, David W. "From Stacks to the Web: The Transformation of Academic Library Collecting." *College & Research Libraries* 74, no. 2 (2013): 159–177. Accessed June 12, 2015. doi: 10.5860/crl-309.

Libby, B. "Odegaard Library." *Contract* 55, no. 2 (March 2014): 52–57.

Lombardi, M.M., and T.B. Wall. "Duke University: Perkins Library." In *Learning Spaces*, edited by D.G. Oblinger, Chapter 17. Boulder, CO: EDUCAUSE, 2006. Accessed October 24, 2015. http://www.educause.edu/research-and-publications/books/learning-spaces/chapter-17-duke-university-perkins-library.

Lowry, A.K. "The Information Arcade at the University of Iowa." *CAUSE/EFFECT* 17, no. 3 (1993). Accessed October 26, 2015. https://net.educause.edu/ir/library/text/CEM9438.txt.

Madsen, D. "James B. Hunt Jr. Library, Designed by Snøhetta." *Architect Magazine*, June 25, 2013. Accessed October 25, 2015. http://www.architectmagazine.com/design/buildings/james-b-hunt-jr-library-designed-by-snhetta_o.

Mattern, S. "Library as Infrastructure: Reading room, social service center, innovation lab. How far can we stretch the public library?" *Places Journal* (June 2014). Accessed September 11, 2015. https://placesjournal.org/article/library-as-infrastructure/.

Monahan, Torin. "Flexible Space & Built Pedagogy: Emerging IT Embodiments." *Inventio* 4, no. 1 (2002): 1–19.

Montgomery, S.E. "Library Space Assessment: User Learning Behaviors in the Library." *Journal of Academic Librarianship* 40, no. 1 (2014): 70–75. Accessed September 11, 2015. doi: 10.1016/j.acalib. 2013.11.003.

Morey, C.R. *A Laboratory-Library*. Princeton: Princeton University, 1932.

Oehlerts, D. "The Development of American Public Library Architecture from 1850 to 1940." PhD diss., Indiana University, 1975.

Raisinghani, M. "Wireless Library Aids student Productivity," *THE Journal* 30, no. 4 (2002): 24.

Randall, R.H. *The Furniture of H. H. Richardson: [Exhibition]*. Boston: Museum of Fine Arts Boston, 1962.

"Rubenstein Library Renovation in Pictures." *Duke University Libraries Magazine*, June 10, 2014. Accessed October 27, 2015. https://blogs.library.duke.edu/magazine/2014/06/10/rubenstein-library-renovation-in-pictures/.

Schwartz, M. "Tomorrow, Visualized," *Library Journal*, Fall (2013) Library by Design Supplement: 1–7. http://lj.libraryjournal.com/2013/09/buildings/lbd/tomorrow-visualized-library-by-design-fall-2013/#_.

Snee, T. "Carver Grant to Help UI Libraries Update Information Arcade," University of Iowa News Services, June 20, 2005. Accessed October 15, 2015. http://news-releases.uiowa.edu/2005/june/062005carver_grant.html.

Thompson, H. H. "Un Ritorno All'antico: The Use of Uomini Illustri in Library Decoration of Reformed Monasteries in the Veneto (1479 to 1503)." Master's thesis, Pratt Institute, 2011.

Van Beynen, K., Patricia Pettijohn, and Marcy Carrel. "Using Pedestrian Choice Research to Facilitate Resource Engagement in a Midsized Academic Library." *Journal of Academic Librarianship* 36, no. 5 (2010): 412–419. Accessed June 12, 2015. doi: 10.1016/j.acalib.2010.06.005.

Van Slyck, A. A. "The Utmost Amount of Effectiv [*sic*] Accomodation": Andrew Carnegie and the reform of the American Library." *Journal of the Society of Architectural Historians* 50, no. 4 (1991): 359–383.

Van Slyck, A. A. "The Librarian and the Library: Why Place Matters." *Libraries & Culture* 36, no. 4 (2001): 518–523.

Watson, Les. *Better Library and Learning Space: Projects, Trends, Ideas.* London: Facet Publishing, 2014.

Wetherold, H. "The Architectural History of the Newberry Library," *Newberry Library Bulletin* VI, no. 1 (1962): 3–23.

Wheeler, H. and P. M. McCauley, "Baltimore's New Public Library Building." *Library Journal* 58, (May 1, 1933): 386–393.

Williamson, W. L. *William Frederick Poole and the Modern Library Movement.* New York: Columbia University Press, 1963.

2

The Visioning Process

Gili Meerovitch

In a time of ever-diminishing resources, libraries are looking for ways not only to repurpose spaces to meet and adapt to current user needs, but also to maximize returns by leveraging the library as a platform for scalable learning space. As resources continue to be allocated toward digital environments, we are witnessing a transition from a focus on content to a growing focus on context. From this point of view, the conversation about reimagining the library's role in learning is no longer limited to the library as a stand-alone unit; rather, it engages all stakeholders in creating an experience that can build a learning network, which establishes communities of lifelong learners.

Developing a shared vision is a strategy for building consensus around the library's future and building support for constructing or renovating the library facility to aptly reflect the institution's approach to learning, research, and engagement well into the future. Metaphorically, the visioning process can be thought of as the preconcert moment, when orchestra members are tuning their instruments so that the performance begins with all parties in harmony. Similar to the orchestra's musicians tuning their instruments, the academic library and its various departments must synchronize, so that when the actual planning and repurposing of library spaces begin, all parties are engaged toward a unified goal. This chapter describes a visioning process that not only discovers what the library aspires to become, but also includes a strategy to bring about positive change to the institution. The process, developed for academic library projects, can be applicable to any library looking to reimagine itself. This strategy is a useful resource that can be applied whether the library undergoes a limited renewal or comprehensive renovation, or anticipates construction of a new purpose-built facility. Regardless of scale, the role of the academic library is undergoing a transition from providing content and service toward a focus on context and impact. The visioning process for the academic library addresses this change with the entire campus in mind.

FRAMING THE CONVERSATION

To begin, one must establish an understanding about how change occurs along a continuum. As higher education evolves, libraries are moving from a model that brought information into the library toward a model that pushes information out to patrons and users wherever they are. Consequently, attitudes toward library content are shifting from stewardship—focused on collecting, acquiring, storing, and preserving information—toward discovery—sharing, digitizing, and publishing new content. Similarly, library services are shifting from skill-based services that are built around collections, with a focus on reference and instruction, toward expertise-based services that are built to support the life cycle of work, with a focus on educational and consultancy aspects. In the latter, services are no longer tethered to the building and can be deployed beyond the boundaries of the physical library facility, both tangibly in the departments' spaces and virtually, for example, when embedded in courses.

To begin the conversation about the library's future, it is important to help an institution identify where it sees the library on such a continuum. For example, when examining library services, a library might find that some of its traditional services are unchanged, while new services are being developed and others have already been transformed into newer and highly progressive models. Recognizing that there can be multiple starting points gives everyone permission to still be in transition. We think of a continuum as a sliding scale that ranges, in this case, from a traditional model on one end to a progressive model on the other, and transitional stages in between. Finding the starting point is an important first step, but perhaps even more critical is understanding where the library aims to ultimately end up, and articulating which direction it will work toward.

WHILE CHANGE IS UNIVERSAL THE SOLUTIONS ARE NOT

While change is universal, solutions are not. Depending on a library's particular circumstances, the approaches can range widely. As the conversation expands from one that is internal to the library to one that is campus-wide, its focus can range from service, workflow, and space utilization to more comprehensive topics, such as scalable solutions to deal with learning outcomes, expanding research capabilities, and outreach to the campus and surrounding community. To direct the discussion, universities can seek expertise from an architectural planning firm that has a deep understanding of academic library typology through project experience. An experienced firm understands that a clearly articulated vision is informed by broader planning issues, and, while a vision can be responsive to a variety of constituents, each of whom have their own priorities, there is also a need to balance programmatic goals, functional requirements, and campus objectives with financial resources and realistic implementation schedules. It is equally important that the firm's assigned team members bring proven experience and expertise in leading participatory processes and are well versed in leading broad constituencies in decision-making processes that build consensus and result in projects that receive the broadest level of support and approval. The job of the consultant is to frame the conversation in terms of strategic thinking in order to foster a mind-set that embraces change. In many instances, it is less of a matter of an ability to change as it is increasing the comfort level of planning for an uncertain future. In addition, understanding the library's present state and its aspirations is essential to a successful visioning process. This understanding presents a strategic opportunity to align the library with the campus's priorities in a way that will maximize a renovation's impact.

The beginning of the process involves making pragmatic observations of how a library facility actually functions. An outside perspective has the advantage of providing an institution with an objective and unencumbered look at what actually exists. That first impression plays a significant role in forecasting what important changes will be required for the library to become better equipped and up-to-date. Several library walk-throughs at different times of the day over the course of a semester or quarter reveal how space utilization affects patrons' behaviors, as seen in routine activities, in entry sequences, and in the interactions between users and library staff. Recognition of what works successfully and commitment to maintaining or even expanding these elements can be a reassurance and mitigate the resistance to change.

THE STEERING COMMITTEE

The steering committee should partake in the visioning conversation to set and prioritize goals for the library's facility. An effective committee includes the representation of all stakeholders, including multiple on-campus departments, schools, groups, administrations, and campus facilities. In certain circumstances, it can also include outside representation of the community surrounding the campus, alumni, and industry partners. To assemble this committee, identify a chair or co-chairs and then select up to 12 members, to keep it productive. To help craft a vision for the future library, it is beneficial to select future-oriented thinkers who network with their respective departments and peers. The committee members are both the conduit to communicate to their respective disciplines and the means to harvest input and feedback from them.

These channels of communication must be constantly active in order to inform the committee's thinking and its recommendations. A well-balanced committee will include representation by the following:

- Primary users: students (undergraduate, graduate, post doc/advanced degree)
- Library users: faculty (be sure to include representatives from both the sciences and social sciences—think of the makeup of your collections. It is important to include representation from all disciplines, regardless of the growth/reduction in holdings in their respective disciplines)
- Library's faculty and staff
- Occupants (nonlibrary units): academic or learning partners, student services, institutes
- Administration (information technology, capital planning and facilities, development, public safety)
- Representatives of the surrounding community

The first step in building a consensus is an invitation that encourages participation and sets a positive tone for a constructive process. The library affects everyone on campus, including those who routinely access its collections and services digitally without ever setting foot in the building. Emphasize that a collective effort, as well as the committee members' insight and guidance, is critical to crafting an exciting and stimulating vision for the library's future.

FUTURE MANDATE

The shared goal is to develop a library building that will be relevant for the next 10 or 20 years and reflect the institution's approach to teaching and learning spaces, research services, and engagement. While it is important to keep in mind what worked well in the past, the focus of the shared vision and strategic planning must remain on the future.

A well-articulated mandate will give the committee a purpose and lead to a focused and effective outcome. It should describe a future library that will serve the next generation of students, researchers, faculty members, and the public at large. Thus, it is important to clearly communicate that the overall strategic planning effort will address a wide range of enhancements to both spaces and services and result in a long-term plan that outlines its priorities for improvements.

When undergoing a renovation, expanding an existing facility, or planning for a new one, it can be tempting to focus on the immediate space deficiencies, current mainte-nance issues, and internal clashes and conflicts. Consultants, who stand outside the orga-nizational dynamics, are often able to ask difficult questions and facilitate constructive conversations around contentious topics. Libraries seeking an outside consultant should look for a skilled facilitator with a deep understanding of libraries, someone who can provide useful analysis and advance discussions toward building a consensus that leads to an actionable plan.

THE VISIONING PROCESS

Once the steering committee has been established and received its mandate, the vision-ing process can be launched with a kickoff meeting to establish a communication plan and reiterate members' roles and responsibilities. A detailed overview of the process is a suc-cessful method of easing any discomfort with planning for change. Establishing a detailed work plan early in the process affords the steering committee, as well as the librarians and library staff, the knowledge of what to expect in the coming months and gives them time to gather information regarding the services the library offers, and plan on participating in meetings, focus groups, tours, and other activities geared toward capturing a snapshot of the current space utilization and conditions of the library. Consultants should share knowledge, creativity, and experiences that can inspire others not only to consider other points of view and think beyond the immediate environment but also to reimagine how available capacity and resources could be utilized to achieve the vision. The visioning pro-cess ought to focus on discovery, evaluation, and analysis. While the discovery includes mapping, benchmarking, and an environmental scan, the evaluation frames the conversa-tion from the perspective of the specific institution, and the analysis can then crack ideas open and begin to delineate the contours of a vision for the future.

LIBRARY MAPPING

A good first step for the actual visioning process is to map out the library as a building typology, identifying the key spaces important to the library and examining the chang-ing attitudes toward library collections, services, and technology. In many cases, libraries already have in place organized working groups that know what the problems are, but did not know how to take the next step. For example, one library recognized the need to address a shortfall of collaborative work spaces but did not know how to go about assess-ing its existing space utilization, balancing the number of individual and collaborative seats, or evaluating spatial adjacencies. By test-fitting a few scenarios, the consultant pro-vided multiple options and addressed spatial implications. In the event that the visioning process stalls, one way to advance the conversation is to examine current trends relating to key topics identified by the library and the steering committee. Additionally, it helps to consider hot topics and major issues that are on the users' minds when they think about the actual value of the library, which should be revealed during the preliminary outreach mentioned earlier. Finally, when engaging with outside consultants, it is extremely helpful to draw on the expanded collective knowledge, experience, and expertise of the consultant team.

BENCHMARKING AND IMAGINING

Examining what other institutions are implementing that is relevant to these trends comes next. This examination might include preparing an environmental scan and presenting images and examples of contemporary spaces that illustrate responsiveness to evolving user needs. During this preparation, one should focus on spaces that are relevant to the key topics identified by the steering committee. Such spaces range from media-rich research environments to scholars' commons, data visualization spaces, event spaces, gathering and exhibition spaces, and so forth. Once specific space usage is identified, the next step of the process should be to benchmark similar spaces in peer and aspirational institutions. Things to compare might include available seat count, the number of group study rooms, the utilization of a room reservation system, and a service model used at points of service. To identify other institutions for comparison, make use of the comprehensive consultant knowledge of the methods and criteria of other institutions.

FACILITIES TOURS/DEFINING CAMPUS CULTURE

Touring completed projects can be beneficial. The consultant can help focus the attention of the steering committee on what the library might perceive as its core structure and point to how the physical environment reflects the library's organizational structure and culture. Once the committee is better informed about the recent trends in academic library spaces and what other institutions are doing, it can begin to evaluate what is applicable for its own project. Campus culture should be an early topic for discussion that centers on the prevalent attitude toward change. It is important to begin the conversation with review-type questions such as, "What expresses, describes, or exemplifies the campus's/library's organizational culture?" or, "Historically, is there a pattern of how change has occurred on the campus in the past?" Through such lenses, examine a recent event—an organizational change or a transition in leadership—and identify the factors that contributed to a successful or unsuccessful change. A keen understanding of the culture is necessary for developing a winning strategy: Is this a culture where change can grow from within or is it led from above? Are changes quick or slow? Are successful changes siloed or networked? Understanding the institutional culture is useful in articulating what specifically is right for the library (not pander to trends), and it can be helpful in crafting a strong and consistent message about the value of building or renovating the library (for a communication plan or development activities, for example).

Thinking strategically about the library's future can defuse some of the resistance to change and build constructive support. Open-ended questions such as, "What are some of the concerns about working differently?" and "What are librarians and library staff members looking forward to?" can keep the conversation focused on the future while providing insight into new opportunities, which, in some cases, can build positive excitement.

ALIGNMENT WITH CAMPUS PRIORITIES

After establishing the core competencies and identifying the desired behaviors to be emphasized moving forward, look to the campus strategic plan or the declared strategic priorities. This might include a host of topics, ranging from providing access to a focus on student success and scholarship, research and innovation, leadership, outreach, and service to the community. Whichever priorities the campus leadership aims toward, they must be infused in and inform the library's vision. For example, if the identified strategic plan aims for student success as its goal, the discussion must address how the library will contribute to engagement, achievement, retention, and completion rates, whereas a goal focused on teaching and learning might be devoted to instruction, research, scholarship, and assessment. A strategic goal of service to the surrounding community, however, could involve outreach and partnerships outside of the library.

Through evaluation and analysis, additional strategic opportunities are uncovered. For example, while working on one library that aimed at becoming a place where scholarship was respected, discussions revealed that while most users and stakeholders recognize the library as a place from which to access content, opinions differed when it came to the library's value. While library faculty and staff perceived its value to be the services the library offered, the users, on the other hand, perceived the library's value as an amenity—a place to do their work and access printers and computers with specialty software. Recognizing this difference of perceived values was an opportunity to examine the library as well as its organizational structure, and consider areas for adjustments, growth, and/or reduction. Positioning the library's value in alignment with its strategic priorities helps focus the thinking on the future rather than on the present, and reframes the conversation around what is possible, rather than on what exists. Broadening the conversation to encompass ideas about services, partnerships, special projects, cross-disciplinary initiatives, and other opportunities allows for the creation of a library that can better serve its community for years to come.

DEFINING THE LIBRARY'S PURPOSE AND AUDIENCE

When the frame of reference has been expanded and the committee agrees on keeping the library in alignment with the campus's strategic priorities, it can begin to build a consensus around the library's primary purpose service model and desired user experience.

To articulate the primary purpose of the library, it is important to first identify the library's primary user group. For most main academic libraries, undergraduate students constitute the largest group of users; however, graduate students and faculty make up the largest majority of intensive users of library resources. When identifying this group, it is important not to lose sight of potential branch libraries, additional campuses, satellite locations, and members of the community at large who are unaffiliated with the campus but might also use the library. Understanding which groups the library serves and recognizing that the library cannot be everything to all of its users are important because they inform the understanding of the library's purpose.

EVALUATING ALONG CONTINUUMS

Identifying the library's position on a continuum between place-based and boundary-free models is another way to facilitate discussion. For example, a primary purpose of a library serving undergraduate students might be to provide resources and information in order to prepare learners for academic and professional success. At the other end of the spectrum, a primary purpose of a library serving scholars and researchers might be to partner with learners and researchers in creating knowledge and to support the life cycle of research. Once the current approach is identified, the direction that the library wishes to move toward in the future can be identified and discussed.

When identifying the future direction of the library, addressing the concerns of those who might be reluctant or wary of anything new is equally important. Use the present environment as a starting point for gathering information about changing workflow. Ask librarians for their observations on how the library "works" today and how they might see their work changing. Look for insights about change in behavior patterns. For example, one research library's organizational restructuring created a greater demand for collaborative work spaces. Studying the impact of new technology on workflow and space needs is also important as the increase of digital communication tools, such as Skype, Chat, GoToMeetings, and Hangouts, can result in fewer large library instruction sessions and a greater demand for smaller rooms to facilitate online webinars.

Identifying where a library falls on a continuum, relative to a number of factors, will inform and dictate what kind of workflow will work best. On one extreme, a place-based library will likely prefer a library-centric workflow with fixed service points and face-to-face interaction, while situating the points of service as destinations. On the other extreme, the placeless library will likely prefer a network-centric workflow, mobile or roving service points, virtual interaction, and meeting the users where the users are. These are ideological scenarios and everyday libraries embody some characteristics of each extreme. Choice is never strictly limited to one of the two options, nor is it a value judgment; the purpose is to recognize how the library works today and what its aspirations are for the future.

Identifying the current place on a continuum will allow the steering committee to discuss and recognize the direction the library wishes to move toward. To align the library's primary purpose with its service model, ask leading questions that focus on behaviors, for example, "How will the librarians engage undergraduates who do not yet understand the role of libraries in collegiate level research?" and "How can the librarians promote collaboration with faculty and administrators?" The conversation of user experience aims to bridge between content and services and to align the primary users with the service model. Here, too, locating the library's position on the continuum informs this discussion.

CRAFTING A VISION

To craft a concise vision statement, the library will need to complete a few exercises in order to narrow its options. First, the library must examine its attitude toward collection development on a sliding scale between broad and generalist on one end and deep expertise on the other. Second, it must identify its primary user attitude toward consumption of information on a scale between random to expert. Next, it should consider its attitude toward the learning and discovery process on a continuum between serendipitous and prescribed, and finally, whether its attitude toward research is more disciplinary or multidisciplinary.

Once the shared vision statement is articulated and defined, it needs to be presented to the campus community in order to test how well it is supported by various users on campus and by the community. This face-to-face engagement can be achieved through a series of on-campus focus groups and open-forum discussions. Questioning, prodding, and encouraging conversations to figure out if the vision is well aligned with users' expectations, and finding what, if anything, is missing require additional attention.

SPACE IMPLICATIONS

Conduct a series of group discussions, centered on library functional space usages to explore the implication and anticipated impact of the vision on space needs. Focus groups should include representatives from campus-wide stakeholders in addition to open forums that include both campus and nonaffiliated community representatives. A web-based survey can function as an additional outreach activity designed to further expand levels of engagement. Drafting survey questions that follow topics and discussion points uncovered in focus groups can assist in collecting information. Several universities have mandated compliance with institutional review board's requirements relative to funding research proposals involving human participants. Alternatively, an informal questionnaire can be conducted via SurveyMonkey, or other open access mobile, web, or social media survey tools. Lastly, host an informational session open to the campus and local community to present what was learned from the stakeholders' input. At the conclusion of the evaluation and analysis, the library can further hone its visioning statement to reflect a refined shared vision.

SPACE PLAN TO SUPPORT THE VISION

To translate the shared vision into an actionable plan, the steering committee must be reconvened to articulate specific goals and priorities that will guide the library's future planning. This process should build on the visioning exercises and continue to frame the conversations in terms of behaviors. The goals should articulate the shared vision by identifying the end results that support the vision. For example, if the goal is to create a welcoming environment for all users and to engage the undergraduate students who do not yet fully understand the role of the library in their academic journey, then one of the objectives of future planning will be to look for opportunities to optimize services for the student body. Outlining the overall objective will in turn inform the planning process to consider measures including improvements to the entry sequence, creating clear wayfinding throughout the facility, increasing visibility of interactions centered on learning activities, increasing visibility of the library and technology services, and addressing issues of physical accessibility.

A future-oriented strategic thinking process can enable the steering committee to identify existing programs that are likely to grow or diminish, as well as identify new programs, units, or functions within the library that may be relocated, as well as nonlibrary groups that could relocate elsewhere, on or off campus. This process of identification allows a clear and organized plan for the vision of the library's space needs.

Prioritizing the goals is a critical key to the realization of any vision. This is particularly true today, as many university libraries anticipate phased implementation as resources become available over time. With limited funding, it is important to aim to maximize the impact of the changes made. Prioritizing should focus on two aspects: the level of importance and the level of urgency. Action items that have the ability to fulfill multiple goals are likely to yield the highest impact. Both important and urgent, these items are typically perceived as having the highest priority for implementation. Action items that are urgent, but not important, can also be considered as high priorities. This is often the case when working with existing and aging buildings. For example, a leaking roof or structural deficiency could be considered a high priority even though it will have a low impact in the advancement of the library's vision.

NEXT STEPS: DON'T LEAVE THEM HANGING

A successful visioning process builds momentum that the library will want to harness. Preparation and planning for the steps immediately following this process help to maximize the energy, excitement, and goodwill that the visioning process yields. Nothing is more disappointing than building up momentum and having it fizzle out because of little to no follow-through on actionable items. Immediate tasks might include detailed programming, additional information gathering, and, if applicable, documenting of the existing space utilization, scenario planning, and devising an implementation plan. Both a clearly articulated shared vision and prioritized goals prepare the library and the campus for the next steps in building or renovating. Finally, the process outlined above illustrates the benefits of engaging with an outside consultant and the numerous advantages of having a non-stakeholder and skilled facilitator, who is well informed about the issues academic libraries are facing.

3

Stakeholder Input

Janette Blackburn

Libraries have long been the bellwether for change in the communities they serve. Traditionally an intellectual hub, the library today is also a place for social interaction. It is deeply engaged with its constituents, melding new functions and spaces for teaching, events, and social activity with more traditional programs.

Although the inclusive stakeholder process, in which project funders, leaders, and users provide input, has long been a constant in library design, the dynamic is changing. As libraries transform themselves to accommodate their new roles as centers of learning and community, engaging an expanded mix of stakeholders is of critical importance. The unique characteristics, cultures, and drivers of each institution mean that there is no one process. Instead, each project and community must create its own path for advancing its vision and gathering stakeholder input.

WHAT DRIVES TRANSFORMATION?
RETHINK TO STAY RELEVANT

As we approach the mid-21st century, the most common drivers of stakeholder engagement are rooted in an institution's desire to rethink and remake its library. While a myriad of issues are of interest to stakeholders, the three drivers that recur most often are:

- New paradigms for services and partners
- Balancing print and digital collections
- Enhancing community and identity

The increasingly blurred boundaries between traditional library services that support access and use of information resources and those of a host of partners in learning, technology, and outreach activities call for engaging a stakeholder group far beyond a library's traditional parameters. Partner organizations in learning, the use of technology, and social/cultural programming may interact and prioritize differently than their library cohorts. While this may require a stakeholder process that includes new expectations for communication and decision making, the process can also forge important new synergies among participants.

Although a library's broad mix of stakeholders may have varying—even competing—aspirations, they can often be brought together around concepts that build community and reflect the institution's identity. For instance, in recent years special collections have transitioned from privileged, rarefied destinations to inclusive, prominently showcased resources that are integrated with an institution's curricular and cultural missions. Their emergence as a primary library destination calls for a framework of support across a broad base of constituents whose complementary needs include teaching, research, events, and exhibits.

RESPOND TO FOUNDATIONAL SHIFTS

Re-envisioning the 21st-century library can be a catalyst for wider institutional or community change. Many libraries' drive for reinvention is triggered by larger institutional factors that require them to rebalance. In these cases, as institutional master plans are prepared to implement strategic moves, stakeholder input will include discussions of values, identity, and future forecasting. Examples are as follows:

- Persistent scarcity of funding may demand a dramatic rethinking of facility and program needs and the forging of new partnerships organizational models.
- Diversity initiatives may expand the range of support services and user environments the library is called on to provide.
- Growth in online learning may require rapid shifts in collections access practices, collections digitization programs, and online support services.
- Economic and environmental pressures may prioritize funding for deferred maintenance and infrastructure improvements over new construction of bigger and better facilities.

While the drivers may vary, the importance of stakeholder engagement in determining a shared path forward does not. Forgoing a process in which collective understanding of project goals and priorities is formed will lead to uneven decision making, a stalled process, and, all too often, a canceled project.

WHO ARE THE STAKEHOLDERS?

The retooled library may include new partners who have had relatively little engagement with library staff, and it is important not to underestimate how broad input must be. Each group of stakeholders brings different expectations and a different understanding of how a successful library will serve them. Prepare to build bridges across stakeholder groups.

Depending on the stage of the project, the level of detail and number of stakeholders will vary:

- Early project stages such as master planning and conceptual design involve large groups of stakeholders and identify values, goals, principles, and trends in user preferences. Input may be gathered in online surveys and open community forums.
- More detailed design phases will involve small task forces that provide input on user needs, operations, and aesthetics. Tools may include review of detailed program spreadsheets, room data sheets, and design drawings.

Resist the temptation to develop a perfect plan before going to senior leadership. Bring them in early to help them understand what a mid-21st-century library is. Allow them the opportunity to participate while ideas are loosely formed and can be shaped to align with institutional strategies. Doing so can help unlock process, build buy-in, and ease approvals.

INPUT SPHERES

Be clear about input roles. Every building project needs to be structured around a core group, a "coordination team" charged with leading the process. This group may have final authority, but more often, it will develop recommendations for final approval by others (e.g., trustees, senior leadership). To keep the team nimble in its approach, it should have no more than five to six individual members.

To facilitate broader representation, the coordination team can be embedded within a larger project team that includes additional stakeholders: faculty, staff, student, alumni, and community representatives. This group gathers, interprets, and prioritizes feedback from its respective constituencies, and provides comment on alternatives and strategies.

Especially for large projects, it may be wise to convene additional issue-based user groups that are likely to represent specialized aspects of the project, such as collections strategy, accessibility, operations and maintenance, and sustainable design. These small groups of individuals work with the project team to define specific attributes and space needs within the overall framework (Figure 3.1).

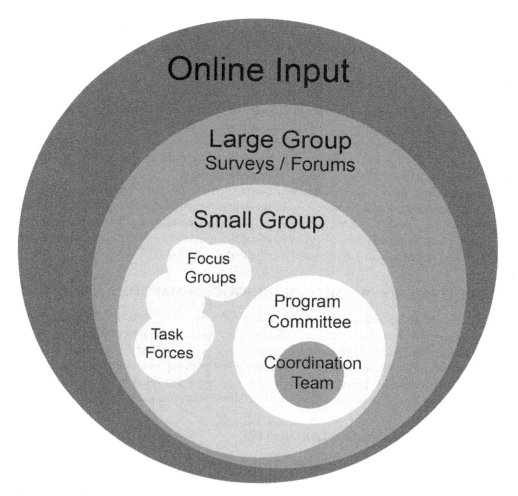

Figure 3.1 Whom to invite? Sample stakeholder participation and topic diagram.

ACADEMIC AND PUBLIC REALMS

The culture and organizational structure of the larger institution the library serves will be a determinant in the stakeholder process. Although there are similarities, there are also distinct differences between public and academic library engagement processes.

The *academic library* stakeholder group consists of faculty, students, staff, administration, trustees, alumni, and donors, with governing agencies and community groups having less direct input. The vision is framed in relation to the institution's academic and research strategy. It is expected that the campus community will engage in intellectual discourse about the project that will be influential to its formation. The institution is free to design the input process as needed to fit with its culture and decision-making structure.

The *public library* stakeholder group is typically much larger and more diverse. Core constituents include patrons (an entire neighborhood, city, or region), staff, civic governing bodies, and donors. As both intellectual and community center, the public library has a central mission framed around public service. A sense of ownership and entitlement among vocal special-interest sectors may need to be balanced with an understanding of what is best for an ambiguous "public good." Public standards and regulations for everything from budget expenditures to space allocation may be significant drivers. Even the public input and communication format may be bound by regulated processes.

MAKE IT HAPPEN: FUNDING

Projects need funding. This means articulating specific and compelling program and building strategies to capture the attention of potential donors. An institution's development officers, trustees, and potential funding sources are important stakeholder groups who should be included in the process from the beginning, so that project principles reflect the aspirations of the institution and funding bodies.

Engage these groups early and often. Invite them on tours of precedent projects to provide context and make connections to the programming and design process. Consider including a program or design workshop as part of a trustee event. This is a simple but powerful way to gain a highly engaged fund-raising group that understands project needs and is invested in realizing outcomes it has helped shape.

CORE ELEMENTS OF A SUCCESSFUL PROCESS: MAP THE JOURNEY

Careful planning will provide the foundation for successful stakeholder engagement and, ultimately, a successful project. Tailor your process to your goals and the stakeholder mix. Design the process from the outset so you have a timeline and defined goal. Think of it as a travel guide for your journey. The route is the pathway of stakeholder engagement and the destination is the completion of your library project. Plan for unexpected stops and side trips along the way, but keep the final destination in sight.

MAKE IT OPEN AND COLLABORATIVE

From the start, design and implement an open and collaborative process. Use the process to harness the richness of different perspectives, create a campus-wide buzz, build buy-in, and secure commitments. Universally (and regardless of scale and aspiration) seek input early and prioritize communication throughout the project. Don't underestimate the need to do this, even on small, seemingly simple projects such as user or staff space furniture upgrades.

MAP WHO AND HOW

Tailor your model of engagement to your constituents and to your institution's culture. It may work best to engage:

- Students through hands-on activities and online surveys
- Faculty through robust discourse around ideas
- Staff through testing ideas against strategy and operations
- Community through captivating imagery that defines an ethos and tells a story
- Institutional leadership through mission-aligned goals, compelling data, and imagery that allows them to build buy-in for approvals and funding

MIX IT UP

Combine stakeholder groups in different ways to find common ground. Overlapping groups of staff departments will identify shared goals that may emerge as priorities and points of buy-in. It will also highlight discrete interests that must be addressed through a more narrowly focused feedback loop.

LEAVE THE BUILDING

The library's "power users" may be easy to reach; they are likely to be vocal and invested in the process. In paying attention to them, do not overlook the more casual, infrequent users. Reach these groups by going where they are. Are they studying in the local coffee shop, dining hall, or campus center? Spending leisure time at the mall or gym? Go find them. Understand how their needs differ from those of power users and what barriers may stand in the way of more robust use.

EMBRACE ITERATION

While forward momentum is important, allow the process to be iterative. Listening, testing, and circling back to evaluate program approach in light of emerging design ideas, and vice versa, will make the final results more complete.

KEEP UP THE PACE

Establish an ambitious but realistic schedule to keep the process moving forward; build in time for brainstorming, testing, and evaluation loops to develop and benchmark nascent ideas. The emergence of common themes from various stakeholder groups will be a signal that you are nearing a milestone in the process. Once these common themes are identified, you are ready to build a design that addresses the values and concerns of the majority of stakeholders. You are also now able to define more focused needs of special-interest groups and a strategy for addressing them. If these common themes are not emerging, it is a signal to slow down the process and seek more and different ways of engagement.

WATCH THE INSTITUTIONAL CLOCK

Be acutely aware of the rhythms of the institution and their impact on feedback. In academic libraries:

- Summer can be a good time for focused work with staff.
- Alumni weekends can provide great opportunities to build community support.
- Fall is the best time to begin initiatives with a campus community refreshed from summer break.
- Grading periods, trustee visits, and commencement are generally blackout dates for seeking input on special projects, as key stakeholders are absorbed in the core work of the academy.

Taken together, the windows for broad community engagement over a calendar year are relatively short. For many institutions, core work needs to be planned for mid-September to mid-November and February to mid-April. As a year-long planning window dwindles to just 18 weeks, the compressed timeline for input can surprise stakeholders and planners.

SCALE UP, SCALE DOWN

Institutional scale: The scale of your institution may also play a big role in determining process. In larger institutions, scale and anonymity may become partners that dilute expectations for input and buy-in. In contrast, stakeholders in smaller communities often exude enthusiasm and empowerment.

Project scale: Small interior renovations with a limited budget and short time frame may make extended user engagement unrealistic. A simple, straight forward process may rely on a few "open house" events and social media tools to maximize input opportunity at a point in the project when it is most useful.

For a large project, such as a new building or major renovation, the process and timeline should be more expansive and iterative. Not only does the nature of the project call for

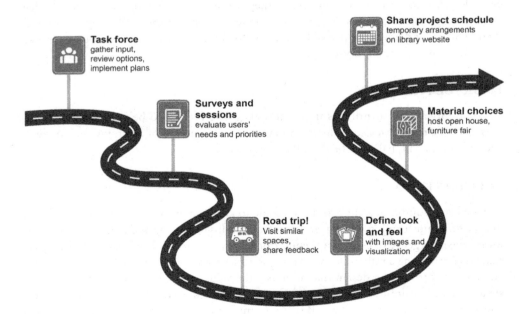

Figure 3.2   Stakeholder engagement road map for small projects.

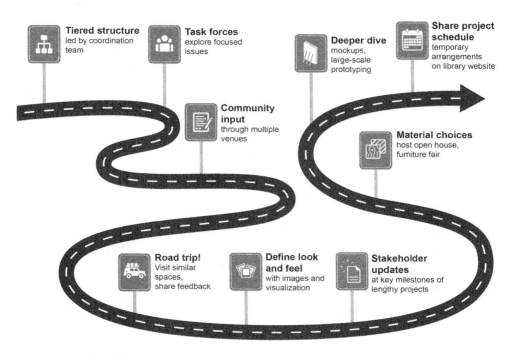

Figure 3.3   Stakeholder engagement road map for large projects.

broader input, but also the passage of time triggers the need to circle back as stakeholders come and go and specifics within the plan change. The number of stakeholders on core committees is also likely to expand, and multiple task forces may be needed to address specific project issues (Figures 3.2 and 3.3).

HOW BOLD IS IT?

Tailor process and participants according to the degree of change and institution-wide significance associated with the project.

Stakeholder input for projects to refresh existing spaces and programs may emphasize a shared vision among the most affected user groups. The input process may be more streamlined than for more transformative initiatives.

Projects that "break the mold" through dramatic transformations of program, partnerships, and spaces are best served by a more intensive effort. Input from a broad community of stakeholders includes iterative cycles of observation, playback, and synthesis throughout the design process.

The stakeholder engagement process for landmark projects—those that aspire to attain national or international prominence for a signature place or program—requires particular attention. On the one hand, public scrutiny of a project may require careful control of message content and dissemination, and on the other, the risk of a well-publicized project implosion is high if stakeholders are not aligned and vested in the project vision.

ENGAGEMENT TOOLKIT

Set the Table

The initial step in successful stakeholder engagement is a deliberate process of gathering input through listening and observation. Venues range from established forums, such as faculty meetings, student government events, or trustee meetings, to interactive sessions designed for specific stakeholder needs. Whatever the venue, these tools and techniques will enrich the process when matched to the appropriate user groups and issues (Figure 3.4).

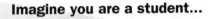

Imagine you are a student...

Your phone chirps letting you know that the folio you requested through the library website a few hours before is available. You use your phone to reserve a media booth – luckily there is one available. You text your project partner and agree to meet in the café at the library.

As you enter the library, a LCD screen shows upcoming artist talks. As you get to the cafe to pick up coffee, you run into your professor, who is also in line. She spends a few minutes helping you go over the outline for your art history paper.

When your project partner arrives, the two of you head to the information point to pick up the folio, then go to the media booth to use the scanner. A touch interface lets you zoom and pan the display of related information and documents indicating a social network of artists.

The librarian stops by the media pod and suggests two other artists who have a similar attitude toward street art. You realize these artists may be useful to your studio course so you quickly drop links and images on your phone. Unrolling the sketch paper the librarian brought, you draw some quick ideas for class later.

With your coffee you go upstairs to a quiet area to write. After you unpack your laptop, the bibliography you had started the night before automatically checks in with the library, showing which volumes are available. After writing for an hour you head to the stacks.

As you leave, a friend stops you and asks about the sketches. When you show him, he recognizes the similarity of ideas to some of the pieces in the gallery. As you rush to class, you make a mental note to come back that night for the artists talk.

Figure 3.4   Sample engagement techniques that could be part of your toolkit.

Take a Road Trip

Building tours are a powerful way to bring stakeholders together and create camaraderie. Visit a range of projects, as no single example will exactly capture your program needs or aesthetic gestalt. Experiencing potential models for a new facility project firsthand will spark an honest exchange of ideas, likes, and dislikes among stakeholders.

Develop Common Language

A successful process rests on the development of a common language. At the outset, develop a glossary of terms that describe activities and special effects. Using terms such as front stage, backstage, flow-by, white space, collision space, and mixing bowl, rather than the technical terminology of programming and facilities to describe space attributes, evokes a more vivid sense of the user experience.

Leverage Interaction

Plan interactive events to fully engage participants and provide meaningful feedback. Effective icebreakers, they will also generate more honest input than an around-the-table discussion by sidestepping groupthink, shyness, and peer pressure. These are especially successful with students, and may also work well with certain staff groups or other subsets of a community.

- **Self-Observation:** Ask users to take photos of activities that are integral to their educational experience at the institution over the course of one day and evening. Use these images to facilitate discussion at the workshop.
- **Experience Vignettes:** Work with users to convey experiences they expect to have in the building through descriptive sentences, drawings, or image tagging. These should be highly descriptive (e.g., "sitting with my friends drinking sustainably harvested coffee from a real mug while watching results from the robot build competition").
- **Image Olympics:** Provide a series of innovation space precedents for users to rank with colored stickers. Focus will be on program elements that should be in the new space. Program elements important to users will be apparent by the number of votes.
- **"What Will You Do?" Exercise:** Ask users to write answers to the question, "What will you do in the new [name of library or space]?" on sticky notes and aggregate them on the wall. Group answers according to themes and ask for comments.

ILLUSTRATE ABSTRACT IDEAS

Storyboards

Storyboarding combines visualization and narrative to develop facility-use scenarios from the perspectives of different stakeholders. Stakeholders now are freed from imagining specific physical places. *How big, how many*, and *what kind* are replaced with *why am I there, what do I want to do*, and *how do I want to feel*. Rewinding the dialogue to these essential questions can unlock new ideas and hone understanding of different stakeholder communities' goals and priorities (Figure 3.5).

Space and Time

Ask stakeholders to envision space needs and map activities over the course of the institution's calendar. Compare and contrast the cycles of the day, week, and academic year. Using diagrams to review space changes of the course of a day or semester in this exercise will help identify the potential for shared and overlapping space uses. Use scenario

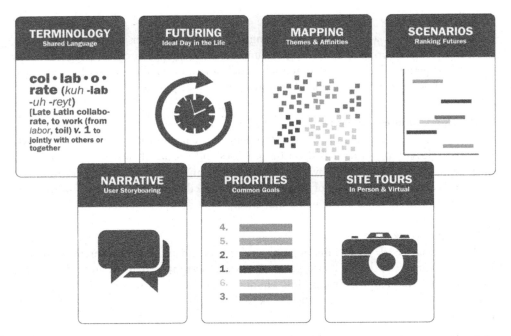

Figure 3.5 "Day in the life" storyboards highlight the use of the facility from the perspective of the various user communities.

planning exercises to map how space might evolve on Day 1, Day 100, and well into the future. By harnessing the thought power of your stakeholders, you'll clarify how programs and, accordingly, space may need to adapt.

Diagrams and Models

Develop maps of relationships between building functions and paths of movement or ask your design consultant to do so. These may be done as a precursor to, or in tandem with, the development of compelling imagery to show what the space will look like. This is an essential step that should not be overlooked as you gather input. By separating program analysis from spatial design, discussion is focused (or refocused) on users' needs. Through these diagrams, stakeholders can explore and articulate important synergies, operational needs, and spatial experiences.

Techniques for mapping space relationships and use patterns are numerous and range from simple "by hand" approaches to sophisticated digital tools. Some effective tools are listed here:

- **Chipping:** Users can reposition color-coded squares, "program chips" scaled to represent area requirements for each space or group of spaces, to explore different space adjacencies. This is a simple and effective icebreaker that facilitates discussion among groups. Planning and design firms may employ 2D and 3D digital versions of this tool. While the digital versions cast stakeholders more as observers, they allow rapid and accurate exploration of complex space models.
- **Heat Mapping:** Design professionals may also assist with development of a "heat map" diagram that conveys data about space use in an easy-to-grasp diagram. This form of diagramming can be used to create a graphic representation of intensity of use, energy output, and traffic patterns (Figure 3.6).

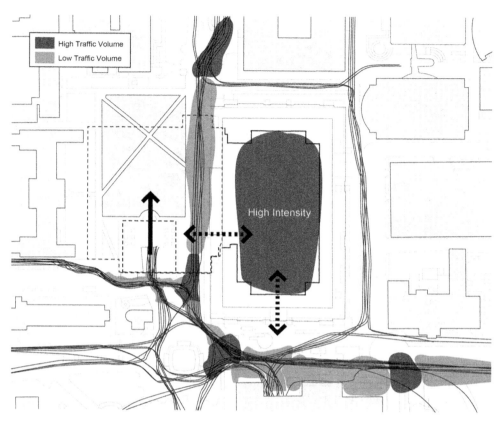

Figure 3.6   In this example of heat mapping, pedestrian activity around a campus library is articulated with high traffic volumes (dark gray) and low traffic volumes (light gray).

- **Bubbles and Blocks:** Stakeholders and design professionals can work together to create quick diagrams and models that show desired spatial relationships and paths of movement. This participatory exercise can use a variety of tools, including white boards, pencils and trace, Legos, blocks, touch screens, and tablets. It is often helpful for scale models to provide furniture and other details beyond the basic building form (Figure 3.7).
- **Cardboard City:** In later project phases, mock-ups and prototypes help stakeholders experience how they will interact in their proposed space. Create a "cardboard city," a full-scale mock-up of one component, or a series of key spaces built from inexpensive materials such as cardboard that can be modified on the spot in response to user input (Figure 3.8).

Stack areas and user seating are the most common library components prototyped for stakeholder input. No matter how experienced your design team is, don't assume they are operating with the same set of assumptions as the library about stack area details.

There are a myriad of options and user preferences that come into play. Invite vendors to furnish your mock-up. Bring in building and equipment product samples for review. Sample shelving units eliminate guesswork and allow library staff to confirm shelf dimensions and spacing and make decisions about accessories and construction details that may be overlooked or misunderstood during the design and construction process.

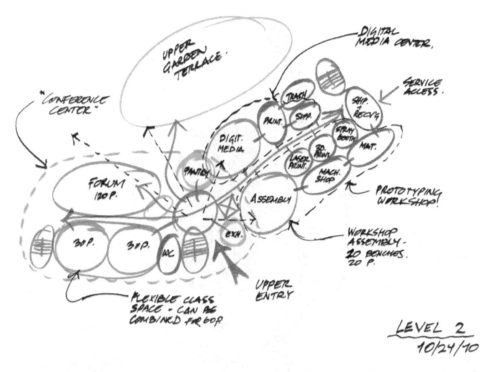

Figure 3.7 Quick freehand sketches are a simple way to explain how a series of spaces can work together abstracted from architectural form and mass.

Figure 3.8 Mock-up of large-scale, experimental classroom.

Furniture fairs are one of the most successful ways to engage and energize large stake-holder groups. Vendors set up samples of short-listed furniture options in the library, where stakeholders are invited to test them out and fill out comment surveys. Not only does this activity clarify furniture product preferences, but it also builds buy-in and positive anticipation for the new space.

SAMPLE JOURNEYS

No two journeys will be the same. The following three case studies illustrate how engagement strategy is mapped to culture, vision, and opportunity.

Cal Poly: Envisioning Incremental Improvements

The Robert E. Kennedy Library at Cal Poly San Luis Obispo undertook a planning process for phased improvements to the library's interior spaces that would enhance the user experience, forge connections between the library and academic partners, and develop a new special collections and archives research center. Improvements were sequenced so that renovations could be funded and implemented as a series of small projects.

The combination of a small steering committee and frequent opportunities for input was effective in defining the project and developing investment over a relatively short period of time. Large groups of stakeholders gathered for workshops formatted with ple-nary, breakout, and playback sessions over two days.

> . . . the meetings weren't so much about sitting through presentations as they were about having genuine conversations about what it's like to be the student who stays until 2AM and then migrates into the 24 hour study room . . . and how it feels walking in and knowing that there's at least one friend there who can help you out with that one finance problem. The library is both an area to accomplish learning and a home in which you identify yourself as an integral part of the Cal Poly community.
> —Student representative to the Building Program Committee[1]

The core group was led by the library dean and included the director of campus facil-ities planning, the CIO, and other key academic leadership. Library staff participated in the development of guiding principles that were used to establish project priorities. Open sessions were held to gather input from students, faculty, the community, and academic partners within the library. San Luis Obispo residents were invited to provide input on strategies for broadening community awareness of the archives' regional history collections.

The library leveraged these activities to create "buzz" about the project and to build community awareness. A widely publicized and well-attended forum in the library coffee shop included real-time social media commentary and streaming video on the library web-site. Design students rethought library space as part of a studio project, with the results exhibited in the library's main gallery.

Teachers College, Columbia: Defining a New Space Type

The planning of the Learning Theatre in the Gottesman Libraries at Teachers Col-lege, Columbia University, entailed creation of new program and space models. This proj-ect gives Teachers College a flexible "black box" learning space that can be transformed for scenario planning, immersive learning, and education research. The use of flexible furniture, lighting, technology, and space definers allows the space to be reconfigured to create a wide range of environments.

The college designated a core group of individuals who will be the program developers, funders, and end operators to define the vision and lead detailed planning. Within the college, stakeholders included trustees, donors, administrators, faculty, and graduate students. The core group developed venues for outreach to a very broad set of constituents, from potential end users of the space to a national cast of education innovators.

The core group held a series of workshops over the course of an academic year to educate the Teachers College community about the potential of this space model and to develop use scenarios. The process of defining space needs began by collecting scenarios of how the space might be used and documenting the scenarios in written narrative and videos of workshop activities. To enrich the vision development process, guest innovators, researchers, and artists were invited to share their stories and participate in the scenario development exercises. Users tested furniture and space definition strategies through gaming exercises that used scale models.

Space design planning began in earnest the following year. For a year, the core team met biweekly, on average, to ensure that the reconfigurable space and equipment toolkit would accommodate the imagined scenarios. The uncharted territory of this project called for an extended time frame to allow ideas to percolate and mature and frequent meetings to address the evolution of program and strategy.

Illinois Tech: Change Catalyst

The Ed Kaplan Family Institute for Innovation and Tech Entrepreneurship at Illinois Institute of Technology was planned with a dual role: (1) to provide interdisciplinary teaching and research space to support innovation and entrepreneurship across the campus and with the Chicago business community; and (2) to provide a new home on campus for Illinois Tech's internationally recognized Institute of Design (ID), which would be relocated from its current location downtown. The project is envisioned as a catalyst for academic growth, specifically the strengthening of interdisciplinary teaching and research activity to support innovation and entrepreneurship. In addition, the relocation of ID entails a dramatic operational and cultural shift. While this project is not a library, it shares the same central themes of the stakeholder engagement process: use of shared, flexible spaces for community, research, and learning, coupled with new academic partnerships and new technologies.

The core planning groups included a coordination team composed of six faculty and facilities leaders, who were charged with gathering input, reviewing options, and delivering final recommendations. The coordination team was a subset of a larger programming and design committee made up of 31 members of the Illinois Tech community, including students, faculty, business partners, staff, and trustees. The stakeholder engagement process included an interactive workshop format that was used to build bridges and foster creative problem solving among disparate groups. Activities that allowed stakeholders to try on user personas and visualize spatial synergies were particularly effective in defining central issues of identity, operations, and flexibility.

Individual input was sought from each of eight college deans and other key academic leaders on the implications of this shared facility for faculty and students in their respective colleges and on the potential use scenarios they envisioned. The deans' input was used to frame conversations with interdisciplinary faculty groups to further shape use scenarios and to invest faculty in the project. Students participated in interactive sessions to define space and program preferences, understand perceptions of campus spaces, and map daily activities, schedules, and paths of travel. Broad stakeholder outreach that engaged business and community leaders was seen as essential to building successful buy-in. Downtown breakfasts were hosted to seek input from and forge bonds with Chicago entrepreneurs, who are important contributors to innovation center programs.

The project completion schedule allowed a six-month window during the academic year to complete all planning phase outreach. More than 400 stakeholders were reached in this relatively short period.

TRAVELING THOUGHTS

What Should You Ask of Your Professional Design Team?

Journeying through the stakeholder engagement process in partnership with your design team is the most effective way to embed your institution's culture and aspirations in the design approach and the final results.

Building and space renewal projects require substantial commitment of institutional resources: time as well as money. Because library space projects are frequently catalysts for larger institutional change, successful projects depend on broad community understanding and support. Architects, interior designers, facility planners, and programmers can be valuable partners in shepherding the rich stakeholder engagement process that is needed to build that support.

As your design team interacts with stakeholders, ask the team to:

- Listen and play back what they hear.
- Observe and recount what they see.
- Synthesize input on activities and experiences and use it to refine program and design.
- Develop a building program that is grounded in needs-based assessment.
- Clarify spatial concepts for stakeholders: size, proportion, critical adjacencies, and movement paths.
- Inspire the crowd with compelling imagery and models that convey the ethos of the environments you want to create.
- Engender confidence in the facts by organizing comparative data and detailed information about space characteristics, performance requirements, furniture, and equipment.
- Educate your community about trends and precedents.

The Project Is Finished. Now What?

Stakeholder engagement does not end with the ribbon cutting. Change, even for the better, can be unsettling. Prepare stakeholders with realistic expectations for Day 1. Today's buildings contain complex systems and technologies that must be commissioned and adjusted. Plan to check in with primary users. Reserve some project funds for the inevitable adjustments and unforeseen opportunities that will become evident once you have occupied the new space for a few months.

Appoint a building assessment and renewal committee to monitor the user experience and shape the building program so it remains vibrant. Engage your stakeholders in a post-occupancy evaluation (POE) to inform building use strategies and your next project.

The POE should consist of a structured survey designed to gather and analyze qualitative and quantitative input from building users about how well it is meeting the project's identified goals. Comfort, functionality, and improvements to performance and service are some topics that might be addressed. Remember that successful buildings are living things: organic change and betterment are essential to keeping your facility relevant.

NOTE

1. "Student Input Is Key in Reimagining Kennedy Library," Robert E. Kennedy Library blog post, April 23, 2014, http://lib.calpoly.edu/outloud/2014/04/student-input-is-key-in-re-imagining-kennedy-library/.

4

Engaging the Services of
Design Professionals

Jack Poling

A time comes in the life of all libraries when the building no longer supports the institution's mission and day-to-day needs. In the postwar decades, American public and academic libraries enjoyed significant attention, mirroring the general expansion of the economy, urban areas, and education. As a result, library construction exploded, and libraries were built across the country to accommodate need. This period represented the first sustained library construction boom since the end of the Carnegie Library era around 1930. Thousands of new libraries were built between the end of World War II and 1975. These buildings were designed to support the traditional mission of the library—to house materials for patron checkout or use within the facility. The extent of what the library had to offer lay within its walls and in library staff expertise. These buildings have come to the end of their useful life, and the mission of the library has evolved. With the evolution of libraries becoming places for community gathering and connection to information that lies outside the building, a third American library building boom is under way.

The need for a new library manifests itself over time through the gradual breakdown in the efficiency and health of the building's systems and the inability of the building to accommodate the library's new and evolving needs. Usually, too, the building begins to appear dated and tired.

When the need for a new or renovated/expanded facility becomes critical, the library needs to embark on the process of funding, designing, and constructing a new or renovated facility. This process is foreign to many libraries (except larger systems, which often have more current building project experience) simply due to the fact that often it has been decades since the library's last significant construction project. The building process involves many aspects, and understanding the required steps helps when embarking on the long path to a successful project.

The building process involves establishing a series of milestones and a properly conceived process with careful attention paid to each stage. Once the need for a new or renovated facility has manifested itself, one of the first steps is to engage the services of a design professional to assist the library in moving forward. The following discussion outlines considerations on how to embark on the process.

In the United States, architects are licensed by each state to protect the public's health, safety, and welfare. The role of the architect is not necessarily to design great buildings, or even beautiful buildings, but to design safe buildings. The safety of those buildings is prescribed by building codes, carefully crafted over time, in response to changing technologies and legislation.

Interior designers are trained to design functional, safe, and healthy interior spaces. They provide broad expertise in understanding space usage, as well as the selection of materials, finishes, and color.

Engineers have specific expertise in building systems. Civil engineers provide site design, including parking and earth structures design and storm water management on the site. Structural engineers design the building's foundations and structure. Mechanical engineers design heating, ventilation, air-conditioning systems, and plumbing systems. And electrical engineers design the electrical systems within the building. Technology consultants are often part of the team to bring their specific expertise to the design of data systems within the building.

Landscape architects design outdoor public areas and work in conjunction with the civil engineer.

Design teams also often include a cost estimator. Sometimes construction firms prepare project cost estimates, or individuals or firms versed in the specifics of the local construction market will bring their expertise to the design team to evaluate the cost-efficiency of various systems being considered for the project.

Typically former or current library administrators, library planning consultants offer deep knowledge of library operations.

In practice, many architects and interior designers have considerable knowledge and experience with library planning and can work in multiple roles on a project. Thus, it can be difficult to know exactly who is best for the task of assisting with moving a building project forward. Often, successful teams consist of architects, interior designers, engineers, library planners, and other consultants, especially on larger and more complicated projects.

One important consideration is that if the scope of the work involves any building design work, however conceptual or diagrammatic it may be, the practice laws of most states require that work be done under the supervision of a licensed architect and licensed engineers. The practice laws of states are easily accessed and are usually stated in a straightforward manner.

In advance of design team selection, the library (or government entity) may choose to consult an architect who can help define the project scope and help write the Request for Qualifications (RFQ) or Request for Proposals (RFP) document. The architect can draw on past experience and understanding of state practice laws to give guidance on the need for architects, interior designers, and/or library planners in an upcoming project.

WHEN TO START THE PROCESS

The process of funding, designing, and constructing a building can be a very long one. Almost all public and many academic libraries are funded by a combination of public and private money, and the process of securing both can be protracted.

Public money is secured in a variety of manners, depending upon the jurisdiction of a public library's locale or an academic library's institutional affiliation. Public libraries are primarily funded by bond or millage monies, generally approved by public vote, or by a (usually temporary) sales tax increase. The process of getting a library project to the ballot takes months, sometimes, years. The science of when to go to the voters can be complicated. Attaining legal counsel will help determine the necessary steps in the process, as well as the requirements, limitations, and opportunities. Each jurisdiction has its own requirements. In general, the steps to get to a vote include preparation (for example, developing a building program, design, and budget) and navigating the legal process, promotion, and the vote. Determining a schedule is best accomplished working backward from the desired date of the vote. Consulting legal counsel or local authorities can help with the regulatory process of getting the project on the ballot. It will also require the library to set aside proper time to promote the project and generate support. A three- to six-month promotion period will allow enough time to conduct a properly conceived campaign but not too long to create attention fatigue. Given the specialized art and skill that goes into developing and launching effective promotional campaigns, libraries often hire campaign consultants who specialize in structuring and leading such efforts. The programming and design effort can also take three to six or more months, depending upon the desired depth of project development and ability of the library to make timely decisions to advance the process. It is important that attention be paid to the timing of the work. Holiday periods and summers (for academic libraries) are typically more difficult times to make meaningful progress.

The selection of a design team should be complete and in place up to a year prior to an anticipated vote for public funding. A good rule of thumb would be to start the programming and design process with nine months to a year to complete the work.

Private fund-raising also takes time. In most instances, the process of raising private funds extends to the end of the construction process and is often completed after the new building is opened. Experienced fund-raising consultants provide invaluable guidance in structuring and executing a successful campaign.

Funding for academic libraries varies greatly, depending upon whether the institution is public or private. The manner in which funding mechanisms are realized is specific to the institution, and care should be taken to understand the funding process and abide by its methods. Many academic libraries also engage in private fund-raising. Their goals and strategies are similar to those of public libraries, although the process is led by college or university advancement and administration leaders rather than consultants.

THE OWNER

The owner leads and executes the project and holds the contract with the design team. An owner can take many forms. Some public libraries are autonomous and have the authority to fund their own projects. Most public libraries are part of larger jurisdictions, and the owner, in such locales, is often the jurisdiction instead of the library. Almost always part of larger institutions, academic libraries are bound by the practice of the institution when considering a construction project.

Given that ownership of the project often has multiple organizations represented, it is crucial to convey who actually makes decisions throughout the process and who has the authority to execute the work on behalf of the governing body. Accordingly, one of the first tasks in any project is the creation of a clear understanding of the project leadership and selection committee (which often continues as the building committee).

THE DESIGN TEAM

The responding firm or team can take many forms. Teams may consist of a single firm with the necessary architects, interior designers, engineers, and planners/programmers available in-house. Teams can also consist of *multiple* firms that collaborate to pursue the project.

When considering design teams, the owner should take care to understand the makeup of the team and form an opinion about what types of teams it will consider. Expertise and experience with library projects are highly desirable, often requisite, and geographic location is a consideration. Design firms with demonstrable library experience may not be local and may come from afar to pursue work. In some cities and regions, multiple firms with ample library experience exist. It is important that libraries gain an understanding of the abilities (or lack thereof) of local firms and determine whether or not firms from out of town or outside the region will be considered. While significant in dollars, the cost of travel for out-of-town firms is usually negligible as a percentage of the total cost of completing a project. Geography should not dissuade a library from considering nonlocal firms. But in consideration of the effort put forth by design teams in pursuit of projects, a library should neither seek nor encourage responses from nonlocal firms if it is not willing to seriously consider them.

THE SELECTION PROCESS

The selection process typically consists of two phases. The first phase involves issuing an RFQ or RFP for design teams to respond to. In the case of public libraries, the RFQ or RFP is typically announced publicly on the government entity's website or through a third-party project announcement database. The second phase involves interviewing a select number of firms. Occasionally (typically a result of local solicitation regulations), the process involves three steps and includes issuing an RFQ, then RFP, and then an interview process.

On occasion, the selection process is completed in a single step, usually involving the solicitation and review of proposals, with selection made solely on the basis of the proposals received. This abbreviated process is rare, and does not afford the library the benefit of the interview process. Arguably the most valuable element of the design team selection process, interviews with a short list of firms gives the library a sense of the personality of the team and what it would be like to work with them.

SCOPE OF WORK

Effective, clear RFQs or RFPs contain as clearly articulated a scope of work as can be developed. The design team will rely on this description of the anticipated project to determine whether to pursue the project and its ability to successfully execute the project if it is awarded the work.

While development of the parameters of the project is often the product of the services being procured, it is important to give as clear a sense of the anticipated work as is possible. This scope description describes whether the project is new or renovation/expansion, the site for the project (if known), whether or not site selection will be a part of the work, the extent to which programming will be a part of the project, the anticipated size of the project (if known), the anticipated budget for the project (if known), and anticipated fund-raising assistance that will be required of the design team.

A clearly defined scope of work will assist the library in obtaining consistently constructed proposal or qualification responses and will aid the library in obtaining easily comparable responses.

RFQs and RFPs

Solicitations for design teams take two primary forms. The form of solicitation is determined in consultation with the library's jurisdiction or institution. On occasion, local law or ordinance will dictate the method of solicitation.

RFQs solicit the qualifications of responding firms or teams relevant to the anticipated project. They allow the library to learn about the composition of the team, the experience of the individuals proposed for the project, and past experience. The RFQ includes as thorough and concise a statement of the scope of the work as can be developed and the terms of the solicitation, including due date, any format requirements (for example. electronic document or hard copy, number of hard copies, or size and length of response), proposed schedule, and any legal stipulations required by the jurisdiction. The RFQ should also state clearly and in tabulated form the information being solicited, and the library should expect that responses be constructed using the same format so that qualification documents can be compared as consistently and easily as possible.

RFPs solicit responses that are more tailored to the specific project. RFPs seek all of the components of a qualifications statement plus additional information illustrating the design team's understanding of the project, approach to the project, work plan, schedule, proposed fees, and other elements that demonstrate more specifically how the design team would work with the library and key stakeholders.

Whether the library is issuing an RFQ or RFP, the library should ensure that the solicitation reaches its intended audience. Many locales have design firms with adequate library design experience to provide a local pool of good candidates. In other instances, local firms may lack this experience, and the library is well advised to look outside the immediate area. The library should take time to research other new facilities and the firms that designed them, search within library organizations and online forums for recommendations on firms of interest, and talk to other librarians about the firms they are considering to invite to respond to the RFQ or RFP. For most public library projects, the solicitation must also be announced publicly, allowing interested firms to respond.

Respect for the design firm's time is also important. Design firms need ample time to research the project, decide whether they will response, and prepare their responses if they choose to pursue it. Generally, three to four weeks is adequate time to complete the process. Less time can add stress to the project and schedule and can, in some instances, dissuade (for a number of possible reasons) qualified firms from pursuing the project.

COST

The cost of preparing a response to an RFQ or RFP can be significant. Architectural and interior design firms and library programmers who have responded to many requests often use templates to prepare a response, which allow them to build on what they have completed in the past. Other firms who have not responded to a significant number of solicitations may have to embark on a more involved process. Larger firms generally have marketing staff that work with design professionals to complete a response. In a smaller firm, the design professionals themselves will likely prepare the response.

It is important to understand and respect the effort put forth in preparing a proposal or qualification document. Firms measure their promotional time in various ways, but the time required to complete a proposal can range from a day or so of work to many days with many people contributing to the effort. Considering that the value of a design professional's time can range from under $100 to $300 or more per hour, the investment on the part of the firm can be significant. Preparation for and attending an interview are even more involved. Marketing efforts for a single library project, measured at cost (materials plus the actual cost of employees' time), can range from under $1,000 to $10,000 or more, depending upon the complexity of the response and costs. Often, travel for firms coming from afar to lend their expertise and experience is a significant cost in the pursuit of a library project.

In almost all cases, unless a design competition (rare in the United States) is undertaken, the cost of the effort is borne by the responding firm or team, and the cost to the library is solely the cost of its own effort to execute the selection process.

EVALUATING PROPOSALS

After the proposals are received, a carefully assembled selection committee will read and evaluate the proposals. The goal of evaluating the proposals is to advance the process to the final step—interviews. Ideally, the library will receive a number of proposals, allowing a level of selectivity for the interviews. The number of responses can vary greatly and is dependent upon the exposure the solicitation gets, the library's ability to contact as many candidate firms as possible, and the general workload of those firms.

The selection committee should evaluate the proposals using an objective set of criteria tailored to the project. After completing the evaluation, often using a numeric scoring system, the selection committee should discuss the nuanced, subjective aspects of the proposals and prepare a short list of firms to be interviewed. This short list ideally includes three or four firms that are unequivocally qualified to execute the project and have demonstrated abilities that are of interest to the library. The purpose of the interview is not to determine whether an individual firm is qualified.

The library must bear in mind that preparation for and attendance at an interview can be an expensive and emotionally intense effort, especially when travel is involved. Various factors can influence whether or not a firm might actually be selected and fairness should be a major factor in compiling a short list. For instance, if ample qualified local firms are interested and there is a desire to work with local firms, do not short-list firms from outside the area. Conversely, if appropriate experience does not exist locally and outside firms have been solicited with requisite credentials, do not short-list unqualified local firms.

The goal of the proposal process is to determine a short list, not a long list, of qualified firms to interview. This list can be difficult to arrive at if the library receives many qualified responses to the RFQ or RFP. But the library should exercise discretion and seek to develop a narrowly defined short list. Decisiveness in creating a concise short list conveys the message to potential design teams that the library is capable of making decisions and moving forward.

When the short list is completed, the library should contact all firms immediately and let them know of the decision. Keeping firms who have submitted proposals informed of any delays in the selection process will go a long way to ensuring a smooth, respectful process for all involved.

THE INTERVIEW

The interview is often the most interesting and most stressful part of the selection process. A small number of firms are invited to make presentations to the selection committee. Some jurisdictions require that these meetings be open to the public. The library should let the selected firms know who, on the owner's side, will be attending the interview and their roles (for example, voting or advisory).

When the short list is created, the library then contacts the short-listed firms immediately. Proper preparation and scheduling time range from two weeks at a minimum to ideally a three- to four-week time frame. Many design professionals have very busy schedules and will not able to collect their team for an interview on shorter notice. The selection schedule is laid out in the RFQ or RFP, and this schedule should allow for an adequate lead time and should be adhered to if possible.

Once this is completed, the library will develop a structure for the interview. Most interviews range from a half hour to an hour and a half and include a presentation and a question-and-answer period. Increasingly, very short presentations are requested, and the ideal interview structure allows for a complete but concise presentation followed by ample time for discussion. In general, an hour to an hour and a half works best.

The interview should not be a restating of the information included in the proposal. This time is best utilized to give the selection committee a strong sense of the nature of the individuals the committee would be working with, team dynamics, the nuances of cultural and personal qualities, and a general and largely subjective sense of how well the library would work with the design team. The structure of the interview is often as loosely organized as asking for a presentation of a certain duration followed by questions and answers. If the selection committee has specific topics it would like the short-listed firms to address, they should be clearly spelled out in the outline for the interview. Often, design teams are asked to address specific questions.

It is common for design firms to arrive at an interview with various sketches prepared or ideas ready to present. It is natural for members of a selection committee to be intrigued by the design of the project. A good presentation will include conceptual discussions of how the firm says it works, show a high level of consistency, and be insightful. If the concepts shown do not coincide with the message of the firm's process or do not clearly address the project's key issues, the meeting can become counterproductive.

QUALITATIVE VERSUS FEE-BASED SELECTION

Local or institutional guidelines often inform whether the selection of a design team is qualitative or fee-based. In some cases, selection processes are required to be fee-based, and in others, they are required to be based on qualifications. Often the actual selection is a hybrid where both qualifications and fees are considered. It is important at the outset of the project to determine and understand the selection requirements of the governing entity.

A qualitative selection process is one that considers the qualifications of a design team, as determined through the proposal and interview process, in making a selection. In its pure form, a qualifications-based selection does not require a fee proposal and the decision is independent of cost.

Fee-based selection takes into account the qualifications of a design team to successfully execute the project, but the selection is made solely on the proposed cost of the work.

In practice, both qualifications and fee are generally considered in selecting a design team, with qualifications being used to narrow the group under consideration and fees being considered to assure that a fair price is being paid for the services of the design team.

An important consideration is to shape the process to appeal to the types of firms and teams best suited to the project. For instance, for a very high-profile project with high aspirations for design and the quality, these aspirations should be apparent in the language of the solicitation. On the other end of the spectrum, some projects and owners have a much more direct, less aspirational vision for their work, or are bound by ordinance to select based on cost. This type of project will naturally attract a different type of response and likely a different type of team. Understanding the aspirations for the project and making those goals part of the language of the solicitation will help ensure that the design team responses are relevant to the project.

Ultimately, the selection of a design firm should be based on a proposal that demonstrates a strong ability to complete the project successfully, adequate directly relevant expertise, a strong interest in the project, and a strong subjective feeling on the part of the selection committee that they will work well with the firm.

COMMUNICATION

As has been noted, the effort put forth by responding teams is significant. Firms and teams pursuing projects understand very well that only one team will prevail, so failure to win the project is common and disappointing. However, that disappointment can be tempered by clear communication.

Aside from the language of the solicitation, constant and timely communication with interested design teams is respectful and appreciated. The RFQ or RFP will outline a timeline. Adherence to the timeline is appreciated, but designers understand that different factors can alter schedules. Stay in touch with interested parties and pass along information relevant to the process in a timely and immediate manner. Respect the design team's time by providing ample time for them to complete responses or prepare for interviews if the schedule does change. And, when decisions have been made, extend firms the courtesy of timely responses.

Finally, be prepared to offer some insights to the successful and unsuccessful design teams on why a team was chosen, what they did well in their proposals and interviews, and what they could have improved upon. It is difficult to receive bad news about something that involves such a significant effort. Providing the firms with constructive feedback and insights is greatly appreciated and will help them learn from the experience and improve their chances of being selected for a future project.

5

Working with the Architect

Pixey Anne Mosley

Working with an architect to turn a remodeling design from vision to detailed drawings used for actual construction is a complex, time-consuming, and iterative process. Depending on the scope of the project, this can take weeks or months to accomplish. During this time, you will be in a relationship with the architect in a role that may not be a natural one for most librarians, that of the paying client for a customized outcome. It is a different type of customer relationship than that of serving customers or engaging an information resource vendor selling a prepackaged product. This is because the purpose is to actually develop the product and will involve both creative and analytical components.

To make the relationship an optimal one, it is important to realize what the inherent motivations behind the relationship are and the expectations associated with the signed contract. Your motivation as the representative of the library is to get the best remodel possible at the lowest possible cost. Unfortunately, the current bargain-focused economy as well as DIY (do it yourself) design shows on television and tips on the Internet can lead one to think the architectural role is optional or offers support for a high degree of flexibility in the project. Individuals new to commercial-level remodeling may be taken aback at how much of the project budget goes to the architect and not understand how costs need to be actively managed during the design stages. When contracting with an architectural team, one is hiring professional experts. Their expertise is there as insurance against making bad decisions, such as taking out a load-bearing wall without reinforcing it, not providing sufficient heating or cooling to an office, overloading an electrical panel, or buying furniture or carpeting that will not hold up to the commercial-style abuse found in most libraries today. However, one should also consider why the architects want the job. It is not simply for the greater good or enjoyment working on a "library," but rather because this is their source of income and how they build a professional reputation. They hope to make a profit on the work itself and hope that it may lead to professional recognition by peers and future business, either within your library or other libraries doing similar remodels. To support this goal, architects may want to incorporate avant-garde or experimental design elements that will set their design apart from that of their peers. Consequently, there is an automatic opportunity for conflict in the design process based on these differences. Similarly conflict may occur based on how each party defines the concept of the "best remodel possible."

While a certain amount of exploration of different ideas will be a normal part of the design process, a key part of minimizing conflict and managing costs will come from having a clear idea of the desired objectives associated with the remodel, understanding priorities, and creating a clearly defined decision-making process. Each stage of the design process has opportunities for input and dialog on different aspects of the plan and for arriving at a mutual understanding of the desired vision. But unlike many processes that are cyclical or iterative, the architectural design process is more linear in nature. Each stage works almost like a funnel, starting with broad ideas and concepts, narrowing down to several different specific options that are then fine-tuned or tweaked to an end product that is used as the starting point for the next phase of design refinement. This means that trying to revisit or change major earlier decisions later in the process can lead to significant delays and increased costs. To avoid this, stakeholder involvement and the decision-making process need to be thought out carefully and are addressed in more detail later in the chapter.

UNDERSTANDING THE DESIGN DEVELOPMENT PROCESS

Understanding the design process and what decisions are implemented at each stage is a critical part of the overall success of the remodel. In this case, success is defined as ending up with a design that functionally and aesthetically matches or exceeds expectations and is completed within a reasonable time frame while staying within the defined budget. The author recognizes that this definition still allows for a significant amount of subjectivity.

The first part of understanding the architectural design process is to become familiar with the terminology often associated with the different stages. These are program design or programming, schematic design, design development, and construction documents. The actual amount of time spent on each of these stages will vary from project to project. Additionally, some architects may blend the meetings and activities in programming and schematic design into a single stage, particularly if the project seems fairly straightforward. A less-complex project with a clearly defined vision and focused scope may move through programming and/or schematic design quicker than one that is more complex with the vision that is still a bit fuzzy or where different stakeholders have varying strongly expressed opinions to put on the table. Conversely, a space remodel with complicated plumbing, electrical, environmental, or structural elements may slow down a bit during the design development and construction documents stages as these elements must be verified and incorporated into the final drawings. Each stage will have its own focus and expectations for stakeholder engagement and decision making.

PROGRAM DESIGN (PROGRAMMING)

The purpose of the programming stage is to verify and supplement the architect's understanding of the entire project as portrayed in the documents used as the basis of awarding the architectural contract. This may mean a meeting or series of meetings to clearly define the affected areas and to discuss detailed purpose, functional needs, and expectations associated with the space. The architects may produce computerized or drawn sketches of the layouts to show proximities or illustrate what will or will not fit in a space or show traffic patterns. At this point, discussions based on these sketches may be more free-form and conceptual than talking about specific finishes or furnishings. This free-form discussion and the manner in which design layouts are put in the table without a lot of detail can lead library stakeholders not to realize that decisions are actually being made as to where specific components will be located.

At the end of this stage, everyone associated with the project should agree on where the various major elements of the design will be located within the larger context of the project and how space will be assigned/partitioned for the various functional needs. For example, this is where the architect locks in whether a particular location will be used for collections, offices, instructional classrooms, or user seating. Drawings will be used to stimulate discussion rather than as a deliverable and will likely be two-dimensional layouts with simple lines for walls and furniture laid out with representative standard mono-chromatic symbols for chairs, tables, and so on. While the elements in the drawings will be proportional, they usually will not include specific dimensions or spatial calculations. Unfortunately, some individuals can find it difficult to visualize or "feel" how this will translate to a three-dimensional environment and will try to seek more definition about details, such as wall textures and colors or specific furniture pieces to better understand what is being presented. This does not mean that ideas of finishes or specific furniture styles cannot be discussed as part of this dialog but decisions on this level of detail are not made as this point in the process. If it helps stakeholders to better understand what they are seeing, it is a useful tool to apply, but with repeated emphasis that these are simply suggestions and not final.

Because the team is primarily looking at the placement of big picture elements and getting a sense of the project wish list, this is not a stage where the budget or cost estimation plays a major role. This is because the budget-related trade-offs come into play more significantly when looking at the design and construction details. For example, in constructing a wall panel, there is typically a cost hierarchy, starting from a glass and anodized aluminum storefront-style wall, then up to a sheetrock wall that goes to the ceiling grid, then up in price to a sheetrock wall with soundproofing that goes to the building structure, and then finally to a "making a statement" option, such as a high-dollar, budget-blowing electrified glass or digital display walls. This is also the stage of the project when initial space inspections should be occurring to identify if there are any environmental problems that will need to be incorporated into the next stages of the design, such as asbestos abatement or code issues such as fire alert/suppression system updates.

SCHEMATIC DESIGN

The next stage, schematic design, will take the decisions from the programming stage and begin to introduce specific design elements of the actual space. The architects will be capturing a more specific sense of the style of furnishings for different areas or types of wall finishes, such as being transparent or opaque and whether soundproofing will be needed. The drawings may start providing more of a three-dimensional representation to give the client a sense of how it feels to move through the space and give a sense of ceiling height and lighting. Often, this is where you will see the artistic "architectural renderings" created that are then used to preannounce the forthcoming project or give an overall sense of the feel of the space post renovation. This is also where significant infrastructure elements will get acknowledged as a component of the project, such as adding a raised floor for providing flexible power and network connections or a dedicated heating, ventilation, and air-conditioning (HVAC) element for special environmental needs.

During this stage, formal documents with drawings summarizing different aspects of the project are usually produced and provided to the library for feedback. That said, the drawings still will not specify all detailed dimensions or furniture details but are focused on capturing the scope and broad perspective of the remodel. As with programming, decisions are still focused on major construction elements or big picture perspective. That said, the budget does begin to be a part of the discussion in terms of preliminary cost estimates that identify major areas where it may be necessary to economize or consider trade-offs to incorporate some high-impact elements. It helps to have a sense of the budget priorities as it will help defuse frustrations and resentment of boring but necessary design requirements, such as HVAC modifications and updates. If there is an institution-level design review board, it may be necessary to provide a copy of the design for approval before the project can continue forward to the next stage of the process. This effectively locks in many of the major design elements of the layout and sets a tone for the detailed decisions coming in the next stage of the process.

SITE VISITS

Often during either programming or schematic design stages for major, large-scale designs, the architects may make arrangements or encourage members of the user team to make site visits to other libraries. There are several reasons for this activity. The first is to see the results of similar remodeling projects to get inspirational ideas for the detailed design process. A good example is a chance to try a particular type of chair or see how well a raised floor or sliding wall actually looks and feels. This also offers the opportunity to learn from other institutions about what they might have done differently in hindsight and how well the design has actually worked out. It also gives a chance for communication to move beyond the abstract in making sure the library and architect are on the same page about their vision.

However, traveling can be expensive, so a library should be careful about choosing where to send individuals to visit and make sure there are aspects about the destination that intersect with the planned remodel. For example, a library team with oversight for a remodeling project that is constrained by an older building structure or limited budget would not get as much out of a visit to the latest award-winning new construction library as they would in visiting a library that had dealt with similar older building constraints in a creative and innovate way. The other drawback of visiting an over-the-top design in a new facility is that it automatically sets one up to be disappointed with the outcome of whatever one can accomplish locally. To keep costs down, one may also want to see if one can take advantage of visiting libraries in the vicinity of American Library Association (ALA) conference venues. Many of the major players in the library architecture and remodeling world are members of ALA and send representatives to conferences to participate in discussion groups and programs. Adding a site visit to a nearby library, while already in the area, helps stretch budget dollars and could be a low-cost way to see more examples from other libraries.

Including the architect in site visits can be particularly useful if there is a design component that the architect is less familiar with, such as a specialized multimedia center, maker space, or preservation lab. It is important that whoever goes on the trip brings back pictures and notes on ideas that can be shared with others. It is also important to realize than not every model implemented at a different library is appropriate for adoption. Libraries have many different organizational structures and specific needs and expectations from users. While some decisions with respect to collections, service desk models, or operations are appropriate for transplanting, others will not be a good fit. That said, if one is taking a new and innovative approach to the design that rejects prior trends in library spaces, visiting other facilities can become nothing more than an exercise in rejecting what one sees.

DESIGN DEVELOPMENT

Often the next stage, design development, is what most people expect when they think about working with an architect. This is where the team starts digging into the details and producing drawings that reflect all the different elements of the project with detailed dimensions and beginning to provide specifications on furniture components. At this point, the architects may bring individuals from specialized fields into the project to represent design issues or concerns with different project components. For a typical extensive library remodeling project, this will include a structural engineer; someone doing audio/video/digital technology components; a team representing mechanical, electrical, and plumbing (MEP) components; an interior designer; and an official cost estimator. These specialties may be represented by an in-house person in large architectural firms or subcontracted to an independent company if the firm is small.

In addition to more detailed and extensive drawings, this is the stage of the process when detailed digital and physical vignettes get created to show how furnishings work together and to provide a three-dimensional perspective of the space to aid in effective decision making. This may include providing samples of possible finishes, such as different flooring options, or arranging for a comparison of different furniture samples. In choosing seating, it is a good idea to arrange for a furniture showroom approach where actual chairs can be seen and tried for comfort by a variety of individuals representing different size and shape needs. When choosing furniture fabrics, ensure durability by using grades defined as standing up to 100,000 rubs or higher. Though low technology, one technique to use when selecting larger furniture elements like desks, mediascapes, or "booth" style collaborative seating is to use mock-up furniture built from less-expensive materials (such as cardboard or plywood). This provides a life-sized version that lets users choose between different sized options for a desk or collaboration-seating unit. Similarly, if individuals are having difficulty getting a feel for how space is going to be partitioned, using painter's tape on the floor to outline the locations of walls can provide a sense of what will go where. Individual architects may suggest other methods for getting a three-dimensional feel for the design.

As one might assume, this is the part of the process where the decisions on the myriad of details associated with the design are finally made. This is the phase where materials and colors for finishes on walls and floors are chosen. Similarly, specific furniture styles and manufacturers are identified and pieces requiring custom design and construction are planned out. At some point, it can seem like decision overload. But it is important to make all decisions in an informed manner. This may mean needing to actually request to see a fixture, such as a faucet or light fixture, rather just accepting a list of manufacturer part numbers or see a picture of a "representative" style. This latter is mentioned based on author's personal experience of discovering once a faucet that was installed with a ridiculously short spout that barely extended out over the edge of the sink bowl and installing a light fixture that required a specific type of bulb that has since been discontinued.

Similarly, this is the phase where it becomes obvious that the cliché about not being able to please everyone becomes a stark reality. That said, one really needs to avoid decisions where no one will be pleased, and this is the point in the process where one needs to have confidence to listen to one's inner voice about concerns and speak up. Taking a wait-and-see approach with the intention of speaking up later will not work.

CONSTRUCTION DOCUMENTS

In some ways, creation of the construction documents is the most critical stage of the design process, though it can also seem to be the most anticlimactic. This is the stage when all the decisions of earlier stages are translated into highly technical drawings and specifications so that a bid can go out to make the remodel happen. In this process, the architects document every single element of the design. Accuracy is critical because the documents are a binding part of the process of hiring contractors for the actual construction. An error in the documentation can mean problems down the line in terms of both cost and delays or having to live with something that one did not want or expect. But it is anticlimactic because most of the discussion and creative part of the process is done and most of the decisions have been made.

Another aspect of the construction documents process is that trying to review the documents to make sure nothing has gone awry can be a *very* tedious task and even overwhelming as one tries to translate abbreviations or technical specifications. In many cases, one will not have the skills to actually understand all of the jargon around the MEP pages or know whether the callout for "coaxial cable to be RG-6 type with 18AWG upper center conductor and 34AWG aluminum braid wire shields" is correct. But one can look at where lighting fixtures are being installed and where telecommunication wiring is being run to make sure they are in the correct locations and that the documents indicate what will be installed and how subsequent site containment and cleanup will occur. If this is one's first time to ever see construction documents, then engage with the architect to get a crash course in reading them, or if one's local institution has an architecture department, consider approaching someone for a quick lesson in understanding how information is cross-referenced between drawings and notes and specification books. If one learns more through reading, then there are books, typically textbooks or field guides, one can use to get an introduction to architectural drawings and design terminology. One well-structured source that includes introductions to components such as walls, ceilings, and acoustic and security systems is *Interior Construction and Detailing for Designers and Architects* by Ballast. To specifically learn more about interpreting the drawings themselves and better understand issues such as how different types of walls are represented, textbooks such as *The Professional Practice of Architectural Working Drawings* by Wakita and Linde can be useful references. Some guides provide useful pictures of what an infrastructure should look like that can be helpful if one is not familiar with the interiors of walls or ceilings. An example of this type of work is the *Field Guide to Commercial Interiors* by Binggeli.

Again, it is important to speak up and ask about anything that raises a concern in your mind even as you respect the professionalism of the architect. Despite having expertise in their chosen fields, architects are as human as anyone and can make mistakes. So if one knows that prior discussions mentioned eight oversized study tables and twelve 4-person cubicle units and sees a reference in the construction documents for twelve oversized study tables and eight 4-person cubicle units, do not wait and think it can be fixed later. Speak up *now*!

ROLE OF THE ARCHITECT DURING CONSTRUCTION

Despite how many eyes look at the construction documents, for a project of any magnitude, there will be at least one mistake that is hopefully minor. This is why the role of the architects does not stop once the actual construction begins, but their role does change. The architect has three primary roles during the actual construction. One is to visit the site periodically to confirm that the contractors are following through appropriately on what was shown in the construction documents. The second is to answer questions from the contractors if there is something in the construction documents that are unclear. And finally, the third is to authorize appropriate changes to the construction drawings. This can be necessary if the contractors encounter something unexpected once they get into the space and start doing demolition. It can also be necessary if a particular finish or element is no longer available by the time construction gets to that phase of the project. It is the author's experience that this latter situation is becoming more common as manufacturers are maintaining smaller inventories and changing styles more frequently, particular for finishes such as tiles, countertops, appliances, or color matching. When this occurs, the architect will explore which comparable products are now available and work with the project team for a mutually satisfactory substitution. This does not mean that the architects will be on site every day, but rather that they will be on-call or checking in periodically, such as monthly, on a major remodeling project. This continued engagement should be clearly documented in the contract.

MANAGING STAKEHOLDER INVOLVEMENT

When working with an architectural team, bringing in other stakeholders within the organization is a delicate balancing act. It is important to acknowledge that there are significant ideas others in the library can contribute to shaping the design. But at the same time, one needs to avoid creating an end product that is such a mash-up of ideas that it brings to mind the blind-man-and-the-elephant story of "a camel is a horse created by a committee" metaphor. One must also manage contributor participation in a way that does not create confusion on the architect's part regarding whose recommendations to follow or set up a future scenario filled with "I told you so" or "if you had just done as I suggested . . ." comments.

Stakeholder engagement should actually begin well before the architectural team is even chosen. It is the nature of the culture in many libraries to want to know what is going on, even within units not directly impacted by a change or an event. For this reason, rolling out remodeling plans in library-wide meetings or with larger management teams for sharing within their units is a good way to initiate stakeholder engagement. As the remodeling or construction project rarely exists where there is an open-ended budget and everyone gets everything they might want, this is an opportunity to begin setting expectations that there will be compromises and trade-offs. One can also begin dialog on the difference between "needs" and "wants." That said, one does not want to totally squash the enthusiasm for the remodel in such a way that individuals are already disappointed before they get started.

It is also important to begin identifying who are the key stakeholders who need to play a role in the detailed design process as the "owners" of the space and will interact more closely with the architects throughout the project. There are also secondary stakeholders who will likely be the individuals working in or using the space on a regular basis and who will be able to contribute specific insights. Among these stakeholders, there will be some who are very engaged in the developmental details and others who take a more relaxed outlook. Similarly, some will tend to get bogged down in wanting to nail down the details to the final design quickly and struggle with the big picture or moving through the design process. Others will want to keep options open for consideration too long. Within this stakeholder group, it is important to discuss up front whether there are any established nonnegotiables before the design process begins. Often these may take the form of a fixed budget, defining a particular space that will be a part of the remodel, or the project scope that will describe the extent of the remodel. This scope could range from a remodeling project that is most going to refresh an area with new finishes and fixtures to a more extensive remodel that guts out an entire area of a building and rebuilds with new infrastructure and layouts in addition to finishes and fixtures.

The other critical issue to address with the stakeholders is the concept of input versus decision-making authority. This is important to clarify to the architects as well. Individuals may feel that as the future occupants or owners of a particular space, they should have final say over the design decisions. However, this can be a problem if the renovation is touching more than a single-purpose, dedicated space or if the space is actually a multipurpose one. In this case, an individual, who is usually in an administrative role, will need to serve in the role of project coordinator and balance competing priorities in distributing the limited financial or space resources associated with the project. Problems can occur if individual stakeholders start approaching the architects directly with their ideas and, in doing so, bypass the internal review and approval process. In this situation, the administrator who serves as the project coordinator needs to reinforce with the architect where and how decisions will be made and help the architect refer individuals back to the process.

CONFLICT MANAGEMENT

If a remodel was only about physical space, a discussion of conflict management would not be necessary. However, remodels are actually about how people interact within the space, and whenever people are involved, there is a high probability of conflict occurring during the design process. This can come from a variety of sources. Unless a library has an unlimited budget in an unlimited amount of space, at some point there will be limits to what can be accomplished as part of the remodel. As decisions are made on what to fund and what to not include or defer to a future remodel, some individuals will disagree. Similarly, individuals will feel that they instinctively know what the design should look like and experience frustration when it takes a different direction. Another source of conflict can come between individuals who will be occupying adjacent or shared spaces. Finally, conflicts can come about from aesthetic preferences, such as one individual wanting blue chairs and another wanting burgundy.

These differences can occur at every stage of the design process and can be expressed in a variety of ways, depending on an individual's personal communication style. Some individuals are comfortable speaking out openly about their preferences and are quick to criticize the design or others' opinions, even in open-meeting environments. Others tend to have difficulty communicating their preferences, particularly in an open-meeting environment, and want to have more private, one-on-one dialogs. While neither style is "wrong" when used inappropriately and not facilitated effectively, the former can be perceived as a bullying behavior and the latter as passive-aggressive behavior.

Although conflict is unavoidable, how it is actually managed is critical to the overall long-term success of the project. This requires being sensitive in validating the feelings and emotions of others and acknowledging openly their contributions and ideas as having value. It is also important to provide a variety of venues so that individuals will have a chance to give input. At some stages, it may be necessary to actually employ formal group facilitation techniques to prevent a small group of individuals from dominating the conversations. It may be important to lay down some ground rules for engagement to help maintain a respectful environment for dialog. Similarly, it may be appropriate for administrators or the project coordinator to coach individuals on being more effective contributors. This may include pointing out to more outspoken individuals how their remarks are being received and encourage more active listening skills or encouraging more reticent individuals to speak up at the appropriate time and be more assertive. It may also require restricting direct stakeholder access to the architect or establishing a formal channel for communicating with stakeholders that includes all project team members.

DECISION MAKING

The design phase of a remodeling project involves an uncountable number of decision-making opportunities. How decisions are reached and communicated can go a long way to reinforcing or undermining the long-term success of the overall project. Similarly, the decision making is a progressive process, with a core framework but intentional deferment on the details as the design options unfold. Some institutions actually have rules or procedures requiring certain portions of the project to have been decided before the project is even approved to proceed and limits on what can be changed during the subsequent design phases. There is some overlap between managing conflict and making decisions and underlying both is the practice of effective communication.

For this reason, it is important to share openly the rationale behind decisions as they are made or revisited. Stakeholders will be more engaged if they understand the reason for the decision, so it is important to explain the "why" behind the decision. The most problematic decisions for some stakeholders to understand are those decisions where there is not a single "right" answer but rather varying degrees of "good" with different pros and cons for each. These decisions can be the most difficult for some individuals to make and communicate and are the most vulnerable to criticism and challenge.

There is a distinct difference between questioning remodeling decisions and challenging or undermining them. The questioning individual truly seeks to understand why a particular decision was reached and will be a staunch supporter once this understanding is achieved. Sometimes this will require extra patience of engaging through one-on-one or small group meetings. It can be particularly difficult to sometimes explain decisions that are based on technical limitations, such as building foundation or structural issues or when the primary deciding factor is budget. The worst possible responses to legitimate questions that seek to understand are "because every other library is doing it this way" or "because I said so and I am the Director."

However, there are individuals in every organization who may cross the line from questioning a decision as part of the process of getting to supporting it and actually disagree with a decision to such a degree that the questioning becomes a formal challenge or venue for attacking the decision. Whatever the motivation, the situation can be particularly difficult to manage, particularly if stakeholders start bonding together or taking sides or choosing public arenas for challenging the decisions. In this situation, it will be important for administrative decision makers to present a united front and be more firm about the expectations and roles of the dissenting individuals. In these cases, ultimatums may be necessary but should be used as little as possible and should be handled separate from meetings that include the architects.

CONCLUSION

In conclusion, the process of getting from a vision for the remodeling project to formal architectural documents used to begin the construction process is a complicated one that requires developing relationships between the architectural team and project stakeholders. Depending on the scope of the project, this stage of the remodeling process can take anywhere from a few weeks to several months to even a year or more. This process requires leaders to exercise and demonstrate both detail-oriented technical skills and interpersonal skills for engaging with a wide range of people. An ability to make thoughtful organizational decisions in a timely manner and effectively communicate them is essential in order to move the project along according to the budget and timetable.

BIBLIOGRAPHY

Ballast, David Kent. 2007. *Interior Construction and Detailing for Designers and Architects*. 4th ed. Belmont, CA: Professional Publications.

Binggeli, Corky. 2009. *Field Guide to Commercial Interiors*. New York: John Wiley & Sons.

Wakita, Osamu A., and Richard M. Linde. 2003. *The Professional Practice of Architectural Working Drawings*. 3rd ed. New York: John Wiley & Sons.

6

Working with the Contractor

Pixey Anne Mosley

Living through the ups and downs of the actual demolition and reconstruction phase of a library renovation is stressful for everyone. Few libraries are in the position of closing their doors for the duration of the construction and must deal with relocated staff members and services, disruptions to user traffic patterns, and in some cases reduced or restricted access to collections. Throughout this process, the relationship that one has developed with the contractor can make a huge difference in the organization's ability to manage the stress and how effectively and efficiently unexpected events are resolved. But similar to the relationship with the architect, the relationship between paying client and building occupant and the contractor is not one that many librarians have experience in addressing. Working with a contractor may require library managers to move outside of their comfort zone in developing negotiation and other conflict management skills and learning the technical aspects and jargon of another professional area.

For a major library renovation project, the contractor's role is often more complicated than it initially appears, and understanding this complexity will improve the engagement between the librarian and the contractor. This is discussed in more detail throughout the chapter, but in simplest terms, the contractor is responsible for daily, on-sight coordination of all of the work associated with taking a project from a set of construction drawings to completion. This involves hiring various specialty trades in subcontracting roles and scheduling them for optimal efficiency, as well as lining up the plethora of inspections associated with commercial construction. Related to this, contractors manage the overall project construction budget and prepare bills and invoices that are submitted to the library. They monitor the safety and professional conduct of the various construction employees and respond to any concerns or complaints. They play a major troubleshooting role in assessing the impact of problems that can develop during a major construction initiative, some of which may require modifications to be made to the drawings by the architects. In all of these roles, they serve as the primary liaison to the library or academic institution in setting expectations, providing updates on progress, and addressing issues of concern.

Another key element to the partnership model lies in understanding the contractor's motivations for wanting to do the project and how success is defined. Just as with the architect, the underlying reason that the contractor wants to take on the project is a commercial one. The contractors want to do a good job but also expect to make a profit on the project and do work that can be a springboard to getting future work with one's institution. To this point, it is in their best interests to do a good job but in the most economical way possible. Many times, the contractor will have provided a fixed price or bid for the job, and changes or problems that lead to going over budget can cut into the contractor's profits for the job or scheduling for their next jobs following the library's remodel. Keeping this in mind can help understand why the contractor may request building access to run crews on multiple shifts or express frustration at what can on the surface appear to be unreasonable expectations in minimizing disruptions and continuing services.

UNDERSTANDING THE ROLE OF THE CONTRACTOR

There is not a single, one-size-fits-all model that describes the contractor's title and detailed responsibilities for every project, regardless of size and scope. Libraries often function within the context of a larger academic or civic institution and may be subject to rules or policies that define the general contractor role at a local level and add an intermediary to the team. For example, some larger academic institutions or city government may assign someone, often called a project manager or project engineer, from a central facilities unit to take on some elements of the contractor role. For less-complex, simpler projects, this project manager may take on all of the general contractor's responsibilities. For larger, complex renovation or new construction projects where it is appropriate to hire an on-sight general contractor, the project manager's responsibilities may include such items as lining up inspections or turning building alarm systems on or off. The project manager may also serve as an expert adviser to the library in better understanding the concerns the contractor may have and make sure the work is carried out in accordance with written, detailed institutional standards for materials and construction.

Depending on the size of the project and level of institutional oversight, there are several different types of individuals who can act in a contractor capacity. Small projects that involve a single contracted service or trade may not need a general contractor. In this case, someone from the library will work directly with the contractor from the relevant trade in defining the details of timing, scope of the work being done, and expectations of on-site workers. This sort of model is most frequently used for short-term projects involving relocations or refinishing, such as relocating furniture or stacks, repainting a wall, or replacing worn flooring through a hallway. However, for more complicated projects it will often be more appropriate to hire a general contractor. For the purpose of this chapter, complicated or complex projects are defined as those involving multiple tradespeople or work having to be done in sequential stages. This could include examples such as a bathroom remodel that will involve inspectors, plumbers, tile layers, drywall installers, painters, and general construction for installing shelving and towel dispensers, or a carpeting project in an area of the stacks that will require relocating books and shelving in order to do an abatement of asbestos in the old tile adhesive under the old carpet before installing the new carpet. Another example might be a reroofing project where the work has to be done in sections. In this kind of project, the general contractor serves as a coordinator to monitor that the multiphase plan is being followed. The general contractor hires each of the individual trades needed for the project and schedules services in a way that makes sure all the various elements get completed satisfactorily. This model also provides a single point of contact if there are questions or problems that arise or changes that must be approved, which can significantly and positively impact a project by minimizing delays or misunderstandings.

It is not uncommon, with the proliferation of DIY (do it yourself) resources available on television and the Internet, for an individual to want to bypass hiring a general contractor and redirect the funds to a more tangible and visible purpose. However, general contractors are experts at dealing with the various trades in their subcontractor roles and will prevent the library from getting cheated through the substitution of a lesser quality product or poor installation practices. Additionally, commercial construction is complicated and subject to a wide range of federal and state regulations and union rules. General contractors are expected to be familiar with these requirements and take responsibility for maintaining compliance with the various regulatory and oversight organizations.

SELECTING THE CONTRACTOR

The process of selecting a contractor can follow several different models. For smaller or independent libraries, it can be as simple as calling up local vendors, placing an order for the work to be done, and cutting a check when it is finished. However, many libraries are part of a larger academic institution or civic (city or county) governmental structure and will be subject to organizational policies in proceeding with the construction part of the remodel. This may require choosing a vendor from a preestablished list of "approved" service providers who have gone through appropriate checks on their business practices and hiring processes.

For larger projects involving multiple trades, it may be necessary to put the project out for a formal cost estimate or binding bid before the contracting process. Within this latter model, there will be different rules about how the proposals are considered. The most restrictive is when the institutional rules require one to use the lowest bid without consideration of any other factors of the proposal. However, even in this model, there are usually provisions for a second layer of protection by verifying that the estimate accurately reflects the scope and checking references on previous projects. At many institutions, the bid process will allow for a more thorough discussion of the proposals and in some cases include interviews with the individual who will be assigned to the project, particularly within the general contractor capacity. At this point, it is critically important to go over the proposal with a fine-tooth comb and make sure that it has addressed all of the appropriate details of the project. In addition to the demolition and construction activities, the proposal should include details about maintaining a safe work environment, demolition and debris removal from the premises, and any staging of the project. The last thing you want to happen is to award the contract only to discover that the contractor did not understand that portions of the building would have to stay accessible during the remodel or that the contractor was responsible for the removal of debris. If something looks wrong about a proposal, speak up *before* the contract is signed off and issued because it is usually very difficult to add expectations after the project has started.

Depending on the project and the geographical location, construction bid pricing may be similar or vary widely. It is important to be wary about bids that stand out as unusually low or unusually high. In some cases of high bids, one is actually paying for the "reputation" of the contractor. Just as name brand groceries or pharmaceuticals are more expensive than store brands or generics, going with a standout trade or contractor who is highly known in the region or even nationally may be more expensive. In a related way, vendors who are trying to break into an area or is in the process of building a reputation for work at the institution may actually take a reduced profit margin for the visibility of the project and getting their foot in the door. As a consequence, so long as they have not underbid to the point of overextending their resources, these vendors may actually be more committed to doing a good job than those who have become complacent as the routine "go to" resource. It is important to make sure that the contractor understands the full scope of the project and to verify that he is not proposing the substitutions of lower-grade products or that he plans to cut corners in other ways.

ESTABLISHING EXPECTATIONS

Once the contractor(s) is selected and agreements detailing the major aspects of the remodel are signed, it is important to engage with the contractor during the construction phase of the remodel as the success will often lie with the details. It is important to keep in mind that parts of the library are about to become a construction zone and it will not be possible to do every "noisy" or disruptive job when the building is at minimal occupancy. Along the same line, contractors can sometimes accomplish an impressive amount of progress when the library is actually closed to the public, but this may require higher costs to accommodate second- or third-shift wages. The following sections detail some areas to explicitly address with the contractors early on in order to save everyone later headaches.

MANAGING DELAYS

Construction ALWAYS takes longer than it feels like it should. There are numerous reasons that timelines slip on remodeling projects, and in most cases, there is absolutely nothing that can be done about the delay. The sources for delays will typically fall into two different categories: material resources and/or labor resources.

Material resource delays come into play when one has an unexpected wait for equipment or parts or furnishings. One aspect of the global economy is that something happening halfway around the world can affect the progress of one's local project. An example of this might be a lighting retrofit that gets delayed waiting for electronic motion sensors backordered from a country with political or military turmoil. Weather can also be a factor, such as in the case of a furniture shipment that is delayed because of severe disruption to shipping lanes by a major hurricane. Delays can also come from discovering a particular product or finish specified by the architect is no longer available and a new replacement product has to be identified and ordered. More manufacturers are not maintaining a deep inventory of materials but have instead gone to a manufacture-on-demand model that requires longer lead time between receiving an order and delivering the finished product. This can affect everything, including carpeting, fabric, furniture, countertops, or cabinetry.

Labor resource delays occur because at certain stages of any remodeling project, one is likely to be competing against other projects in the area for a limited pool of individuals with a particular expertise or certification. For example, during some remodels, such as updating an elevator system, there are several points where official inspectors have to review the work and give approval for the next stages to continue. It can sometimes take several days to get this scheduled and accomplished. To others watching the project from the outside, it appears that the progress has stalled for no apparent reason. One can also run up against institutional priorities or politics in the assigning and pulling of resources. This occurred to the author when the institution decided that the president's house on campus needed repainting prior to the arrival of the new president at the same time that the region was experiencing an unusually wet, rainy spring. This meant that on every sunny day for approximately a month, ALL painting crews on any project around campus were moved to the president's house project. But this meant that individual smaller projects experienced delays and missed their own deadlines.

When encountering delays like these, nothing is accomplished by getting frustrated or angry or taking it out on the contractor. Instead, one has to learn to laugh at the situation and maintain a sense of perspective. But it is important to establish up front with the contractor the planned timeline for the project and milestones to watch for in gauging the actual progress. The key to managing the frustration caused by delays is to understand the reasons behind them and be able to communicate this information appropriately to stakeholders living within or displaced by the construction zone. For this reason, one should establish expectations on receiving updates if something unplanned is occurring. However it is important to keep expectations reasonable and not to go overboard in trying to micromanage the project and expect daily progress reports. A good rule of thumb is to ask for and expect an update if something is more than a week off of schedule or if work ceases for a week or more. This also provides an opportunity to praise and express appreciation to the contractors when they reassure you that they have already looked at the timeline and are working on how to get back on schedule.

SAFETY EXPECTATIONS

Another aspect of undergoing construction that will need to be clarified with contractors is how the staff and public will be kept safe during the completion of the work. Depending on the particular project, this may be a simple and straightforward process or a very complex one. Maintaining a safe environment is the responsibility of everyone, and it is important to encourage both the library staff and the contractor to watch for unsafe practices and report them appropriately through predefined channels so that issues can be addressed with appropriate managers or contractors.

For some projects, safety issues are less complex and simply involve such issues as restricting access to the construction area, transporting construction materials in or transporting demolition debris out through a staff or public space, and making a material data sheet available for paints or cleaners being used. With the increase in environmental concerns and restrictions, such materials have become less hazardous and usually will only require special accommodations for staff members with a high level of medical sensitivity such as being pregnant or having a compromised immune system. This does not mean that there will not be complaints at an odor being unpleasant, but that the odor itself does not create an unsafe environment or represent a health hazard. If they know that some components of the work will be noxious or particularly noisy, contractors should expect to provide additional information and cooperate with institutional safety officers if needed to calm staff fears. Similarly, it may be appropriate to set aside funds to purchase earplugs or other hearing protectors and dust masks for those individuals who wish to use them.

Safety issues on larger remodels can be very complicated, particularly if they involve large areas of space that include or are adjacent to high-traffic areas or involve toxic materials. When addressing adjacency, the use of caution tape on a project that is taking more than a few days will become ineffective at keeping people out. In this situation, it may be necessary to put up more substantial barricades of fencing or polyvinyl sheeting to protect against trespassing into the construction envelope. Concerning issues of mold or asbestos removal, the best thing to do is to bring in an outside expert and hold open question-and-answer sessions that will allow individuals to be engaged in a fact-based discussion. These experts can come from an institution's larger oversight office for health and safety or from local government representative that monitors and conducts inspections and can describe the actual risk associated with the work and efforts that will be taken to protect everyone's safety. It may still be necessary to plan for the identification of some on-site alternate work locations that are removed from the proximity of the construction area for the handful of employees who cannot move past the fear-based mind-set. Administratively, this is a better long-term option than creating a precedence of allowing an individual to simply work from home on the basis of construction zone anxiety.

Another aspect of safety that must be established with the contractor deals with the situation where a space, closed off to the public, must remain accessible for library employees. This could include situations such as having to page items for users when the project limits public access to the stacks or where staff members must go through the construction zone to get to their offices. In the former case, there should be a way to clearly identify the library employees in the space. One good option is the use of a particular color of safety vest. It is also important that staff be attired appropriately; often this requires closed-toe shoes and long pants as opposed to shorts and sandals. For the administrator who has a role in the project oversight, it is a good practice to keep at hand a change of shoes or and protective footwear in addition to one's own safety vest, hard hat, and so on. To aid staff access through the construction zone, the contractor should use signage, caution tape, and even temporary barricades to define a pathway and clearly communicate to staff members that they are to stay on the path, in which case safe attire is less critical. One key to maintaining safety standards is to empower and support the contractor to evict anyone from the space, public user or library employee, if they are not following protocol.

One last safety issue to discuss with the contractor is accountability of the crew to model safety practices while in the presence of or visible to any library employee. It is a common practice that employees who are engaged in construction every day can get a little casual about some safety measures, such as making sure someone is holding a ladder before getting on it or standing above the "Do Not Stand" rung. However, it does represent an increased risk to the project and undermines confidence that the construction crew is doing a good job. As the internal point person, the library's administrative project coordinator will quickly hear about it, often from multiple individuals. For this reason, one should establish with the contractor what the reporting mechanism should be for the issue to be addressed promptly and the construction employee to stay compliant with the safety protocol.

SIGNAGE

It is important to clarify with the contractor who is responsible for updating signage relating to the construction. It is best to let the contractor be responsible for all signage that establishes the perimeter of the construction zone, either through caution tape, plastic barriers, or temporary walls. Similarly, signage designating the terms of occupancy in the construction zone in context of safety equipment such as hard hats, hearing protection, or respiratory masks should also be the responsibility of the contractor. However, the library is generally better able and equipped to anticipate the signage needs for library users and redirect them to the appropriate resources. In addition to signs, a library may want to develop an explicit marketing and communication strategy for getting out the information about the disruptions due to construction to users before they arrive at the library. This can be done through bulk e-mails, social media, periodic updates on the library and institutional websites, and so forth. However, it will be important to emphasize accuracy and build in with the contractor sufficient lead time to implement the communication strategy and create official looking signage.

WORK SCHEDULES

It is important to establish up front when construction employees are expected to be in the building. Few library projects have the budget to employ around-the-clock or nighttime-only construction work. That said, there may be some phases of the project that lend themselves to working an evening or double shift schedule to get specific tasks accomplished within a particular window of time. When this occurs, the contractor should be held as the accountable party for the security of the building and collection. This means giving him or her the access to bring the construction employees into the building but not providing key or swipe card access to each individual construction employee. Where possible it is best to accommodate schedule adjustment requests from the contractor. In addition to executing the project in an efficient manner, it puts one in a better position to ask for later trade-offs, such as not allowing any loud construction during the period immediately prior to and during final exams.

TIME-SENSITIVE DECISION-MAKING

No matter how thorough the planning activities associated with the remodel are, there will always be something that happens that will require a decision to be made within a tight timeline. Just as with emergency planning and building evacuation drills, it is important to define the emergency decision-making process during the early stages of the project before it is actually needed. This aspect of construction is also why most contractors will want to set aside a portion of the construction budget for a contingencies line. For most minor changes, this budget line will be sufficient to absorb the unexpected problems and make the decision-making process easier. If contingency funding is not fully utilized during the project, unused amounts can go toward a few extras at the end of the project, such as purchasing some carpet squares for future replacement of stained areas or artwork for additional decorative elements. When making any decisions that add to the cost of the project, it is critical to document them appropriately. For schedule changes, this may simply require an e-mail confirmation of the request. For changes with significant budget impact, one may need to work within an online system such as IMPACT or E-Builder and register the approval for the change as part of the formal project documentation.

Some decisions will actually need an immediate or extremely short turnaround of few hours. However, these decisions are likely to be fairly minor ones that do not need a significant level or engagement with stakeholders. Typical examples might be a request from the contractor to continue working a longer schedule, keep a crew working across a weekend in order to get through a particular task, expand the construction envelope a little further than expected, or receive approval to proceed to the next phase earlier than anticipated. In this case, the decision is primarily reached by the administrative project coordinator.

Other decisions will need a response to the contractor within a short timeline, between a few days and a week, and offer more opportunity for consulting with key stakeholders. Examples of this might be when a particular color of countertop or tile is no longer available and the architect offers two or three options for substitutes. Another example could be where the construction is proceeding and during a walk-through everyone realizes that something small but important was overlooked in the construction drawings, such as door stops, corner guards, or book truck bumpers/standoffs for walls. In these cases, one does not have the luxury found in the earlier architectural design phases of canvassing a large group of stakeholders for their opinions and negotiating for consensus. But one should have time to take options and samples to designated stakeholder representatives and bring them into the decision-making process in choosing the design elements.

Finally, some decisions may be more complex with greater impact on other aspects of the project. An example of this may be the discovery of an unexpected source of asbestos within the construction envelope, previously undetected damage, or violations of updated building codes. In these cases, one generally does not have the option of ignoring the issue and hoping that it goes away or just closing the door and pretending it is not there. Often, the "surprise" must be addressed for the project to proceed and initial approval given but the budget shortfall must be made up somewhere else in the renovation project. In this scenario, one is more likely to have time to bring the issue to more of the stakeholders and engage in dialog on how to approach the necessary adjustments. This may mean having to choose more economical finishes or defer the purchase of some accessory items that could be added later as new funds are made available in the future. Generally, it is easier to eliminate something from a project than to take steps that require the architects to come back into the picture to make major changes to the official plans or documents. However, depending on when the shortfall is identified, the options on what can be eliminated or changed may be limited because of ordering lead times and cancellation/restocking penalties.

CONCLUSION

In conclusion, providing service and working through a major remodeling experience are not generally classified as "fun." But the hope is that the improvements associated with the end result will make the memory of the discomforts fade quickly. In getting there, one key to creating the best possible construction experience lies in establishing clear and open communications with the contractor toward the accomplishment of the shared vision established in the construction documents. Another key is to clearly establish the decision-making process for addressing, documenting, and communicating minor and major changes through the course of the remodel.

7

Library Programming

Daria Pizzetta

Library planners and architects say they *program* libraries. This is often a confusing statement for librarians because library programmers do not determine what classes, lectures, or other programs occur in the library, nor do they determine collection needs. *Programming* refers to decisions made about the spatial needs of the facility being designed or renovated. A successful program will weigh the variables of cost, quality, and quantity in a building project and will manage expectations so that a list of priorities can be established. When properly done, a library building program will provide adequate information to develop a statement of probable hard costs that can be used, along with the building program, to inform the administration or the community as to the vision and the cost of a new or renovated library building. It can also provide valuable information when selecting a new building site, if not already identified.

If you are thinking of doing a building project, consider attending the American Library Association annual conference and follow the building track. Both the Library Leadership and Management Association and the Public Library Association sponsor informative programs at annual conference on building library facilities. These programs are presented by design professionals, architects, interior designers, and library planners, along with their library clients, and offer a balanced perspective. Attending these programs can inform you about the process and results of good planning.

A good way to kick off the programming process is through a benchmarking trip. Visit other libraries, especially newly constructed or renovated facilities, and see what spaces and building systems they have incorporated into their plans. Ask the librarians about their experience with the building process and what they would change, if they could. Remember too that some of their decision may have been made years ago. Document your visit with photographs or by videotaping your tour. Keep notes on what you like about each library and more importantly about what you do not like. It is also wise to ask about building costs and the overall project budget, which will include costs such as land acquisition and professional design fees. The contractor's schedule of values for a building project, if available for comparison, can be a tool for evaluating how your budget might be applied and what elements of the building are most costly.

The first meeting between the library design committee and the programmer should be an information-gathering session, not a public presentation of findings or ideas. Whether this is a new building or a renovation project, it is helpful to provide the following documents to the library programmer during the initial meeting:

- Plans of your existing facility
- Departmental lists
- List of collections and collection counts
- Current seating counts by type: reader seating, lounge seats, computer stations, group meeting rooms
- List of staff positions
- Current list of all events that take place within the library facility (classes, lectures, meetings, study group schedules, and so forth)
- Door count and circulation statistics
- Operating hours
- University or state guidelines that mandate space per students or patron
- University or municipal guidelines for material and systems requirements
- Land survey of selected site if available (this is for a new building project only)

Programmers often distribute questionnaires to the library administration, staff, and selected patrons to solicit facts and opinions on the operations and needs of the library. Programming questionnaires focus on the three major spatial groupings within libraries: patron areas, collection areas, and staff areas. The responses to the questionnaires should be compiled and evaluated so that common ideas and concerns are documented.

In lieu of questionnaires or for smaller facilities, it can be sufficient to interview the library director. At a minimum, the programmer should gather the following information, prior to any committee workshop or presentation:

- What population will your library serve? Is the population growing or declining?
- Are you a stand-alone facility or part of a multibranch system? If so, are you the main facility? How does this facility fit into a multicampus/multibranch system?
- Whom do you see as your peer institutions? What is it that they provide that you would like to duplicate?
- What is your projection for collection needs? Is your collection growing or declining? Is the format of the collection changing so that it affects your library's spatial needs? Will there be materials stored off site?
- What technology needs are anticipated?
- What are your group meeting needs?
- What is the culture of the library?

Furnished with this general information, the programmer can prepare for the first workshop with the design committee. Workshops are full-day or multiday hands-on work sessions in which each group is asked questions about their goals and visions for the library spaces and is presented with the programmer's findings and recommendations. These sessions are invaluable in gaining consensus, ensuring that differing points of views and priorities are discussed and resolved early in the planning process.

BIG PICTURE ISSUES

It is important that the programmer act as the leader in guiding the design committee to understand the big picture issues. What is the reason for a new building or a renovation? Is there an overarching deficiency that needs to be addressed? Has the building simply outlived its usefulness and can no longer provide the infrastructure to support modern technology, protection for the collections, and gathering spaces for patrons? Is this a project that will allow for expanded square footage or that will be kept within a limited building envelope?

Develop the project goals, identify what are the most important services for the library to provide, and delineate what the library can do better. Define what message about the value of the library on your campus or within your community the program can highlight. If this were an "elevator speech," could you easily give five responses to the statement, "The building we plan and design must _____."

Three of the most important issues that the building program must establish include right sizing the building, creating flexibility within the building envelope to accommodate change (and this include advances in technology), and planning for energy efficiency.

RIGHT SIZING

Everyone wants to see his or her facility built to be right-sized. If there is too much space, you will have problems filling it, and the library will not seem welcoming, not to mention the problems with upkeep. If there is too little space, you will have to make concessions as far as the events held at the library and the size of your collections. As part of the spatial programming exercise, it is important to create a sample schedule for a year's activities at your library. This will help to determine the types and numbers of classrooms, program spaces, and meeting rooms that your library will need. Create user scenarios that follow patrons through a typical day at the library. Scenarios will help the programmer and the committee understand the frequency of patron visits, the duration of patrons' stay, and how patrons circulate through the library.

Insist that your library programmer provide sketches showing how each room can be configured and reconfigured, how furniture and equipment will be placed, and how people and materials circulate through each space. Visualizing the use of each space and its many configurations will confirm that it is the appropriate size. These program sketches should be reviewed with the committee and also other members of your staff, as one group may observe a potential alternate use or flaws in how each space is set up.

To properly plan for your collection, the programmer will need an accurate count of your materials. If you are planning to weed the collection, especially getting rid of obsolete media formats, this is the time to do so. Determine what formula will be used to calculate your book stack capacity. In an academic collection, allow 1½" per book, while in a public library 1" per book is sufficient. A children's department uses ½" per book to calculate its collection needs. Also, calculate the desired openness on your shelves. On opening day, the shelves should not be crowded, but contain space so that there is room for growth. The programmer will also wish to discuss with you the various options for shelving sizes and the appropriate aisle widths for your book stacks.

FLEXIBILITY

Over the course of the life of your building, you will at some time want to move collections, reconfigure spaces, or modify technology. The initial building program can anticipate change by building in flexibility. The programmer should present options for the inclusion of a raised floor system that will allow you to easily relocate power/data outlets and their associated cabling and underfloor air distribution systems. While wireless computer network (Wi-Fi) has solved the issue of needing to include hundreds of data port throughout a library, electrical power still requires somewhere to plug in, and a raised floor system is key to providing this flexibility. It is also important to plan for oversized conduits and panel boards for the support of technology. Flexibility needs to extend to thinking about both the walls and the furniture. Consider how many of your walls need to be solid partitions and if any of your programs can be held in open spaces or segmented by open movable wall systems or simply surrounded by book stacks. The furniture that supports collaborative areas, learning commons, and classrooms should be considered as a kit of parts that can be easy assembled into new configurations. It is important to understand the difference between spaces that require scheduling and spaces with a single purpose. Some committees may approach developing group spaces as if selecting from a Chinese menu. Instead of working from the assumption that a certain number of group spaces are needed, the programmer instead should examine how to schedule group spaces for their maximum use. In an academic library, spaces used for classrooms by day can become study labs or collaborative work areas by night. In a public library, group study rooms can host morning book clubs, after-school tutoring, and collaborative study groups at night. The importance of projecting schedules for all spaces cannot be overemphasized, as it will lead to providing flexible right-sized space.

Further to understanding how spaces should be scheduled, you also must review your policies on the use of these spaces by the patrons. If you have no written policy on the use of group spaces, this is the time to develop one. Establish the limit of the number of times one group can meet per month or week. Outline your policy for a reservation system or first-come- first-serve rules. Determine if there will be a charge for the use of the space and if there is a difference in payment for not-for-profits versus for-profit uses in a public library. If meeting space is to be accessible to the public when the library is closed, the programmer will need to know this, as it will affect its placement when adjacency diagrams are developed. Will rooms be reserved for specific age groups even when those age groups are in school? What is the library's quiet use policy? As abstract as this may sound, these decisions affect space size and flexibility.

Establish how the largest meeting room will be used. What is the frequency of use for this room? Is there an alternate place for meetings or presentations of this size within the community? If you determine that you need an auditorium, the program will outline how much theatrical equipment, lighting, sound, and AV systems will be needed. Can your children's department use this space for puppet shows, or will the intimacy of that experience be affected?

ENERGY EFFICIENCY AND SUSTAINABILITY

The building program should define whether the building project will seek a Leadership in Energy and Environmental Design (LEED) rating and to what level. Silver, gold, and platinum are the levels of certification. Regardless of seeking a LEED rating, as stewards of the earth for the next generation, every effort should be taken to make the building as energy-efficient and sustainable as possible. Many municipalities now require LEED ratings for projects of certain budgets, while many universities embrace sustainability on a policy level. To meet today's building codes, the heating, ventilation, and air-conditioning (HVAC) system and building envelop must adhere to strict energy consumption and thermal resistance guidelines. The program should define the various methods for energy efficiency such as the use of air-lock vestibules, the solar orientation of rooms that require natural lighting, and methods for reducing power usage (the use of occupancy sensors, the R-values of exterior walls, etc.). The program should define a variety of sustainable options such as the use of recycled and natural materials and options for the use of geothermal or photovoltaic power systems. Even at this early stage, the program document can be used to project the LEED rating that can be obtained by including a preliminary evaluation of the LEED points system. (For more on sustainable design, see Chapter 9.)

WORKSHOPS

After the benchmarking visits and the initial information session, four workshops are needed with the committee to complete a programming exercise. A sample agenda of points to cover in each workshop is outlined in the listing below.

Workshop 1: Understanding Your Needs
- Discuss needs, objectives, and project goals.
- Report on information gathered from the programming questionnaire.
- Discuss benchmarking visits and observations.
- Define all activities that will take place within the library.
- Define environmental and sustainable goals.

Workshop 2: Program Definition
- Develop a written program, including all charts, diagrams, and schedules.
- Define area dimensions of spaces and discuss flexibility of layouts.
- Establish specific mechanical/electrical/plumbing, technology/AV and acoustical needs.
- Review site evaluations and context.
- Discuss project budget.

Workshop 3: Program Refinement
- Update program charts and data.
- Confirm program; build a consensus.
- Review space diagrams.
- Review alternatives for accommodating program.
- Develop cost model.

Workshop 4: Design Options
- Illustrate space planning and internal functions of building using adjacency diagrams.
- Develop building and site options, or internal layout test fits.
- Prepare conceptual project cost estimates.
- Evaluate options and select the most desirable one.

VISUAL TOOLS

Each programming workshop will utilize slightly different visual tools. Generally, workshop one will utilize idea boards and photographic images. However, the remaining tools used to conduct workshops consist of program boards illustrating each of the potential spaces within the new or renovated building, study models that convey three-dimensional ideas about the size and shape of rooms, massing models that explore options for the general layout, and massing of the facilities, as well as its orientation on the site, if a new building. Cost models delineating total project costs and photographic image boards conveying the character and qualities that may be achieved in the library should also be provided for detailed review and discussions. These tools help the programmer and committee to communicate and explore various programmatic options. This level of information is extremely beneficial in the initial stages of a project in order to ensure that the program accurately depicts the pragmatic, aesthetic, and financial aspirations of the library.

THINKING IN BLOCKS OF SPACE

As mentioned earlier, library buildings can be thought to contain three types of spaces: patron space, collection space, and staff space. A building program should be organized to group like spaces together and/or be organized by departments, but there needs to be further subsets to outline the needs within each group. For instance, patron spaces will include not only all reader seating areas but also spaces for group activities such as meeting rooms, group study rooms, lecture rooms, or auditoria. Contemporary building programs now include maker spaces, best described as laboratories for creative activities where collaboration and socialization can occur while working on digital, art, and technology projects.

A perfectly programmed library achieves a balance among patrons, collections, and staff spaces. Not long ago, this was done by using a formula of thirds. However, as library service models began to change as a result of advances in technology, trends to provide expanded community programs, and economic cutbacks, this formula is no longer applied. This is why each campus and community requires an in-depth study to determine its needs.

PATRON SPACES

When considering patron spaces, think of the variety of seating choices you can provide. Library users like choice. They should be offered areas within the library that provide traditional reader seats with large table areas for spreading out materials. They should also be offered study room for small groups and collaborative learning, and comfortable lounge seating, even somewhere to put their feet up. Think about how patron seating will be placed throughout the library. Will there be a large formal reading room or will seating areas be dispersed based upon a department structure or coordinate with material locations? At this point, the library should develop a policy on its technology and computer usage, much like the one needed for the use of meeting spaces.

The provision of appropriate seating and service areas is necessary in all libraries. However, academic libraries require specialized accommodations. These include research rooms, group meeting rooms, group study rooms, language labs, and private study carrels. By attending to these needs, the architectural design can greatly assist researchers with their academic pursuits. Finally, the academic library's extended schedule of hours results in the need for improved nighttime lighting, both in the interior and the exterior and, at times, increased security measures and continual climate control for patrons.

Other patron areas to consider include lobby space, display areas, food services, and toilet facilities for patron use. Define the process of how patrons will check out and return borrowed materials, as this affects the spaces provided for both the patrons and the staff.

COLLECTIONS SPACE

A general trend within collections is to provide fewer books that circulate more frequently. The programmer should ask about the impact of eBooks, online access, and subscription-based services to understand if the library can decrease the size of its collections. Academic libraries still must coordinate the need for multiple copies of books with the university's curriculum. Another trend to discuss is the use of lower-height shelving units. Lower book stacks improve sightlines and give staff better visual control of the library. Lower book stacks also allow natural light to penetrate further into the library. Both of these strategies will impact your square footage needs. (For more on lighting, see Chapter 10.)

If the library contains any special collections, government documents, or collections with unusual formats, the programmer must know this. Special collections areas have growth potential and have the most stringent requirements for security, temperature, and humidity control. Periodicals require specialized storage units, while other collections may require folio shelving units or file cabinets for nonprint collections. Dimensions for such units vary greatly and the proposed shelving or storage units must be outlined in the program document.

COMPACT SHELVING CONSIDERATIONS

Libraries occupy large and valuable real estate on campuses and urban areas. More and more institutions are considering how to house lesser-used books, freeing up valuable space for their expanding patron space needs. A program exercise should evaluate if remote storage of lesser-used materials would benefit the campus or community. Another consideration should be if any part of the collection could be stored on compact shelving units. If so, consider if these items will be accessed by staff only or if your users will need to access this material. Who has access to the compact storage units will determine the complexity of operation of the compact units, their placement within your building, and their height. It is generally recommended that compact units only be accessed by the staff, but can be used in limited quantities for open collections, such as government documents. The weight of compact units is also a determining factor to their placement. Compact storage units require structural reinforcement to support their weight, as their load is twice that of standard book stacks.

STAFF SPACES

Librarians are usually so focused on public service and what they can deliver for the users that the last spaces to be considered (and the first to be reduced) in a building program tend to be the staff areas. Build for the future staff, not the present one. This includes building for new patron-oriented service points, not big hunkering service desks. The most current staffing models liberate librarians from behind their desk and allow them to circulate throughout the library, providing assistance. Do not tether the staff to a single service point; position them in movable, adaptable service desks throughout the facilities.

To correctly provide for staff spaces, it is important to know what is called for in your employment contracts. Is there an agreed to office size for each of the librarian classifications? Are there other contractual requirements for staff lounges, pantry areas, lockers, or toilet facilities? You should also consider where staff meetings would be held. For a large staff, is there an adequate meeting room where you can gather as a group?

Libraries must address the needs of their staff by providing well-designed workspace, ergonomically correct workstations, and proper environmental conditions. The staff should determine whether they would work most efficiently if placed together within one large workroom or divided into departmental offices. An open plan layout provides for easy interdepartmental communications, the sharing of equipment, and the efficient flow of materials. Staff spaces should be planned so that all staff members have access to windows, acoustics have been considered, and a balanced HVAC system provides pleasant work environment.

THE BUILDING PROGRAM DOCUMENT

A thorough building program is used as by all building consultants, including the engineering team, to determine what systems and equipment go into a building. Think of this as your architect's and engineer's road map through the project and also as a checklist to evaluate the success of the planning efforts when the building is completed. Simply providing a list of rooms and their square footages is not a thorough program. A thorough building program outlines the type of mechanical, electrical, and technology systems that are to be included in the building's design. It outlines the temperature and humidity controls for each space, its security system, and the type of fire suppression system. The program should also include a preliminary evaluation of the applicable codes for the building's location and an evaluation of the LEED rating (or sustainable goals) if the building is seeking one. A sample table of contents is provided in Figure 7.1.

PROGRAM DATA SHEETS

A common method for documenting the individual requirements of each room is to utilize a program data sheet. The program data sheet will identify a room's name and uses, primary adjacencies, interior characteristics and finishes, mechanical and electrical needs, and furniture and equipment needs. The program data sheet is used as a checklist during the design process to assure that the library's specific requirements are being met. The program data sheet is a necessary item for developing a statement of probable cost, as this is the document that defines the interior finishes. The program data sheet shown in Figure 7.2 is a good outline for defining the details of each room.

Written descriptions, known as narratives, should be developed to outline the needs of site development, parking, building elements, structural assumptions, mechanical/electrical/plumbing and fire protection requirements, technology requirements, AV, security, acoustics, and environmental goals, along with a furniture budget. These narratives can then be used to start discussions with your board, your community, and your municipality or university as to the functions of your desired building, as well as the cost and timeline for completing your project. The programmer should have the support of qualified engineers to outline these requirements.

CODE EVALUATION

Even at this early stage, the architect will be able to determine the likely building code requirement for your building. This outline should be included within your final program document. Your local officials interpret all codes, so you must first determine which national, state, and local codes apply to your project. You will want to know which occupancy and fire protection classification will be applied to your building. This classification will be influenced by the size of your building, the number of floors, and the adjacency to

Space Program Table of Contents

1.   **Introduction**
     Overview
     Process
     Participants

2.   **Space Program**
     Patron Spaces
     Collection Spaces
     Staff Spaces

3.   **Program Criteria**
     Overview
     Detailed Room Criteria

4.   **Critical Relationships and Adjacencies**
     Bubble Diagrams
     Stacking Diagrams

5.   **Planning Criteria**
     Aesthetics
     Adjacency and Circulation
     Barrier Free Access
     Mechanical/Electrical/Plumbing/Fire-Protection Systems
     Automation
     Theater System Requirements
     Security
     Acoustics
     Floor Loading
     Signage
     Applicable Codes

6.   **Finishes, Furniture and Fixtures**

7.   **Appendix**
     Preliminary Code Analysis
     Preliminary Zoning Analysis
     Phasing Diagrams
     Bibliography
     Drawings and Renderings

8.   **Cost Information**
     Statement of Probable Cost
     Preliminary Furniture Budget
     Preliminary Equipment & Soft Cost Budget

Figure 7.1   Sample Program Table of Contents. Used with permission from Daria Pizzetta, H3 Hardy Collaboration Architecture.

other structures. The building codes will determine everything from the number of toilet fixtures to the number of fire stairs in your building. The classification will influence the building materials you use, especially in the exterior walls and fire partitions. It is important that these needs are outlined in your building program as they will affect your gross square footage and potentially the building's construction cost.

IDENTIFICATION

ROOM NAME	ROOM #	PROGRAM CATEGORY

SIZE

# OF ROOMS REQUIRED	# OF OCCUPANTS	NET AREA (SF)	SPECIAL HEIGHT NEEDS

SPECIAL REQUIREMENTS

PREFERRED DIMENSIONS

USE

PRIMARY ACTIVITIES   SECONDARY ACTIVITIES

FREQUENCY
DAILY
CONTINUOUS
INFREQUENT
_____ / DAY WK   OTHER
MO   YR

ACCESS
24 HOUR
PUBLIC
SERVICE
OTHER

RELATIONSHIPS

ADJACENCIES   PROXIMITIES

FLOOR LEVEL LOCATION   ISOLATION
B   1   2   3   EVERY SOUND   YES   NO
VISUAL   YES   NO
SPECIAL REQUIREMENTS

CHARACTERISTICS

CEILING HEIGHT	CEILING FINISH	FLOOR FINISH	WALL FINISH	ACOUSTIC TREATMENT
8'-10'	ABSORPTIVE	WASHABLE	WASHABLE	NOISE
10'-12'	TRANSPARENT/REFLECTIVE	SEALED CONCRETE	PAINT	NOISE GENERATOR
12'-14'	ACOUSTIC TILE	CARPET	TACKABLE SURFACE	NOISE SENSITIVE
15'-18'	DRY WALL	VCT	DRY WALL	MINIMAL
VARIES	SKYLIGHT	WOOD	ACOUSTIC PANELS	MEDIUM
OTHER	EXPOSED	CERAMIC TILE	CERAMIC TILES	HIGH
	SHAPED	SPRUNG	GLASS	ACOUSTICAL DOORS
	OTHER	SHEET VINYL	SHAPED	ADJUSTABLE ACOUSTICS
SPECIAL REQUIREMENTS		OTHER	KEROSEAL WALLCOVERING	OTHER
		ACCESSORIES	MIRROR	
			CHALK/WHITE BOARD	

MECHANICAL AND ELECTRICAL

LIGHTING	HVAC	PLUMBING	ELECTRICAL POWER	SECURITY	COMMUNICATION
NATURAL LIGHT	FIXED TEMP 68-78	HOT WATER	110V/20A/1 PHASE	KEY LOCK	TELEPHONE
FLUORESCENT	A/C - ROOM CONTROL	COLD WATER	208V/40A/3 PHASE	CARD ACCES	PUBLIC ADDRESS
INCANDESCENT	HUMIDITY CONTROL	COMPRESSED AIR	CONVENIENCE OUTLETS	ALARMED DOC	INTERCOM
TASK	AIR FILTRATION	GAS	AUDIO CLEAN POWER	CLOSED CIRCUIT 1	NETWORK TYPE____
RECESSED	SPECIAL VENTILATION	SINK	2 PLEX OUTLETS ON	OTHER	VIDEO/CABLE
TRACK	BALANCED AIR SUPPLY	DRINKING FOUNTAIN	EACH WALL (GFI)		DATA CONNECTION
BLACK-OUT ABILITY	ODOR CONTROL	OTHER			AUDIO SYSTEM
DIMMER	SEPARATE SYSTEM				OTHER
QUIET	NC____		SPECIAL REQUIREMENTS		
OTHER	OTHER				

GENERAL COMMENTS/REMARKS

DATE _____

Figure 7.2 Sample Program Data Sheet.

THE MATHEMATICS OF SPATIAL PROGRAMMING

One-third of the gross square footage of your building will be unusable for patrons, collections, programs, or staff. This space is referred to as the "unassignable" space and is used for the wall thickness, corridors, mechanical/electrical room, data closets, and spaces for vertically run ductwork. No one likes thinking about this space in the programming phases, but without it, your building is not usable. It is shocking how much square footage this takes up. To determine the mathematical formula for this space, you cannot simply multiply your programmed square footage by one-third. Instead, you must multiply the net square footage by 1.5. For example, a 100,000 net square foot library requires 150,000 gross square feet to equal two-thirds net to one-third gross square feet. A tested method for assigning square footage for mechanical and electrical spaces is to assign 8 percent of the building gross square feet to the mechanical/electrical closets.

THE USE OF ADJACENCY DIAGRAMS

Once the spaces of a building program are defined, the programmer can work with the committee to create adjacency diagrams, also referred to as bubble diagrams, which establish options for the placement of departments in a floor plan and in a stacking model. The floor plan will establish the horizontal relationships of the spaces, while the stacking model shows how spaces relate vertically. Bubble diagrams will allow the committee to evaluate a variety of layout options, without developing detailed floor plans. The diagrams will also allow you to understand the ideal size of the floor plate and will help to determine code classifications and resistance rating that the building will be assigned.

KEEPING TRACK OF IDEAS

During programming, many ideas will be generated as to what your library will contain, what it might look like, and what sets it apart from other facilities. The easiest and most efficient way to document the decision-making process and keep track of all ideas is to record the proceedings. An app called audionotes easily connects to your workbook or iPad and can be used for recording. If the programmer uses presentation boards and they are marked up with notes, photograph them. As an appendix to the final document, the programmer should provide copies of all presentations and document discussions with minutes of each meeting. Participants at meeting should be given the opportunity, prior to finalizing minutes, to review them for accuracy.

8

Principles of Good Design

Jody Lee Drafta and Traci Engel Lesneski

Good library design results in spaces both that are functional and that feed the human spirit, often without their inhabitants fully understanding what draws them in to these spaces and causes them to linger. Important components of good design include the scale of the space and the furniture that supports it, the curated use of color and texture, spatial and visual variety, and the qualities of natural and electric light. Carefully choreographing these aspects results in inviting spaces that resonate with people and support their well-being.

INTERIOR NAVIGATION

A primary step in creating human-centered spaces involves addressing interior navigation and spatial sorting, or zoning. Zoned space is interior space that is separated into areas defined by their use and noise level. Successful navigation and zoning enable users to visually read an interior space and place themselves within a cognitive map upon entering a building. Visual connection to the exterior orients people in the context of the building and helps them understand its overall footprint and scale. Clearly defined paths that lead to resources and services make the building more intuitive to navigate and highly sought areas easier to perceive and access.

Visual and physical impediments can restrict access to a library's space. For example, tall shelves placed near the building entry may block sightlines into the interior. Likewise, large, immovable service desks present a visual and physical barrier to library users. Reconfigurable and flexible service points are more adaptable and psychologically accessible to patrons.

Visual cues to the primary paths through the interior space help orient users within the building. For example, McAllen Public Library's new main library, located in a converted Walmart (in McAllen, Texas), uses a decorative wood ceiling to mark the main path and enables the visitor to navigate the building with confidence (Figure 8.1).

Some of the design tenets discussed in this chapter were adapted from Traci Lesneski's article "10 Steps to a Better Library Interior: Tips That Don't Have to Cost a Lot" (*Library Journal*, August 16, 2011).

Figure 8.1   A Walmart store-turned-public library employed intuitive way-finding cues of patterned wood ceilings and orange accents to mark the primary circulation paths and service zones and break down the vast space. Photo credit: Lara Swimmer.

THE IMPORTANCE OF ZONING

It might seem intuitive that library users who want to work in silence go to a designated quiet area, and all patrons wishing to collaborate will place themselves alongside those doing similar work. In reality, seating choices vary. The socially understood norm for library behavior has traditionally been quiet and isolated work. Today, libraries support multimodal learning and myriad functions. As a result, various kinds of public and private areas support collaborative or solo work. Aligning a space's functional requirements with its design and location within a building creates an implicit understanding of how users should conduct themselves within the space. It is important to consider the likely activities that will take place within a building to avoid conflicts in patrons' expectations for privacy (visual and acoustic), sociability (how much human interaction is desired), and acoustics (ambient noise versus silence). Zoning places quieter activities in a part of the building that is naturally quiet (for example, away from high-traffic areas). Visual cues help signal quiet behaviors. For example, spread-out furniture discourages collaborative work. Likewise, zoning clusters spaces and activities likely to generate noise together and provides visual cues that give patrons permission to be animated.

A well-designed library building can be adapted to meet changing service needs. A wide-open floor plan with very few walls offers a simple solution. Although this strategy allows the building to be easily reconfigured, it can cause confusion for library users and staff if the building is not zoned by activity, use, and acoustic requirements.

Avoiding conflicts in acoustic expectations among building users requires an understanding of the sources of sound within the building. The most obvious source is airborne noise such as speech or music, but sound can also come from structural vibrations (for example, the moving parts of mechanical equipment sending vibrations through the floor) and impact (for example, footfalls on a hard floor). Skillful zoning accounts for these sources. Zoning a quiet space next to a noisy mechanical room will almost certainly create unhappy occupants unless the sound transmission is properly dealt with.

Most people tolerate noise when they expect it. Zoning the building's interior based on the level of activity and likely generation of noise helps clarify designated areas and improve a building's usability and comfort.

LIGHTING SHAPES A SPACE

Building users tend not to notice well-designed interior lighting. Alternatively, poorly designed lighting is apparent and can ruin an interior (or worse, our productivity and well-being). Lighting an interior is both a science and an art. It takes science to understand how lighting works and to provide the right amount of light for the task. It takes art to provide lighting that makes the space not only functional, but also beautiful. A room's lighting may technically meet the basic requirements for safety yet create an environment that is uncomfortably bright, or that renders colors poorly, creating a disquieting space.

Multiple considerations go into good lighting design, including determining the color temperature (whether the light appearance is warm or cold), energy consumption, the intensity of light appropriate for the function, the elimination of glare, the quality of light, source of light, use of daylight, and more.

Two key factors have an impact on lighting for library buildings. The first involves the variety of lighting used. Many libraries use only ambient lighting, resulting in a flat interior space. Just as variety in color and texture creates a more interesting garden, combining different types of light sources and fixtures helps provide a more pleasing interior space. The most successful library interiors use a tiered approach to lighting—mixing ambient (overall) electric light with daylight, task light, and accent light—rather than simply flooding a room with a one-size-fits-all approach. Because light touches everything in a space, poor lighting can disintegrate careful design decisions regarding other aspects of the building, such as color and furniture.

Figure 8.2   St. Cloud Minnesota's public library incorporates daylight to enhance the library's interior, reduce energy use, and improve the productivity and well-being of its inhabitants. Photo credit: Lara Swimmer.

The second factor involves the amount of light used. Many library buildings are over-lit, wasting energy and operating dollars, tiring our eyes, and creating uncomfortable spaces. Varying light levels throughout an interior allows our eyes to rest, saves energy, directs attention to particular areas, and cues behavior. For example, lower ambient light levels in a quiet reading area with supplemental task lighting cues library users to respect the intent of a quiet area.

Daylight harvesting can greatly enhance a lighting strategy. Even when views may not be particularly lovely, bringing daylight into an interior will have marked positive impact. Access to daylight improves the mood, productivity, and well-being of building users and can contribute to energy savings through reduced reliance on electric light. Building occupants' ability to mark time by noting the changes in daylight quality, shadow, and weather also contributes to user comfort and cognitive function (Figure 8.2).

See Chapter 10 for more information about effective interior lighting.

VISUAL AND SPATIAL VARIETY

Humans are hardwired to value visual and spatial variety in their surroundings. Consider a forest, as an example. It offers an abundance of visual textures (for example, moss, berries, leaves, roots, bark, tree canopy, filtered sunlight, and animals) and types of spaces (for example, a hollow ground, nest, cave, and perch in a tree). This diversity provided security and sources of nourishment for our ancestors. We find innate comfort in a visual and spatial variety that reflects nature, and are more likely to spend time in spaces that achieve this variety (Figure 8.3).

Figure 8.3   The children's area at Madison Central Library uses scale, texture, and color—and whimsy—to create a vibrant and engaging space for people of all ages. Photo credit: Lara Swimmer.

Appreciating nature's design does not mean we must duplicate the colors and textures found in nature. It means that just as a forest has ground cover, mid-ground plants, and a tree canopy, so too should a library interior have varying layers of texture and interest. Consider a typical bland convention center conference space, often a nondescript box void of natural light, with putty-colored walls and floor and a flat ceiling with ubiquitous fluorescent lights. These types of spaces quickly become unsettling to be in. While that discomfort could be attributed to many things, from uncomfortable seating to the lack of fresh air available or daylight, often it is the result of our innate need for visual and spatial variety.

Legibility and variety play a significant role in determining how much building users engage with a particular space. Balancing these elements with finesse helps users feel at home in the space, in body and mind.

Views outside or within spaces contribute to visual variety. Offering open views into other spaces greatly benefits building users. Being able to lengthen one's visual perspective while working provides a hither-and-yon rhythm that advances concentration. Looking into the distance implies a spatial unfettering, which the mind mimics as it unfurls to study and write. Visual connectedness to, and layering of, adjacent spaces reinforces understanding of the space and provides a more interesting tapestry for contemplation. Research into work space wellness suggests that the health of our eyes depends upon the ability to work the eye muscles between long and short views.

Views to the outdoors have even stronger positive effect. Windows and access to daylight allow awareness of the passing of time. A space without any exterior views may encourage focus to a certain extent, but over an extended basis, it can produce anxiety and be distracting. Without views to the outdoors, people have nothing to measure the arc of their energy, stamina, or growing fatigue against.

THE EFFECTIVE USE OF COLOR

Color permeates our culture on many levels and in many ways—in fashion, product design, interior design, and even the food we prefer. Whole fields of study are dedicated to the psychology of color and its effects on physiology, concentration, and memory. Color profoundly influences our attitudes and behavior. Designers in all fields forecast color trends. These trends influence everything from the products we buy to the clothes we wear and are linked to such things as the economy and overall mood of a nation.

Strategic use of color can direct attention toward a building asset and away from an interior liability. Color can create boundaries within a space. Color can signal how users should behave. It can add warmth, liveliness, or gravity. Moreover, especially when applied through paint, color is easy and inexpensive to change, allowing a refresh of library interiors over time.

Successful use of color requires understanding context and contrast. For example, a library may have windows that reveal a lovely view. The goal would be to enhance enjoyment of that view rather than detract from it. A common misstep with windows is creating high contrast through the application of color. A dark color might be applied to the adjacent walls to call attention to the view, when in actuality the contrast between a bright window and dark adjacent surface detracts from the view. Our eyes must constantly adjust between the dark wall and the bright window, which tires them and diminishes our appreciation of the view.

As editing brings clarity to good writing, so does use of color. Too many disparate colors in a space without regard for context (for example, scale of space or competing visual aspects) results in a disjointed, chaotic appearance.

A further use of color in libraries is to help define spaces that will prolong concentration. Color can aid in making that purpose clear. It can influence the kind of movement and volume of noise appropriate in a space. It can foster concentration and help determine whether the space reads as transitional or a destination. Like light, color can flatten out a space, or it can add a visual momentum that brings depth and quiet. Color can enter consciousness before almost anything else does because one can perceive it at a distance and without detail. Like zoning and lighting, color helps prepare user expectations for the experience ahead.

THE ROLE OF FURNITURE

Far from being an accoutrement layered on top of an already-defined space, furniture is integral to the space's design, functionality, and overall success. Furniture should be selected while the interior architecture is taking shape, so one informs the other. Furniture selected only with regard to function will lead to a space that feels soulless.

Furniture layout signals the intent of a space. As with zoning, furniture plays a role in cueing behavior by either encouraging or dissuading various activities within a given space. For example, areas designated for quiet, individual work should not include conversational layouts of lounge furniture, but rather individual seats that are not easy to move into collaborative layouts. Conversely, an area meant for creative collaboration should be furnished in such a way that prompts and supports this behavior, with flexible furniture and brainstorming accessories.

We spend a large percentage of time indoors, often seated on furniture that does not support our health and well-being. Furniture manufacturers are increasingly offering more and varied furniture pieces with ever more customization possible to ensure that users can find the right fit for their bodies. Focus upon getting people to be more active in their daily lives has led to a multitude of sit-to-stand work surface products in the furniture market that did not exist a few years ago. In an effort to better support wellness, adjustable work surfaces are gaining popularity for both staff and public spaces in libraries.

As furniture products can support well-being and comfort, so too can the layout. Consider a typical mall food court—typically a sea of tables corralled by a low wall. The first tables to fill are typically those at the perimeter, near the wall. The next to fill are those near some other anchoring device, such as a column. People generally do not like sitting in the vast sea of tables without some sort of anchor nearby. In a library, this phenomenon might translate into a sea of furniture purporting to be a lounge. It is not enough to overload a space with furniture. That furniture must also be arranged to create a sense of comfort and resonate with the interior's design intent. A complementary mix of furniture styles, configurations in layout, and variety of experiences will reinforce comfort, while simultaneously contributing to visual variety and user choice.

New Jersey's Seton Hall University Walsh Library provides an interesting case study in how students use library furniture. Walsh Library contains traditional study carrels for individual use, arranged in a single-file line, each carrel facing the back of the next, parallel to a perimeter wall of windows. When seated in a carrel, views to the left are to the out-doors; views to the right are to the interior of the library (Figure 8.4).

This layout does not seem to satisfy the students, who have taken to changing the carrel arrangement regularly. Using one simple pivot maneuver, they spin the carrel's user side toward the perimeter wall. This shift changes several things at once: light, privacy, proximity to other scholars, and spatial/physical entitlement. With the carrel turned and facing out from the wall, light pools from the window behind onto the desk surface. The carrel occupant faces the library interior, like a bar patron who takes a far corner seat in order to better see who enters the bar. Just like a poker player who holds his cards close to his chest, the student keeps his computer screen private behind carrel's sides. This position discourages conversation and equalizes the power balance between the student sitting and working and the person standing or passing by. It offers a fascinating microstudy of space, privacy, furniture placement, direction, and control.

Figure 8.4   Students at Seton Hall University rotate wooden carrels to create greater privacy and a sense of owned space while they work. Photo credit: Jody Lee Drafta.

CONCLUSION

This chapter has discussed basics of library good design: the proper use of lighting, color, acoustics, way-finding, and furniture placement. These are all skills that can be picked up through reading, from conversations with other librarians who have completed a renovation or building project, or by working with a library design firm. Whichever route you choose to go, understanding and applying these principles will help you to create a library space that all users will find welcoming.

9

Sustainable Design

Mary M. Carr

The building sector accounts for up to 41 percent of the nation's energy use, 38 percent of all CO_2 emissions, 73 percent of electricity consumption, 13.6 percent of potable water use, and 40 percent of raw materials.[1] Commercial buildings alone, including facilities such as libraries, account for up to 18 percent of the nation's energy use and up to 17 percent of publicly supplied water used in the United States.[2] Globally, the world's ecological footprint has been running in a deficit since the 1980s.[3] Faced with these and other facts, the United States, albeit reluctantly, has begun to take steps to reverse these negative trends. At the same time, the term *sustainability* more and more has been used in the sense of human sustainability on planet Earth, our common home. The concept of sustainability now permeates all sectors of our economy, including building design.

Librarians have long been concerned about sustainability. There are a variety of special interest groups dedicated to this topic in library associations at the state, national, and international levels. On June 28, 2015, the American Library Association's concern about sustainability culminated in a resolution on the importance of sustainable libraries. Among other points, the resolution "recognizes the important and unique role libraries play in wider community conversations about resiliency, climate change, and a sustainable future and begins a new era of thinking sustainably in order to consider the economic, environmental and socially equitable viability of choices made on behalf of the association."[4] Concern about sustainability must turn into action.

Sustainable design principles, as outlined by the U.S. General Services Administration, include the ability to:

- Optimize site potential
- Minimize nonrenewable energy consumption
- Use environmentally preferable products
- Protect and conserve water inside and out
- Enhance indoor environmental quality
- Optimize operational and maintenance practices[5]

To this set of six principles, the author adds a seventh—durability and flexibility.

There was a period of time in the 1960s and 1970s when buildings were constructed with the idea that they need not last a long time. Out with the old and in with the new.

Architectural styles change, codes change, building materials change, and library needs change. Why expect a building to last? That notion runs counter to sustainability principles. It is important to value old buildings that are structurally sound; and it is important to build or renovate so that the building will last and be functional for a long time. Many libraries have now adopted this philosophy. The District of Columbia Public Library's building program for a neighborhood library is a case in point. One of the elements mentioned in the program is "Flexible space to accommodate future changes."[6] Consider this when arranging spaces and deciding where to place less-flexible elements such as walls and utilities. What use will this space serve now? What might it serve later? How might this affect the design?

The principles, listed earlier, provide an outline for what remains of this chapter. But before looking specifically at some of the strategies associated with these principles, it is important to consider several other key concepts integral to sustainable building design.

THE INTEGRATIVE PROCESS

Conventional building planning, design, construction, and operations processes most often failed to recognize that buildings are complex, holistic systems. As a result, building systems were not likely to work well as an integrated whole. If there were system problems, solving one problem might create another elsewhere, resulting in inefficient buildings and unnecessary costs.

Today there is recognition that a building functions holistically, so that is the way it should be planned, built, occupied, and even deconstructed. The integrative process requires close cooperation of the entire design team, including architects, engineers, landscapers, contractors, librarians, library users, and others, at all project stages, always considering the entire building and all of its systems together. The process emphasizes connections and communication throughout the life of a project. Although integrated design is most often applied to new construction or renovation, using these principles at every phase of the building's life cycle reduces negative impacts on the environment and on the health of the building occupants.

THE ROLE OF THIRD-PARTY CERTIFICATIONS

Essential to the integrative process is the use of third-party certifications, standards, and ecolabels. It is important to be familiar with these "Good-Housekeeping Seals of Approval," although they can be confusing in both their number and variety. The project team, if planning a new building, major renovation, or an upgrade in the building's operations and maintenance, may elect to follow a third-party building certification process. Within those certifications, the planning team will need to pay close attention to a variety of standards, as well as building product certifications and ecolabels. Even if the planning team is looking at a simple remodel or is designing a project that will not undergo building certification, the many standards and product certifications need to be considered carefully. Most architects, as well as many other building experts, will be familiar with the vast array of green standards and certifications.

Perhaps the best-known third-party building certification is LEED (Leadership in Energy and Environmental Design). LEED is a system developed by the U.S. Green Building Council (USGBC) "to measure and rate the environmental performance of buildings, building interiors and even entire neighborhoods."[7] Libraries often seek LEED certification when building or renovating. LEED awards points for excellence in areas including energy usage, water efficiency, use of recycled materials, and indoor air quality. The total points are totaled and fall within four certification levels: Certified, Silver, Gold, and Platinum. Many architects, and even a handful of librarians, are LEED-accredited professionals.

Another building certification system applied to commercial buildings is Green Globes, which also provides assessment tools for the design of new buildings or significant renovations, the management and operations of existing buildings, and interiors. Administered by the Green Building Initiative, the rating system was introduced in the United States in 2005. Originating in the 1990s in the United Kingdom, Green Globes is derived from the BREEAM (Building Research Establishment Environmental Assessment Method) standard. The certification levels are One, Two, Three, or Four Globes.[8]

Certification of the structures is only part of the certification, standards, and labels puzzle. Various professional associations involved in building practices create their own standards. For example, ASHRAE is self-described as a global society that focuses "on building systems, energy efficiency, indoor air quality, refrigeration and sustainability within the industry, through research, standards writing, publishing and continuing education."[9] Supporting the governance of standards and certifications is the International Standards Organization. In addition to a myriad of professional standards, there are also codes and standards enforced by state and local governments.

There are also standards and certifications against which products can be judged. When it comes to certifications, third-party building product certifications and ecolabels have more credibility. The number and types of ecolabels for building products is dizzying. There are third-party certifications for nearly every building product imaginable. What makes these products sustainable is that they:

• Are made from salvaged, recycled, or agricultural waste products
• Conserve natural resources
• Avoid toxic and other emissions
• Save energy or water
• Contribute to a safe, healthy environment by not releasing significant pollutants into the building; by blocking the introduction, development, or spread of indoor contaminants; by removing indoor pollutants; by warning occupants of health hazards in the building; by improving light quality by helping to control noise; and by enhancing community well-being.[10]

Some third-party certifications and ecolabels are familiar; others are not. For instance, the FSC (Forest Stewardship Council) label is familiar to many. Be sure to investigate the ecolabel to determine what group or association sponsors it and whether or not the label is legitimate. Some labels may sound good, but are really just corporate or organization marketing claims to make the product or products sound "green." For a complete list of the growing number of ecolabels, consult the comprehensive Ecolabel Index website: http://www.ecolabelindex.com/. There is also a greenwashing index available online to help sort out true sustainability claims from those that are not: www.greenwashingindex.com/.

LIFE CYCLE AND COST CONSIDERATIONS

It is important to explore one more item before turning to the elements of the building itself. The integrative process is closely tied to life cycle considerations. Everyone associated with the building planning must consider the total cost of facility ownership throughout the entire life span of the building, from planning to occupancy, to deconstruction, and all its uses in between. Given today's building planning, it is prudent to consider a 100-year life cycle. Building up and tearing down is part of a throw-away culture, which is the very antithesis of sustainability and something the United States can ill afford.

Given a building's expected life span, life cycle cost analysis becomes particularly important. If buildings are to remain occupied for many years to come, considering project alternatives that fulfill the same performance requirements becomes ever more important. Alternatives will likely differ with respect to initial cost and recurring or operating costs. These costs, particularly the cost of operation, must be considered in total in order to select the alternative that maximizes net savings. For instance, glazing windows might have a high initial cost, but given what that might save in ongoing heating and cooling costs, it might well make that choice a prudent one. In other words, given recurring and nonrecurring costs, the sustainable choice is likely less expensive.

Green building need not be simply utilitarian just to meet the sustainability challenge. Lance Hosey, in *The Shape of Green: Aesthetics, Ecology, and Design*, argues that "design is shape with a purpose." He asks architects and building design teams to consider cost, performance, and aesthetics, all equally, to arrive at green design through aesthetics rooted in nature. Hosey contends that green techniques can be divided into two categories: "those you see and those you don't." Visible *green*—form, shape, and image—can have a great impact on both conservation and comfort. The second, *invisible green*, which includes considerations such as embodied energy, material sources, and chemical content, is a more familiar agenda, partly because these factors are easier to regulate and measure.[11]

OPTIMIZE SITE POTENTIAL

Siting is the very first consideration for a new library building or a significant addition. Even if the project only involves remodeling interior spaces, there are considerations regarding the library's site and its outdoor spaces. Proper site selection takes into consideration environmental concerns such as ground water, storm water flow, wildlife habitat, the amount and the direction of sunlight, and the exposure to wind. The perfect location for a green building will take advantage of natural ventilation and renewable energy sources, cut energy costs, reduce water consumption, and minimize the environmental impact upon the land. If an addition is planned, the orientation of that addition should be considered. Even if considering a remodel, it might be possible to place windows in such a way to take advantage of higher solar heat gain in winter.

If site selection is possible, an academic or a corporate library should be in the heart of a campus or, in the case of a public library, in close proximity to other public services, including public transportation. Alternative transportation should be encouraged with room for plenty of bike racks and preferred parking and plug-ins for electric vehicles.

Reducing the size of the parking lot, or at least not enlarging it when adding an addition, is a sound approach. A parking lot leaves less land for landscaping, poses storm water management issues, and soaks up the sun, potentially creating a heat island effect.

As buildings, roads, and other infrastructure replace open land and vegetation, the urban areas become warmer than their rural surroundings, forming an urban "island" of higher temperatures.

Roofs are large areas that absorb the heat of the sun and contribute to the heat island effect. Depending on the climate, consider adding a green roof or a reflective roof to the library. A green roof or a rooftop garden is a vegetative layer grown on a rooftop. Green roofs provide shade and remove heat from the air through evapotranspiration. This reduces temperatures on the roofs' surfaces and the surrounding air. Green roofs also reduce storm water run-off. The Ballard Branch of the Seattle Public Library sports 18,000+ low-water-use plants on its green roof. The plants provide the library with insulation, while reducing the water that otherwise would run into storm drains.[12]

A reflective or cool roof is made of a highly reflective type of paint, sheet covering, tiles, or shingles. Although not as delightful as a rooftop garden, a reflective roof also reduces the heat island effect. High solar reflectance, or albedo, will reflect some sunlight and heat away from a building, thus reducing roof temperatures. In addition, a high thermal emittance plays a role, particularly in warm, sunny climates. These properties "help roofs to absorb less heat and stay up to 50–60°F (28–33°C) cooler than conventional materials during peak summer weather."[13] The Richard Riordan Central Library (Los Angeles), which houses the third largest collection of books in the nation, now has a reflective roof, turning the library into a leader in sustainability in Los Angeles. The roofing saves $32,000 annually, contributes to the occupants' comfort, helps to efficiently maintain the temperature and humidity levels needed for the library's rare book collections, and lessens the city's urban heat island effect.[14]

Landscaping, even with a minimum amount of space, should be xeriscaped. Xeriscaping is a method of landscaping that is now used everywhere. It emphasizes water-conserving techniques, including the planting of native and drought-resistant plants, mulching, and efficient irrigation, if needed.

When designing or redesigning the landscape, it is first necessary to ask questions. What is the landscaping to be used for? Will it be an active space or a quiet, contemplative area for reading and meditation? Is this a teaching space? Will there be a community garden? Will there be grass? For what purpose? Can it be mowed easily with a manual mower? After these questions have been answered, it will be easier to properly design the areas to be landscaped for minimal maintenance and select plants that can reduce the amount of water needed. While saving precious water, it is also possible to save time and money.

Some buildings include green walls as part of the "landscaping." Green walls are also known as vertical gardens or ecowalls. A green wall is often part of the exterior of the building, but it can also be a part of the building's interior. The plants on a green wall receive water and nutrients from within the vertical support structure instead of from the ground. A green wall has several environmental benefits ranging from energy savings to reducing greenhouse gas emissions to enhancing the urban ecosystem that entices bees, butterflies, and hummingbirds.

One of the elements of the landscaping design to consider is a community garden. For example, the Glencarlyn Library Community Garden in Arlington, Virginia, is a teaching garden maintained by the Master Gardeners of Northern Virginia in partnership with the library. The goal of the garden "is to provide resources for Arlington residents to learn how to create gardens in both the suburban and urban landscape."[15]

MINIMIZE NONRENEWABLE ENERGY CONSUMPTION

It is important to note that this entire topic of energy is highly complex. When remodeling or renovating an existing library, the first step is to do an energy audit. The baseline knowledge gained from the audit will help to determine what strategies will be most cost-effective in designing or re-designing the building and its systems. The goal in passive solar buildings is the optimal balance of mass, glass, and insulation for a particular site and building design. Strategies to consider in passive solar design for a building project include:

- The collection of solar energy through properly oriented, south-facing windows
- The storage of this energy in "thermal mass," comprising building materials with high heat capacity such as concrete slabs, brick walls, or tile floors
- The natural distribution of the stored solar energy back to the living space, when required, through the mechanisms of natural convection and radiation
- Window specifications to allow higher solar heat gain coefficient in south glazing[16]

Library buildings need to be more than simple "boxes." In a case study of two libraries, the Whetstone Branch Library and the Karl Road Branch Library, both of the Columbus (Ohio) Metropolitan Library, the DesignGroup investigated whether the passive solar design features of the Whetstone Branch were, in part, responsible for the significant difference in energy use by two public library buildings of similar size, plan, and program use. Indeed, they were.[17] The new LEED Gold Billings Public Library's solar array is another example. It produces "more electricity than is needed in the library building at any given moment. The excess power flows out onto the grid and the city receives a credit on its power bill for the library."[18]

Depending on the climate, a heat pump (air-to-air or geothermal) may be something to consider. When it is cold outside, a heat pump extracts the outside heat and moves it inside. When it is warm outside, it reverses direction and acts like an air-conditioner, removing heat from the building. In many cases, heat pumps can compare favorably dollar for dollar with other ways to heat. Planning and careful cost comparisons given the area climate and energy costs are a must. As an example, Meriden (New Hampshire) Library installed a ductless heat pump system to help patrons stay cool in summer and to provide heat in winter, reducing reliance on the oil-fired furnace.[19]

Once the design team has considered all of the possibilities for using renewable energy, the team can consider supplementing these sources with high-efficiency furnaces and air-conditioners. It is also possible to couple the use of high-efficiency equipment with *extended comfort zones*. An extended comfort zone involves controlling the type of air that circulates in a building. In hot weather, an extended comfort zone uses warm, dry air and as much natural ventilation as possible. In cold weather, conversely, it combines warm walls, floors, and windows with cool air. Savings by doing all these things vary, but all studies reveal significant reductions in energy use.

To add to the complexity, but also efficiency, for buildings big or small, programmable monitoring and control technology are essential. In libraries, it is desirable to install automated systems that monitor and adjust temperature, humidity, ventilation, and lighting and enhance the occupants' comfort, as well as save money. Hennepin County's Roosevelt Branch is one such library that has benefited from the installation of a web-based, control appliance.[20]

Occupancy or motion sensors are also important for energy conservation. Occupancy sensors are devices installed in certain areas to turn lights and other equipment on or off in response to the presence (or absence) of people. There are other sensors that control lighting based on the amount of daylight available in their coverage area. There are other, more sophisticated, sensor units that offer a variety of adjustment capabilities. It is now possible to integrate sensors into a building's automation and control system. Sensors are available for small office areas and large, open areas. There are also sensors specifically designed for bathrooms, stairwells, and hallways.[21]

ENVIRONMENTALLY PREFERABLE PRODUCTS

Environmentally preferable products are also referred to as environmentally friendly, eco-friendly, sustainable, renewable, or green products. These are products that inflict reduced, minimal, or no harm on ecosystems or the environment. These products are recyclable, biodegradable, renewable, or organic. There is no aspect of the library building's design that does not use sustainable products. For instance, within the LEED building materials section, points are heavily concentrated in several areas: low-emission products, products with recycled content, FSC wood products, and locally sourced materials. Dr. Martin Luther King, Jr. Library at San Jose State University, which was awarded LEED Silver, O+M (Operations and Maintenance) in 2012, has been recognized for its use of recycled and vintage materials.[22]

Protect and Conserve Water Inside and Out

Water conservation at the library can serve several purposes. It can help the library be socially responsible, reduce its budget, and practice water conservation all at one time. The library, depending on its building project, can incorporate swales, rain water collection, underground recharge tanks, and other storm water management techniques on the outside. Inside the building, the library can include waterless urinals and low-flow toilets in restrooms and water restrictors on faucets and showerheads. Consider installing water fountains with bottle fillers throughout the library.

Bozeman Public Library landscaped with water conservation in mind. A storm water management system is used for irrigation. This system is used so that city water does not need to be used to keep the library landscaping green. The library adopted a "streambed theme" in its parking area medians, which is also part of the library's water conservation strategy. The river rocks were placed in such a way as to allow rain and snowmelt to soak into the ground, rather than to become runoff that goes into the city storm sewer. The stream beds also provide for snow storage in winter.[23]

Green roofs or eco-roofs also address the problem of rapid storm water runoff from impervious surfaces. Fifty thousand square feet of green roof was added to the Golda Meir Library in 2011. This addition became the largest green roof on a public building in Wisconsin, and the fourth and the largest green roof at the University of Wisconsin—Milwaukee.[24]

ENHANCE INDOOR ENVIRONMENTAL QUALITY

Indoor environmental quality (IEQ) is the term that covers conditions inside a building, including air quality, lighting, acoustics, and thermal heating, and how these conditions affect the building's occupants. In addition to improving their lives and protecting their health, better IEQ can make the building more inviting for patrons to frequent, while increasing the building's value and reducing liability for building owners.

Personnel costs often rival a building's operating costs, so strategies that protect or improve employees' health and productivity can have a large return on investment. IEQ goals focus on providing healthful and comfortable environments for occupants and minimizing the risk of building-related health problems.[25] In the case of libraries, IEQ is a definite factor in promoting good service and attracting patrons to the library facility.

Much has been written about IEQ. This is a complex area with a wide range of issues. Many standards and codes are involved—far too many to mention in this chapter. The Whole Building Design Guide underscores the need for an integrated design approach and suggests the following measures for attaining good IEQ in buildings:

- Facilitate quality IEQ through good design, construction, and operating and maintenance practices.
- Value aesthetic decisions, such as the importance of views and the integration of natural and human-made elements.
- Provide thermal comfort with a maximum degree of personal comfort over temperature and air flow.
- Supply adequate levels of ventilation and outside air for acceptable indoor air quality.
- Prevent airborne bacteria, mold, and other fungi through building envelope design that properly manages moisture sources from outside and inside the building, and with heating, ventilating, air conditioning (HVAC) system designs that are effective in controlling indoor humidity.
- Use materials that do not emit pollutants or are low emitting.
- Assure acoustic privacy and comfort through the use of sound absorbing material and equipment isolation.
- Control disturbing odors through contaminant isolation and removal, and by careful selection of cleaning products.
- Create a high-performance luminous environment through the careful integration of natural and artificial light sources.
- Provide quality water.[26]

Dighton Public Library conducted an indoor air quality reassessment program in 2013, not connected to a renovation or remodeling project. The program covered the library's ventilation, microbial/moisture concerns, carbon monoxide levels, and particulate matter concentration. The report included the program's assessment methodologies, standards and codes, and approved levels, and made nine recommendations to improve the library's indoor environment, making it a healthier, safer, more pleasant place to be. The recommendations were often simple, such as cleaning or replacing carpets, adding walk-off mats, or changing air filters. Humidity levels were also a concern.[27] Evaluations of indoor environmental quality can include elements, in addition to those in the Dighton indoor air reassessment, such as indoor water contaminants, temperature, gases, vapors, chemical agents, and lighting.

Mold is a particular issue for libraries. Mold spores are everywhere—in the air and on surfaces. It has been on the Earth for millions of years. Left to grow, mold can be very damaging to books and papers in archives, libraries, and document collections. There are also potential health issues that must be considered because there are more than 100,000 species of mold. Some are very toxic. Mold will grow in places with too much moisture, such as leaks in roofs, pipes, and windows, or where flooding has occurred. Mold grows well on a wide variety of surfaces including, but not limited to, wood, paper (think print library resources here), and cardboard. It also grows well in a variety of media, including paint, insulation, drywall, carpet, fabric, and upholstery. In other words, mold can grow, given favorable conditions, almost anywhere inside and outside the structure.

It is best to make certain that a mold or molds do not develop. Make sure the building has a proper air exchange and humidity level. Following Environmental Protection Agency guidelines, keep indoor humidity below 60 percent (ideally between 30 and 50 percent) relative humidity.[28] Finally, it is important not to overlook simple things to improve the air quality including the addition of MERV (Minimum Efficiency Reporting Value) filters, doormats, and plants.

Indoor lighting is another aspect of IEQ that can and should be considered in any building project. For information regarding daylighting and indoor lamination, see Chapter 10.

OPTIMIZE OPERATIONAL AND MAINTENANCE PRACTICES

There are a variety of ways to optimize operational and maintenance practices. Commissioning is one of them. ASHRAE Standard 202–2013 defines "commissioning" as a "quality-focused process for enhancing the delivery of a project. The process focuses upon verifying and documenting that all of the commissioned systems and assemblies are planned, designed, installed, tested, operated, and maintained to meet the Owner's Project Requirements."[29] The term "commissioning," borrowed from shipbuilding, means that the building is ready for use.

There are a variety of processes, including commissioning (new buildings), retro-commissioning (for systems in existing buildings), recommissioning (for existing buildings that have already undergone commissioning), and enhanced commissioning (an extended, year-long process for new buildings that tracks the operation of building systems). Commissioning is not something to consider at the end of a building process but needs to be integrated as early as possible into the building, renovation or remodel project. When considering a new building, the commissioning agent should be part of the predesign, design, construction, occupancy, and operational phases of a new building. The commissioning agent should be contracted directly to the building owner as a third-party independent representative to ensure unbiased performance of the systems being commissioned.

Commissioning and enhanced commissioning of new buildings employ a whole building commissioning process, and, as the term suggests, looks at the entire building, including the building envelope, the HVAC, electrical, special electrical (fire alarm, security and communications), plumbing, and fire protection systems. St. Helena Branch Library, Beaufort County Library at Penn Center (South Carolina), a LEED-certified building, underwent this process. In this case, the commissioning agent provided fundamental services for LEED compliance. This included an owner's project requirements workshop, the creation of the owner's project requirements, and commissioning plan and commissioning specifications. The agent led precommissioning meetings, wrote functional test procedures, witnessed testing and balancing, witnessed manufacturers' equipment start-up, witnessed and supervised functional performance tests, prepared the final commissioning report, and uploaded all documentation to USGBC LEED Online. The library did not choose to do enhanced commissioning.[30]

Mitchell Park Library and Community Center in Palo Alto, a LEED Platinum Library, performed enhanced commissioning on a major renovation. As described on the library's site, "Enhanced commissioning is a process to test all the major environmental and safety systems such as heating, cooling, lighting, and security, prior to opening the building. Baseline performance levels are set for each one and will become the means to measure the on-going energy performance of the building." The library replaced the outdated library and community center with an all new, LEED-certified combination library and community center. The building was not only commissioned before occupancy, but the building's systems were monitored for 10 months after occupancy to ensure that the systems were performing at peak efficiency.[31]

The University of Missouri's Miller Nichols Library provides an example of retro-commissioning. The overall goal of this project was to "test and adjust existing control and HVAC systems to increase performance and reliability in order to meet the operational needs of the facility."[32] Through the retro-commissioning process, the library identified needed repairs and made them, assuring proper HVAC operations.

All buildings should have an operations and maintenance (O&M) plan, whether or not the building is new or newly renovated. An O&M plan includes all aspects of running a building over the course of its useful life. Because of the far-reaching nature of O&M, a well-designed and properly executed program is critical to the overall success of a sustainably designed facility. According to the Whole Building Design Guide for *Sustainable O&M Practices*, such a program should:

- Set demanding performance goals on both a daily and ongoing basis
- Measure performance so that the building can be benchmarked against other buildings
- Adjust to changing occupant needs by modifying the HVAC, lighting, electrical telecommunications, safety, housekeeping, and building automation control systems, as needed
- Repair, upgrade, and recommission building systems to ensure that they are working to meet current needs
- Extend the useful service life of materials and equipment, for example, reupholster furniture and use carpet squares
- Prevent disruptive failures in the building and its systems
- Promote greater productivity[33]

Sustainable cleaning programs are essential to maintaining indoor environmental quality. They comprise three parts: a green cleaning program, a sustainable purchasing policy, and a sustainable equipment policy. Green cleaning focuses on products, equipment, and methods that have fewer harmful health effects on building occupants and visitors and less negative impact on the environment. Adopting a sustainable cleaning program is not dependent on constructing a new building, launching a major renovation, or even doing a minor remodel.

One example of a green cleaning program is that used by the Dubuque Carnegie-Stout Public Library's program. It was implemented as part of the library's silver certification in the LEED for Existing Buildings in 2012. The library was built in 1901 and is on the National Historical Register of Historic Places. The green cleaning program includes procedures for cleaning products and equipment, hard-floor and carpet maintenance, the handling and storage of cleaning chemicals, and staffing and training.[34]

Waste management can be summed up in three words: reduce, reuse, and recycle. Dubuque Carnegie-Stout Public Library also has a waste reduction policy that goes well beyond recycling. That is the norm. It focuses on reuse. It covers how the library handles hazardous materials such as light bulbs that contain mercury. It also addresses the steps to be taken to avoid sending discarded items to the landfill, and to include the donation of computers and participation in a program that advertises equipment and furniture no longer needed to organizations within the state.[35]

Part of Concordia College's waste management policy is a student printing system in the residence halls, computer labs, and the library. The system tracks paper usage and manages printing. Its focus is reducing the paper and supplies used. The reduction saves paper, ink, and associated costs. In the library, the system decreased paper use by almost 20 percent.[36]

Waste management can be done in any library, whether or not there is a building project. On the other hand, if there is a building project, whether new, renovation, or remodel, there too waste management can be practiced. Northland College, a liberal arts college in Ashland, Wisconsin, is an example. The college renovated its library in 2008. When the project was completed, Dexter Library became the first LEED Gold building in Wisconsin. To receive a Gold-level certification, the renovators controlled "not just what they built, but what they threw away. 75% of the construction and demolition waste was diverted from landfills. These materials were either recycled or reused, reducing the burden on landfills and the demand for virgin resources."[37] Waste management, like other elements discussed in this chapter, needs to be practiced during a building's entire life cycle, from design to construction, operations, possible renovation, maintenance, and finally demolition.

Libraries are purchasing more and more of their resources digitally. On the surface it would seem that the digital versions of resources would be more sustainable than the paper versions. However, in the title of a 2014 article in the *Huffington Post*, the conclusion is clear: "Print or Digital: It All Has an Environmental Impact."[38] Depending on how long the library owns the computers or eBook readers and how often they are used, sometimes print and sometimes digital is more sustainable. Therefore, it is best to select library resources and their formats based upon their use, being sure to factor recycling the technological devices or the print materials into the library's waste management policy. The changing nature of library resources is certainly one good reason to build flexibility into a building or renovation project.

FINAL CONSIDERATIONS

Libraries are community centers and learning laboratories. Precisely because of these roles, Deborah Turner, in her paper titled "Sustainability and Library Management Education," which was published in the *Journal of Sustainability Education* (December 26, 2014), suggests that library and information science educators should support sustainability efforts by "incorporating sustainability concepts into the Library and Information Science curriculum. . . . the paper argues and provides ideas for integrating sustainability into a course focusing on management, offered, and frequently required, by most American Library Association accredited LIS programs."[39] Of course, the reason for embedding sustainability into such a course is to introduce sustainability concepts to the largest number of new librarians graduating from library schools. Sustainability is that important to librarianship that most library students should be exposed to the tenets of sustainability.

In turn, librarians who manage libraries as community and education centers should model sustainability to the communities they serve.

As a living laboratory, the library can provide information about its building online and within. For newly built or renovated libraries, it is possible to offer tours or post signs and hand out flyers that lead people on a self-guided tour of the library's green features. As one example, Rosemary Garfoot Public Library in Cross Plains, Wisconsin, was the first green library in the state. Its renovated Carnegie Library received LEED Silver. The library's flyer highlights the library's green features, including a rain garden, a circulation desk made from trees harvested from the library site, shelves and columns made from wood recycled from the site, carpeting made from recycled materials, entry mats made from recycled tires, low-flow toilets and waterless urinals, and many other features.[40]

The Fayetteville Public Library, Blair Library, completed in 2004 as LEED Silver, introduced the state of Arkansas to green building. Because the concepts of green building were new to both state and local officials, the library's project team worked with both to gain their approval of innovative building practices. A green roof, waterless urinals, underground cisterns, a construction waste recycling program, daylighting in reading rooms, and material harvesting from the site for reuse were some of the sustainable practices that the project team chose to include in the library building program. An undulating roof above clerestory windows in the main reading room and the central hall of the second floor "recalls the natural forms of the mountain ranges to the south. Visitors are presented with views to the natural world to consider and reflect upon during their visit, reinforcing the goal of creating a new relationship with the land."[41]

In 2010, the library became a "test bed for new technology in an effort to support local economic development." The 60 solar panels installed on the library's roof initially provided "power to the library using a commercially available inverter. After six months of collecting production data, the library will test a highly efficient, state-of-the-art silicon carbide inverter developed by Arkansas Power Electronics International (APEI), a small Fayetteville-based company that specializes in developing technology for power electronics systems, electronic motor drives, and power electronics packaging."[42] The project is funded by an International City/County Management Association Public Library Innovations Grant with support from the Bill & Melinda Gates Foundation.

As an educational piece, the library placed a kiosk in the library's lobby that displays real-time energy production data and provides educational information on solar power. The real-time data is also available online: http://www.solrenview.com/cgi-bin/CGIhandler.cgi?&sort=pvi_IDs&cond=site_ID=316. The library also hosted a public presentation of its solar test bed project.

Green inventions are revolutionizing the way the world generates energy, recycles waste, and protects the planet. If it weren't for such green innovation, there would be no solar panels, wind turbines, or hybrid cars. Solar panels improve, and so do wind panels and hybrid cars. Meanwhile, there are new inventions that add to the sustainable options that project teams have when considering how best to build, renovate, or remodel. For instance, in 2014, a University of California, Berkeley research team developed a new type of building skin. The skin self-regulates a building's temperature without electronics. "Instead of walls, the membrane wraps around a building, filled with micro-scale valves and lenses that open and close as they sense light, heat, and humidity. It works with no power at all—not even PV solar panels—and keeps the temperature comfortable and light bright inside."[43] Meanwhile 3D printers are being used to "print" building structures in China. More innovations will inevitably follow.

The arc of sustainable building is toward more sustainable libraries and more sustainable communities. It is important for librarians to recognize this and be an example and leader in "wider community conversations about resiliency, climate change, and a sustainable future," as the American Library Association resolution stated so well. As a librarian, it is important to stay abreast regarding issues of sustainability. Consider all aspects of the particular project carefully. Start early, including all who will work on the building on your design team, and design a library that will rest easily and well within its community.

NOTES

1. U.S. Green Building Council, "Green Building Facts," http://www.usgbc.org/articles/green-building-facts (cited August 13, 2015).
2. *The Guardian*, "Water Shortages Are Coming. It's Time for Us to Act," http://www.theguardian.com/commentisfree/2015/mar/12/water-shortages-are-coming-time-to-act (cited July 30, 2015).
3. M. Williams, "SFGate Home Guide: Difference between a Carbon Footprint and an Ecological Footprint," http://homeguides.sfgate.com/difference-between-carbon-footprint-ecological-footprint-78732.html (cited January 31, 2016).
4. American Library Association, "Resolution on Sustainable Libraries," June 28, 2015, http://www.ala.org/aboutala/sites/ala.org.aboutala/files/content/governance/council/council_documents/2015_annual_council_documents/cd_36_substainable_libraries_resol_final.pdf (cited August 13, 2015).
5. U.S. General Services Administration, "Sustainable Design," http://www.gsa.gov/portal/content/104462 (cited July 30, 2015).
6. DC Public Library, "Library Building Program," http://dclibrary.org/node/616 (cited July 30, 2015).
7. U.S. Green Building Council, "What Certification Level Is Your Project," http://www.usgbc.org/content/leed-cert-levels (cited July 30, 2015).
8. Green Globes, "The Practical Building Rating System," www.greenglobes.com (cited July 30, 2015).
9. ASHRAE, "About ASHRAE," www.ashrae.org/about-ashrae (cited January 25, 2016).
10. BuildingGreen, "What Makes a Building Product Green," http://www2.buildinggreen.com/what-makes-a-product-green (cited August 13, 2015).
11. Fast Company Design, "A Case for Why Design Must Be Beautiful," http://www.fastcodesign.com/1672322/for-green-design-to-have-a-chance-it-should-be-beautiful (cited July 30, 2015).
12. Seattle Public Library, "Ballard Branch: Environmental Features," http://www.spl.org/locations/ballard-branch/bal-about-the-branch/bal-environmental-features (cited July 30, 2015).
13. United States Environmental Protection Agency, "Heat Island Effect: Cool Roofs," http://www.epa.gov/heatisland/mitigation/coolroofs.htm (cited July 30, 2015).
14. Climate Resolve: Inspiring Los Angeles to Meet the Challenges of Climate Change, "A Cool Upgrade to the Central Library: An LA Icon's New Cool Roof," http://climateresolve.org/central-library-cool-roof/ (cited July 30, 2015).
15. Arlington Public Library, "Glencarlyn Branch Library Community Garden," http://library.arlingtonva.us/events/garden-talks/glencarlyn-garden/ (cited July 30, 2015).
16. National Institute of Building Sciences, World Building Design Guide, "Passive Solar Design," https://www.wbdg.org/resources/psheating.php (cited July 30, 2015).
17. Green Energy Ohio, "Benefits of Passive Solar vs. Traditional Design," http://www.greenenergyoh.org/benefits-of-passive-solar-versus-traditional-design/ (cited July 30, 2015).

18. Montana Renewable Energy Association, "System Profiles: Billings Public Library," http://www .montanarenewables.org/profiles'system-profiles/ (cited July 30, 2015).

19. Arch Mechanical Contractors, Meriden Library, Meriden, NH, http://www.arcmech.com/ meriden-library-case-study/ (cited July 30, 2015).

20. MAMAC Systems. "Case Study: Hennepin County—Roosevelt Library," http://www.mamacsys .com/case_study_hennepin_county_library.htm (cited July 30, 2015).

21. Green Seal. "Green Seal's Choose Green Report: Occupancy Sensors," http://www.wbdg.org/ccb/ GREEN/REPORTS/cgrsens.pdf (cited January 26, 2016).

22. San Jose State University, Administration and Finance Division, Facilities Development and Operations, "King LEED 4 Materials & Resources," http://www.sjsu.edu/fdo/departments/ maintops/sustainability/king_lib_leed/kingleed4mr/ (cited July 30, 2015).

23. Bozeman Public Library, "Landscaping Around the Library," http://www.bozemanlibrary.org/about/ green/landscaping.php (cited July 30, 2015).

24. University of Wisconsin—Milwaukee, "Green Roof Project," http://uwm.edu/libraries/facilities/ roof/ (cited July 30, 2015).

25. U.S. Green Building Council, "Green Building 101," www.usgbc.org/articles/green-building-101-what-indoor-environmental-quality (cited January 26, 2016).

26. National Institute of Building Sciences, Whole Building Design Guide, "Enhance Indoor Environmental Quality (IEQ)," https://www.wbdg.org/design/ieq.php (cited July 30, 2015).

27. Massachusetts Department of Public Health, Bureau of Public Health, Indoor Air Quality Program, "Indoor Quality Assessment, Dighton Public Library," http://www.google.com/url?sa=t&rct=j&q=& esrc=s&source=web&cd=1&ved=0CB4QFjAAahUKEwilzIHXxuDGAhUDFpIKHTD FA94&url=http%3A%2F%2Fwww.mass.gov%2Feohhs%2Fdocs%2Fdph%2Fenvironmental%-2Fiaq%2F2013%2Fdighton-public-library-reassessment-april- (cited July 2015).

28. United States Environmental Protection Agency, "A Brief Guide to Mold, Moisture, and Your Home," http://www.epa.gov/mold/preventionandcontrol.html (cited July 30, 2015).

29. National Institute of Building Sciences, Whole Building Design Guide, "Building Commissioning," http://www.wbdg.org/project/buildingcomm.php (cited July 30, 2015).

30. Whole Building Systems, "St. Helena Branch Library at Penn Center," http://wholebuildingsystems .com/projects/st-helena-library-beaufort-sc/ (cited July 30, 2015).

31. "Enhanced Commissioning," https://www.cityofpaloalto.org/forms/mplcc/info_dots/enhanced commissioning.html (cited July 30, 2015).

32. sys-tek, "University of Missouri, Miller Nichols Library," http://www.sys-tek.com/markets/20-higher-education/92-university-of-missouri-miller-nichols-library-retro-commissioning.html (cited July 30, 2015).

33. National Institute of Building Sciences, Whole Building Design Guide, "Sustainable O&M Practices," https://www.wbdg.org/resources/sustainableom.php (cited July 30, 2015).

34. Carnegie Stout Public Library, "Sustainability," https://www.dubuque.lib.ia.us/index.aspx?NID=301 (cited July 30, 2015).

35. Ibid.

36. Concordia College, "Waste Reduction," https://www.concordiacollege.edu/about/sustainability/ campus-operations/waste-reduction/ (cited July 30, 2015).

37. Northland College, "Dexter Library, Sustainability Features," http://www.northland.edu/dexter-library (cited July 2015).

38. Huff Post Green, "Print or Digital: It All Has Environmental Impact," http://www.huffingtonpost .com/omega-institute-for-holistic-studies/print-or-digital_b_4860403.html (cited July 30, 2015)

39. *The Journal of Sustainability Education*, "Sustainability and Library Management Education," http://www.jsedimensions.org/wordpress/content/sustainability-and-library-management-education_2014_12/ (cited July 30, 2015).

40. Rosemary Garfoot Public Library, http://www.rgpl.org/ (cited July 30, 2015).

41. Building Green, "Fayetteville Public Library," http://www.buildinggreen.com/hpb/overview .cfm?projectid=713 (cited July 30, 2015).

42. ICMA, "A Library Spurs Economic Development," http://icma.org/en/icma/newsroom/highlights/Article/100460/A_Library_Spurs_Economic_Development (cited July 30, 2015).

43. FastCompany, "No More Air Conditioners: This 'Skin' for Buildings Keeps the Inside Cool with Zero Energy," http://www.fastcoexist.com/3035428/no-more-air-conditioners-this-skin-for-buildings-keeps-the-inside-cool-with-zero-energy (cited July 30, 2015).

10

Lighting Fundamentals

Carla Gallina and Traci Lesneski

Light invigorates life and defines space. Without light we would not see color, texture, shade, and shadow; in fact, without light we would not see at all. Designing interior and exterior library spaces requires artistic vision, physiological insight, technical skills, and design collaboration. Successful libraries are more than visually interesting spaces; they are places that nurture the health and well-being of people as they research, study, read, teach, listen, and relax. The health and well-being of library staff and patrons depend on a balance of good architectural design, ventilation, and lighting. Quality lighting evolves from the careful integration of daylight and electrical light to reduce glare, improve our visual acuity, boost our psychological and physiological comfort, and mark time throughout the day.

This chapter on lighting is a snapshot in time. The lighting basics presented here are derived from lighting physics and library design strategies, which are effectively timeless concepts. References to energy use, energy goals, and system performance are based on information that is current as of this publication. Be aware that energy codes, code details, performance data, lighting system technologies, and relative system costs are continually changing. These should be reviewed and updated during the predesign phase of each project.

LIGHTING BASICS

Light is fundamentally a perception; it is a psychological, physiological, and personal experience. Technically, light consists of wavelengths of radiant energy that stimulate our visual system. It is often referred to as visible light, and most healthy eyes respond to radiant energy with wavelengths between 380 and 760 nanometers. Visible light changes by wavelength as shown in the spectrum in Figure 10.1.

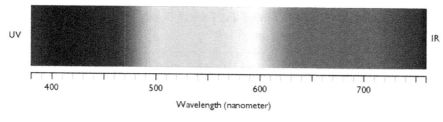

Figure 10.1 Visible light spectrum.

THE LANGUAGE OF LIGHT: NONTECHNICAL VERSION

Ballast. An electronic device required for high-intensity discharge (HID) light sources such as fluorescent. Ballasts provide a high voltage to start the lamp and then return to the appropriate voltage for the lamps to operate. Ballasts are specific to lamp type.

Candela. SI unit of luminous intensity.

Color Rendering Index. A measure of the degree of color shift that occurs when an object is illuminated from a light source other than the sun.

Color Temperature. The absolute temperature (kelvin) of a black body radiator having a chromaticity equal to that of the light source.

Controls. Automatic or manual devices that switch lighting OFF and ON.

Daylight. Indirect light from the sun such as north light, light monitors, and light shelves. Daylight is also achieved through south-, east-, and west-facing windows when sunlight is not present.

Direct. Lighting from luminaires that is distributed downward or is specifically directed.

Direct/indirect. Lighting from luminaires that distribute both direct and indirect light.

Driver. An electronic device that provides an interface between input power and output into the LED. Some drivers convert AC to DC, provide filters for "dirty power and power factor corrections, and allow for dimming.

Efficacy. Lumen per watt.

Foot-candles (fc). A measure of illuminance incident on a surface such as a table or a wall.

Grazing. Accent light that illuminates a surface at a sharp angle. Typically used to accentuate texture.

Illuminance. Light intensity incident on a surface measured in foot-candles. Note that illuminance is measured in micro-units just before the light reaches the surface. Because it is not yet reflected light, illuminance (fc) cannot be seen.

Indirect. Lighting from luminaires directed such that light is reflected into the room from a surface such as the ceiling or wall.

Lamp. Light bulb or light source.

Light source. An emitter of light. Electric light sources include fluorescent, incandescent, and LED lamps. The sun is also a light source.

Lumen. SI unit of luminous flux. A measure of the flow of light emitted from a light source.

Luminaire. A complete system of light fixture housing shielding, reflector, suspension, lamp, ballast, LED array and so on.

Luminance. A measure of light reflected from a surface. Think of it as illuminance x surface reflectance. Luminance is the reflected light that we see.

Lux. The metric equivalent of foot-candle. One foot-candle equals 10.76391 lux.

Sunlight. Direct light/radiant energy from the sun through a window or skylight.

Transformer. An electronic device that transforms high voltage to low voltage. Typically 277 V to 12 V.

Wall Wash. Accent light directed to illuminate a wall from top to bottom. Ideal for flat walls.

COLOR AND COLOR QUALITY

The color that we see when viewing an object varies by each individual's response to the wavelengths of radiant energy produced by each light source. The visual sensation of color occurs when light passes through the various ocular media of our eyes and strikes the retina. The ocular media filters the wavelengths and the intensity of radiant energy, which affects how an object is perceived.

Objects reflect specific wavelengths of light in a diffuse or scattered pattern. We perceive white paper as white because it reflects and scatters most wavelengths of radiant energy, and we perceive black paper as black because it absorbs most wavelengths of radiant energy, scattering very little light back to the observer. A green leaf reflects and scatters radiant energy in the wavelength spectrum between about 490 and 580 nanometers and absorbs most of the radiant energy in the violet-to-blue and yellow-to-red regions. When observed under a light source that does contain radiant energy in the 490 to 580 nanometer region, the leaf will not appear to be the green that we would expect it to be, or that we would perceive it to be, if illuminated with sunlight or another full-spectrum light source.

The color of an object is dependent upon the light source. We see variations in an object's color when it is illuminated from incandescent, fluorescent, and solid-state light sources and from daylight. While almost every electric light source contains the full spectrum of radiant energy, the relative intensity of radiant energy in each region of the spectrum varies due to the technology of creating the light and/or the technological manipulation of the wavelengths to increase a sense of brightness. For example, the human eye is most sensitive to wavelengths in the green region surrounding 550 nanometers. Light sources such as fluorescent and light-emitting diode (LED) that appear to be very bright will likely have a spike of energy in this region as in the spectral distribution graph shown in Figures 10.2A and 10.2B.

The lighting industry has two methods of describing the color properties of light sources: color temperature and color rendering index (CRI). Color temperature is measured in kelvin (K) as referenced in the context of warm white (3000K) (Figure 10.2A) and cool white (4100K) (Figure 10.2B). Warm white light sources contain more energy in the red

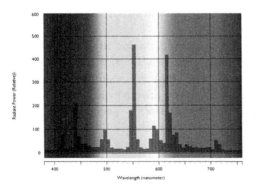

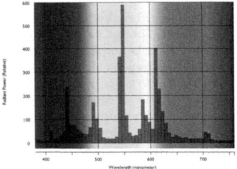

Figures 10.2A   Warm white (3000K) light.   **Figures 10.2B**   Cool white (4100K) light.

spectrum and cool white light sources contain more energy in the blue spectrum; both light sources contain energy in the full spectrum, refer to Figure 10.2.

The CRI is a measure designed to predict how well a light source will render color. It is a measure of the degree of color shift that occurs when an object is illuminated from a light source other than the sun. It predicts the probability of perceiving an object's color in the same way that it would be perceived in sunlight. The CRI for sunlight is 100 percent, which equates to a CRI of 100; the CRI of incandescent is 98, and the CRI of fluorescent and LED ranges from 70 to 90. CRI is not dependent upon color temperature; 3000K and 4000K fluorescent lamps have CRI of 70 to 90.

HOW WE SEE LIGHT

The key to understanding the principles of lighting design is realizing that we only see light that is reflected from surfaces. And the way in which light interacts with surfaces is fundamental to the perception of architectural spaces. White or lightly colored surfaces reflect light; dark surfaces absorb light. Directing light onto reflective walls and ceilings will generate an impression of a brightly illuminated space, even though the actual light levels at the center of the room may be quite low. Directing light onto dark walls or ceilings will consume a lot of energy due to surface absorption and will not result in perceived brightness. Illuminating reflective walls and ceilings is a fine strategy for reducing the contrast between interior surfaces and large daylight openings.

LIGHT QUALITY

The quality of lighting in interior and exterior spaces boosts our psychological health, improves our ability to complete tasks, and enhances our experience of the surrounding environment. Achieving light quality involves eliminating glare, balancing contrast, correcting color, and adjusting intensity. If you eliminate glare, you will reduce fatigue and your eyes will be more efficient at lower light levels. This physiological phenomenon occurs because when glare is eliminated, our eyes are not required to continuously adapt from intense light to ambient or task light levels. Because our pupils are not constantly changing size, fatigue is reduced and the constant pupil size allows our vision to be more efficient at lower light levels.

Illuminating interior surfaces further reduces fatigue by balancing the luminous contrast between tasks, surfaces, and windows. Illuminating the walls and ceiling will also result in the perception of a fully illuminated space even though the ambient light level may be quite low. Color-corrected light that is appropriately directed will accentuate and enhance architectural details and way-finding. Visually interesting spaces include a balanced mixture of ambient, task, and accent lighting to add highlights and soft shadows that shape objects and render texture; and it is key to designing interiors spaces that are interesting but not distracting.

AMBIENT LIGHT

Ambient lighting is commonly referred to as the general lighting in a room or space. It can be designed by using electrified lighting systems such as suspended linear luminaires, decorative pendant luminaires, or recessed luminaires, and it can be designed by introducing and controlling the daylight from windows, skylights, light monitors, light shelves, and clerestories.

Ambient light for a room can be developed from direct lighting systems, indirect lighting systems, or a combination of both. Direct ambient light is distributed downward from recessed or surface-mounted luminaires. It is primarily selected to illuminate spaces with low ceilings (9'-0" above the floor or lower) and is best used in combination with other luminaires that focus light onto the walls. Directing all light downward onto horizontal surfaces may result in a technically appropriate light level for horizontal tasks, but it will cause distracting shadows on faces and writing surfaces and may cause the room to appear dark unless the wall surfaces are also illuminated. It should be noted that with the increased use of electronic reading devices, illuminating horizontal surfaces such as table tops is becoming less important than illuminating vertical surfaces such as computer monitors.

Illuminating walls is one method of achieving indirect or reflected light in a room. Other methods of indirect lighting include suspended luminaires that illuminate the ceiling, light from north-facing windows, and reflected sunlight. In contrast to direct lighting, a system of indirect ceiling lighting will eliminate shadows and reduce object definition. Lighting systems that consist of only indirect light from suspended luminaires will become monotonous without the introduction of direct light. From a human comfort point of view, we need contrast and variety. An ambient lighting system that combines direct and indirect light will yield the benefits of both systems.

Light from the sun is dynamic. Introducing daylight or reflected sunlight into the ambient lighting design will benefit the human need to mark time, will reduce the requirement for electric lighting, and will reduce energy demand. While direct radiant energy from sunlight has psychological advantages during the winter in northern climates, daylight is a better source for interior illumination as it is provides less heat gain, less damaging ultraviolet light, and significantly less glare. As a rule of thumb, the daylight from a window will penetrate into unobstructed space 2.5 times the window height. Strategies for using the sunlight to add indirect ambient light into a room include reflecting the sunlight from light shelves, light scoops, and vertical fins.

Using ambient lighting as the sole source of illumination in libraries is slowly losing momentum. From strictly an intensity-based point of view, appropriate light levels for a library range from 10 foot-candles (fc) for walking around to 50 fc for reading small paper–based print. Because of the wide variety of spaces in our libraries, illuminating the entire library for the most detailed task will significantly overilluminate many more casual task areas. Consider book stacks as an example. Due to light losses within the shelving and the physics of vertical illumination, the ambient light intensity required to illuminate book spines to 30fc is much higher than the ambient light intensity required to illuminate a computer table to 30fc. Locating computer tables in an ambient zone designed for book shelves will be distracting to those using computer monitors.

In an effort to reduce energy, designers should avoid reducing ambient light levels at the expense of light quality and lighting interior surfaces. This will result in the perception of a dark interior space and likely lead to costly reconfigurations to install overhead light fixtures and table lamps.

TASK LIGHT

Task lighting differs from ambient lighting in that it is located near or directed toward a specific task such as casual reading, computer research, conference discussions, media listening, media viewing, and making things. Task lights are often incorporated into the shelves of staff workstations and under cabinets in workrooms and lounges. They can also be freestanding table lights or floor lights, integrated in media displays, attached to collection book shelves, or suspended directly above workstations, seating areas, or tables. Reducing ambient light levels and adding task lighting where it is needed is an excellent strategy for maintaining light quality, introducing visual variety into the library and reducing lighting energy demand.

ACCENT LIGHT

Accent lighting sits at the top of the lighting hierarchy in that its purpose is to direct attention to the special nature of objects, people, and surfaces, and it is used to introduce sparkle, color, and variety into spaces. Light is one of the most effective means of directing attention as our eyes are naturally drawn to illuminated objects and surfaces. If light is used to direct attention to an object, the illumination of the object must be brighter than its surroundings. A rule of thumb for the intensity ratio of surrounding surfaces to accented objects is 1:3.

Accent light is often used in libraries to illuminate special architectural features, new books displays, retail shelving, and way-finding signage. In library galleries and public assembly rooms, accent lighting is used to illuminate art installations, lecturers, musical ensembles, and theatrical performances. Color temperature, CRI, light intensity, light angle, glare shielding, and lighting controls are important considerations when adding accent lights.

EXTERIOR LIGHTING

Library lighting does not stop at the door. In addition to traditional exterior spaces such as library entrances, staff entrances, book drops, book pickups, loading docks, pathways, and parking lots, libraries are developing exterior spaces such as reading and gathering plazas, children's gardens, and sculpture gardens. Each of these areas will have specific lighting criteria for public safety and lighting criteria to develop a visually interesting environment. The actual tasks vary, but developing ambient and accent lighting in exteriors spaces is similar to, and equally as important as, developing ambient and accent lighting in interior spaces.

When designing lighting for the exterior, the most basic criteria should include minimizing lighting pollution such as light trespass, glare, and sky glow. Light trespass is the light that is emitted horizontally beyond the site boundaries and vertically into the sky. Accentuated at night, luminaire glare can become disabling and disorienting if not properly shielded. Envision high-beam headlights from on-coming traffic. Sky glow is a result of light emitted into the sky and reflected off atmospheric particles. Sky glow can be particularly annoying to star gazers, astronomers, and pilots and can be disorienting and debilitating to wildlife.

LIGHTING AND ENERGY DEMAND

Energy efficiency has long been an integral part of the lighting design process. In the late 1960s and early 1970s, energy demand within commercial buildings was escalating and ultimately outpaced energy production. In 1973, U.S. energy production and distribution declined to a catastrophic level when the Organization of Petroleum Exporting Countries increased oil prices and reduced oil exportation. The American Society of Heating,

Refrigerating and Air-Conditioning Engineers (ASHRAE) responded by drafting Standard 90.1 with full support of the Illuminating Engineering Society of North America (IESNA). Published in 1975, ASHRAE/IESNA Standard 90.1is the basis of federal and state energy codes and policies in use today.

The metric used in energy codes to calculate full electrical demand is called lighting power density (LPD). This metric accounts for the rated light socket demand of every luminaire that is hardwired into the building. In the process of developing lighting energy goals, operational energy should be considered along with LPD.

Operational energy is a realistic method for understanding and determining actual (or predicted actual) energy use. The operational energy of a library will take into account the number of hours that the library is open, the operation of automated sensors that switch lights OFF when rooms are vacant, and dim or switch OFF lights to compensate for daylight. Energy codes based on ASHRAE/IESNA 90.1 2010 include a small LPD modification for daylight compensation; it is included in the overall building energy model. But lighting energy codes have not yet embraced a method for calculating operational energy even though the same codes require automated controls to switch lighting OFF when the building rooms are not occupied. One method for calculating and/or understanding operational energy in your library is to install data loggers in utility rooms, storage rooms, private offices, restrooms, and others to document the number of hours that the lighting is switched ON or OFF during a typical day.

LIGHTING CONTROLS

Energy codes require basic automated lighting controls to switch lighting OFF in all spaces within a library except where life safety might be compromised, as in mechanical and electrical rooms and along egress paths. Automated controls are of two forms: overall building management systems that switch all lights OFF and ON relative to a defined operating schedule and local controls that sense daylight, occupancy, and vacancy. Automated lighting controls are required by energy codes because the best way to save lighting energy is to switch the lights OFF. It is common in libraries for all of the lights in public areas to be controlled by the overall building management system with local control devices in staff offices, workrooms, meeting rooms, utility rooms, and restrooms.

OCCUPANT AND VACANCY SENSORS

Occupant sensors switch the ambient lighting in a room ON when a person enters the room and switch the lighting OFF when the room is no longer occupied. Appropriate locations for occupant sensors are storage rooms, janitor rooms, restrooms, and rarely used nonpublic corridors. Vacancy sensors require the occupant to manually switch ON the lighting in a room, and they automatically switch the lighting OFF when the room is no longer occupied. These are appropriately used in offices and meeting rooms. Where daylight is available, vacancy sensors provide the occupant with an option to switch ON the electric lighting or to work via the available daylight without switching ON the electric lighting. In meeting and assembly rooms, vacancy sensors allow users to operate advanced dimming controls based on presentation and discussion requirements in lieu of a single ON/OFF control of the lighting. In these rooms, vacancy sensors are still required by code to switch the lighting OFF when the room is no longer occupied.

DIMMING CONTROLS

Dimming controls in meeting and assembly rooms must be easy to understand and easy to use. Pushbuttons, intensity risers, and ON/OFF buttons should be clearly marked. If a room has many zones and the controls are complex, as in rooms with dividers, a simple map that identifies the zone controlled by each pushbutton should be appropriately (and permanently) located near the control panel. One rule of thumb is that if the system is too complex for an untrained user to operate, then it is too complicated to be maintained and modified by facilities personnel.

DAYLIGHT COMPENSATION

Daylight compensation controls are not only a good idea; they are also required by ASHRAE-IESNA Standard 90.1–2010. Daylight compensation controls sense the amount of daylight present within the daylight zone (typically 15 feet from a window) and dim or switch the electric lighting OFF and ON based on the intensity of daylight present. It can be very disturbing to occupants when the lights suddenly switch OFF. While dimming ballasts, dimmable drivers, and dimming controls add significantly to the first cost of the lighting installation, facilities managers should encourage daylight dimming over switching for the comfort of users and staff.

WIRELESS CONTROLS

Wireless technology has been introduced into lighting control devices such as occupant sensors, vacancy sensors, dimming controls, and daylight sensors with some success. The advantage of wireless lighting control devices is a significant reduction in copper control wire, which will, in theory, reduce construction costs. However, one must not forget that wireless devices require lithium batteries. After an average service life of 10 years, the batteries will begin to fail and most control devices do not have indicators to identify a battery failure. If the lights simply do not switch ON, as in the case of occupant sensors, facilities manager will get the call that "the lights no longer work" and they will troubleshoot the issue unit they discover that the battery has failed. If a daylight sensor fails, it will likely not be noticed by the library staff or patrons and therefore not reported to facilities. In this scenario, the electricity that would be saved by dimming or switching the luminaires OFF will be lost. As for switching controls, if the system requires a remote handheld device to control the lights, consider how you will safeguard it as that handheld control device can easily become lost.

LIGHTING AND BUILDING MAINTENANCE

Maintaining the architectural and lighting systems in libraries requires lighting technologies that have long life, manual mechanisms that are durable, and building surfaces that can be easily refreshed. With the expanding use of LED lighting systems and wireless lighting controls, increased attention has been directed toward the service life of traditional light sources, transformers, and ballasts relative to state-of-the-art electronic and solid-state devices. There are two ways that manufacturers report service life: the rated life of light sources is identified as operating hours with multiple caveats attached (refer to LED sidebar) and the expected life of ballasts, transformers, drivers, and batteries, which is typically reported in years. Lamp and ballast manufacturers are improving the service life of the traditional lighting technologies; in fact, T8 fluorescent lamps rated for 84,000 hours are surpassing the reported life of solid-state LED typically reported to be 50,000 hours (L70). The service life of each of these systems is not insignificant and each system has its drawback. While the 84,000-hour service life of T8 fluorescent may be longer than the service life of LED, T8 operates at a higher energy demand. The energy savings for LED will cause 50,000 hours to seem like a better choice, but L70 means that at 50,000 hours the LED array is operating at 70 percent of its full light output and 100 percent of its energy demand.

STATE-OF-THE-ART LED

Solid-state LED lighting systems have evolved from novelty color-changing accent lights to respectable ambient and task lighting systems. These systems are attractive to owners for two reasons: "they use less energy than traditional light sources" and "they last forever." The technology and reliability of LED lighting systems have improved significantly over the earliest versions that began to appear in the late 1990s. As of 2015, LED technology, efficacy, stability, and cost to own are still evolving.

Types of LED array versus remote phosphor. Two types of LED systems stand out in the many options available: LED arrays and LED remote phosphor. Arrays consist of a circuit board with LEDs attached, typically round with a symmetrical pattern or linear with a linear pattern. The LEDs in the array are exposed, providing light distribution primarily in one direction. The color characteristics are based on the technology and manufacturer of the specific diode. Remote phosphor LEDs as of this writing are only available in a round configuration appropriate for accent lights or downlights. The system consists of reflective chamber with an encapsulated LED chip located at the bottom. A remote lens, located at the top of the chamber, is made of color-correcting phosphors with color-rendering capabilities up to 90 CRI. Remote phosphor systems typically include reflectors to provide various lighting distributions such as 15 degree, 25 degree, and 40 degree. These systems will appropriately replace incandescent halogen light sources when they become available at a competitive price.

Efficiency versus efficacy. Efficacy in lighting systems is defined as lumen per watt, or light output per unit of energy used. Different from efficiency which is a measure of the energy lost in a system, efficacy is more like miles per gallon. Efficacy is the metric that the lighting industry has accepted as appropriate for evaluating the performance of LED. This metric assumes that the LED does not have a reflector that will reduce the light output, and it assumes that the LEDs are not shielded, which will also reduce the light output. It is important to understand that as soon as the LED array or module is installed in a housing with shielding and reflectors, the efficacy of the LED will change and the lighting system must be evaluated for luminaire efficiency, not LED efficacy.

Replacement lamps. Every quarter, lighting manufacturers introduce new replacement lamps made with LED arrays. These are typically in the shape of common incandescent light bulbs with screw-based sockets, but linear fluorescent LED replacement lamps are becoming more available. This is a very large market for lamp manufacturers. Consider how many incandescent and linear fluorescent luminaires are currently operating in residential and commercial buildings. Be aware that replacement lamps do not operate the same nor are their operating characteristics the same as those installed in luminaires designed specifically to house LED. Be certain to read and understand all of the packaging caveats and claims regarding service life and energy demand of replacement LED lamps.

Service life. It is not true that LED lighting systems will "last forever." Not only do they fail; but also they fail in a very concerning manner. The current (2015) methods of rating LED life is L70, L80, or L90. The lighting industry developed this rating system based on the time it takes for an LED array to reach a light output that is 70 percent, 80 percent, or 90 percent of its original light output. A rating of L70, 50,000 means that at 50,000 hours the light intensity from the array is 70 percent less than the original intensity, and at the same energy consumption. It also means that the luminaire has not gone dark or "burned out" as we typically understand lamp failures. The library staff and patrons may find that visual tasks have become increasingly more difficult but this is not reported to facilities as a lighting failure because the luminaire is still producing light.

LM-80 is a system developed by the IESNA along with a system called TM-21. LM-80 is similar to the L80 in that it equates to 80 percent light output at the tested and reported life. TM-21 takes the LM-80 data of an LED light source, and uses algorithms to make a prediction of the service life. While this is a complicated formula, it yields a very important bit of data, that is, how long the lighting system will provide 90 percent of the initial light output. Ninety percent is an important benchmark because this is the amount of light that a fluorescent system will lose over its rated service life of 30,000 to 84,000 hours.

Maintenance. Perhaps the most important question to ask when considering LED systems is how to replace the array or remote phosphor module when it burns out. In early vintage LED luminaires, and in some current small-profile LED "stick" luminaires, the LED array is integral to the housing; meaning, it cannot be replaced. LED luminaire manufacturers are resolving this by installing LED arrays and modules that can be removed and replaced. Be aware that LEDs are still evolving and the array technology or the exact array installed at the time of construction may not be manufactured when the LED array or module reaches its end of service life. As of this writing, stocking LED arrays and modules in the same manner that we stock traditional lamps is a very expensive proposition.

Manual technologies will include luminaires and lighting controls that are handled, touched, or manually operated. Luminaire lenses removed for routine maintenance should be of glass or a quality acrylic material such that they do not crack or become brittle over time. Luminaires located where they can be operated or adjusted by the public should have components such as switches and adjustability mechanisms that are strong enough to withstand severe pressure and abuse. Luminaires located on book stacks must be firmly attached to resist hands-on downward pressure from both children and adults. Children and young adults may view luminaires attached to book stacks as a playful source for "chin-ups" while adults may use them for stability as they bend down to retrieve books from lower shelves.

The skills and resources required for building maintenance must be explicitly understood by all project team members to ensure a successful outcome. Energy-efficient lighting strategies, for example, rely on high light reflectance throughout the interior in order to reduce the numbers of luminaires required for appropriate illumination. As a result, white or pastel surfaces should be used if possible and periodically repainted. In some areas, the lightly colored surfaces are at odds with the high use of the library, requiring increased attention to maintenance. Periodic repainting will be an important part of the library's operations going forward.

HOW TO DEVELOP LIGHTING CRITERIA

There are no set rules for developing the lighting criteria for libraries. Public, private, academic, research, and specialty libraries located in various climates and latitudes throughout the country, all have unique conditions and criteria relative to how the library is used, operated, funded, and maintained. Each library will require a unique set of design criteria based on its type and location parameters.

The minimum criteria for energy demand, lighting controls, and exterior light trespass will be found in local and national energy and building codes. Enhanced criteria for these can be obtained from voluntary programs such as the U.S. Green Building Council's Leadership in Energy and Environmental Design certification. The most accepted standards for light levels in libraries are those developed by the IESNA and documented in the most recent *IESNA Library Lighting Recommended Practice RP-4–2013*.

In general, specific light levels for libraries are not included in codes. The exceptions are for life safety. Spaces without windows are required to have 10 fc measured 30 inches above the floor per the International Building Code. Stairs are required to have 10 fc measured at the center of the tread per the American National Standards Institute. National and state elevator codes enforce specific light levels at the elevator threshold, within the cab, in the machine room, and in the elevator pit. Local health codes enforce various light levels for surfaces where *food for sale* is prepared as in cafés and coffee shops. And, the National Fire Protection Association enforces minimum light levels for egress paths from buildings, at egress door thresholds, and in areas of refuge.

The first criteria that you must set will be to identify who will be designing the lighting system for your library, because lighting can be designed by architects, interior designers, engineers, or lighting consultants. Your selection should be based on the lighting professional's knowledge of light quality, quality lighting systems, and technical lighting. If you do not select the architect as your lighting designer, then the design professional that you do select should have a synergistic relationship with the architect and interior design team and should be someone who appropriately addresses the library's desires and concerns.

By understanding the basic design process of architects and lighting professionals, you will be able to narrow down the number and types of design criteria that apply to your facility. The process begins with identifying user demographics and the way the library will be operated followed by reviewing the architectural design and layout. At this point, the design team will develop an interior and exterior roadmap to assign zones for ambient, task, and accent lighting; to develop appropriate light quality goals; to address architectural aesthetics and way-finding; and to identify locations for public art and special events. Luminaires and light sources will be reviewed for performance, glare control, efficiency, energy demand, durability, maintainability, and installed cost. Lighting control requirements for meeting rooms, audiovisual rooms and public assembly will be identified and documented. Codes and lighting recommendations will be reviewed for minimum light levels, lighting controls, energy demand, and life safety. And the selected lighting and control systems will be tested to ensure that minimum code requirements are achieved.

Table 10.1 provides a list of questions and directions that will help you identify and document the light criteria applicable to your library. By identifying the questions that relate to your library, you can build a set of criteria to move forward with your lighting.

Table 10.1   Questions and Comments for Developing Lighting Criteria

Library Basics	
Who uses this library?	The demographics of staff and library users will determine the basic requirements for light quality, way-finding, durability, security, and vandal resistance.
What is the right perception of our library?	Consider library imagery derived from words such as "dynamic," "conservative," "traditional," "homey," "loungey," "colorful," "artistic," and so on.
What level of flexibility is required?	Planning for flexibility is an exercise in planning for the future. Ultimate flexibility means that all furniture, equipment, book stacks, and kiosks will be designed to be moved. Minimal flexibility means that the library will be less likely to be reconfigured and will be more cost-effective.
What is the task?	Each task in a library is illuminated differently. Identifying the task will aid in developing the appropriate lighting.
Light Quality	
Will the luminaire cause glare?	Indirect luminaires and direct luminaires with proper shielding will reduce or eliminate glare.
How is the luminaire shielded?	All direct luminaires should be shielded to obscure the light source. Diffuse or textured glass is the most durable for small luminaires. Diffuse or textured acrylic is appropriate for large linear or pendant luminaires.
Does the proposed lighting system include lighting walls and ceilings?	Illuminating the ceiling and the walls will create a perception of brightness even if the overall ambient lighting is low.
When is CRI important?	The CRI of light sources used to illuminate art, people as in speakers or presenters, archival texts, color samples, and graphic displays should be 90 or higher. CRI of 80 is appropriate for ambient light in most library spaces.
Does the lighting design reduce contrast?	Balancing the lighting on ceilings and walls with local task lighting will reduce visual contrast and eye strain.
Does the lighting system compensate for daylight?	Adding lighting to the ceiling and walls reduces the contrast between bright windows and interior surfaces.

Light Quality	
When is direct light appropriate?	Direct light increases light levels on horizontal work surfaces. Distracting glare and shadows on faces and tasks result from improperly shielded direct luminaires.
When is indirect light appropriate?	Indirect lighting reduces light contrast on vertical and horizontal surfaces, softens shadows, and reduces glare. Low light levels and high energy demand may result. Ceilings must be 10'-0" or higher.
When is direct+indirect lighting appropriate?	Direct + indirect lighting provides all of the benefits of direct-only and indirect-only systems. Ceilings must be 10'-0" or higher.
Where is accent lighting used?	Accent lighting is used to highlight architectural features, special objects, surfaces, signage, way-finding paths, lecturers, and performers.
Does the lighting system come in at the right cost to own?	Lighting costs are in balance if the quality of the luminaire justifies the associated cost. Consider special luminaires for public spaces and lower cost commodity luminaires for storage and utility rooms.
What is the right intensity of the lighting?	Light intensity will vary by task. Industry standard for light levels will be found in the Illuminating Engineering Society of North America's *Lighting Recommended Practice RP-4–2013*.
Lighting Controls	
Are occupant sensors or vacancy sensors more appropriate for the space?	Occupant sensors switch lights OFF and ON. Vacancy sensors require manual ON and automatically switch lights OFF. Vacancy sensors should be used in rooms where daylight is available and/or where local dimming controls are required.
When should wireless lighting controls be used?	Wireless lighting controls eliminate the requirement for copper control wire, reducing the first cost of the library. Wireless controls require lithium batteries that will eventually fail. Ensure that the device has a reporting system to alert facilities when the battery fails.
When should automation be used for controlling task lights?	Task lights should always be controlled with local vacancy sensors.
Why use expensive dimming ballasts and controls for daylight compensation?	Dimming ballasts are used for daylight compensation to reduce the distraction of lights switching OFF and ON.
Are local dimming controls required?	Local dimming controls are appropriate for meeting rooms and assembly rooms in which the primary use is for lectures or performance.
Is the local dimming control panel easy to understand and use?	Local dimming controls should be labeled for ease of use. In complex rooms such as rooms with dividers, a zone map that identifies the control button should be posted near the control panel.
Energy Demand	
How will reducing overall building energy demand affect light quality?	If the lighting system is properly designed, reducing the overall building energy demand should not affect light quality.

(*Continued*)

Table 10.1 (Continued)

Energy Demand	
Which will save more energy: occupant sensors or vacancy sensors?	Vacancy sensors give the occupant a choice to not turn ON the lights. Occupant sensors always turn the lights ON when a person enters the room.
Is incandescent halogen lighting appropriate?	Incandescent halogen light sources are appropriate in locations where CRI is critical, and where the frequency of use does not justify the first cost of installing LED. When using incandescent lamps always install a dimmer for control. By setting the dimmer at 90% of full light output or less, the life of an incandescent lamp will be extended by 300% to 400%; i.e., a lamp rated for 5000 hours will operate up to 20,000 hours.
Energy-Efficient Building Systems	
How do mechanical systems affect lighting?	Traditional variable air volume (VAV) mechanical systems are fairly simple to coordinate with lighting. Chilled beam systems have very specific cadence requirements and will affect the cadence of the lighting system. This coordination typically means that more light fixtures will be required with a chilled beam system than with a VAV system.
Do ceiling types affect lighting and energy?	Ceiling reflectance will affect the ambient light level of the room, in particular if the lighting system is indirect. The higher the reflectance, the more light will be returned to the room. A space without ceiling should have a very high reflectance paint. More light will be lost in open structure ceilings than it will with a ceiling tile.
How does the library interior affect the lighting efficiency?	Interior surfaces with high reflectance values such as white or pastels will reflect more light back into the room than darker surfaces, which absorb light.
Maintenance	
What is the rated service life of the light source?	The service life of all lamp types varies by manufacturer. The design team should provide a summary of the most current technologies for review.
What is the rated service life of the lighting electronics?	The service life of all lighting technologies varies by manufacturer. The design team should provide a summary of the most current technologies for review.
What is the lamp and ballast compatibility?	Most fluorescent manufacturers warrant their lamp with their ballasts for five years. Lamp and ballast manufacturers warrant their products as a system; i.e., the lamp warranty and the ballast warranty will each be void if the lamp and ballast are not from the same manufacturer.
Where is the transformer/ ballast/driver located?	Ensure that transformers, ballasts, and drivers are located in the luminaire such that they can be easily removed and replaced.
Will the luminaire collect dust and dirt?	All suspended luminaires and luminaires with lenses will collect dust and insects. Ensure that lenses are durable and can be easily removed for cleaning.
Is it possible to replace the LED array?	Not all LED arrays are replaceable. Ensure that they can be easily removed and replaced when they fail.
Is the luminaire easy to relamp?	It is if it can be reached with a ladder, if the lens is toolless, and/or if the hardware screws and pins are captive.

CONCLUSION

The lighting industry is in a state of flux. In the past decade, advancements in solid-state LEDs and fluorescent and halogen technologies and performance have changed the way that facilities managers, engineers, and lighting professionals evaluate and discuss lighting systems. And future advancements will continue to shape the way we think about lighting technologies. These advancements have drawn attention away from the most important and most basic criteria for evaluating a lighting system and that is light quality and psychological well-being.

As we continue to debate the intrinsic value of energy saving and long-term maintenance, we must remember that a system that does not provide the right light for the right space is not sustainable. It will ultimately be overridden by the basic human need to be able to read, write, and be productive. People, not managers, designers, or code officials, will add lighting as required to perform and function as desired within the library environment.

BIBLIOGRAPHY

1. David L. DiLaura, Kevin W. Houser, Richard G. Mistrick, and Gary R. Steffy. 2010. *The Lighting Handbook, Tenth Edition, Reference and Application.* Illuminating Engineering Society of North America, New York.

2. J. P. Freyssinierr, J. Taylor, D. Frering, and P. Rizzo. 2009. Considerations for Successful LED Applications. Proceedings for China SSL 2009, 6th International Forum on Solid State Lighting, October 14–16, 2009, Shenzhen, China, pp. 206–209.

3. Illuminating Engineering Society Library Lighting Committee. 2013. *Recommended Practice for Library Lighting, RP-4-13.* Illuminating Engineering Society of North America, New York.

4. Alan Hedge, William R. Sims Jr., and Franklin D. Becker. 1995. "The Effects of Lensed-Indirect and Parabolic Lighting on the Satisfaction, Visual Health, and Productivity of Office Workers." *Ergonomics* 38(2): 260–280.

5. Alliance to Save Energy. 2013. "History of Energy Efficiency." January 2013. Alliance Commission on National Energy Efficiency Policy. https://www.ase.org/sites/ase.org/files/resources/Media%20 browser/ee_commission_history_report_2-1-13.pdf.

6. Bruce D. Hunn. 2010. "35 Years of Standard 90.1." *ASHRAE Journal*: 36–46. https://www.ashrae.org/ resources--publications/bookstore/90-1---celebrating-35-years-of-energy-efficiency.

7. Lighting Research Center. "Correlated Color Temperature." Rensselaer Polytechnic Institute. Accessed September 29, 2015. http://www.lrc.rpi.edu/education/learning/terminology/cct.asp.

8. Lighting Research Center. "What Is Color Rendering Index?" Rensselaer Polytechnic Institute. Accessed September 29, 2015. http://www.lrc.rpi.edu/programs/nlpip/lightinganswers/lightsources/ legal.asp.

9. Traci Engel Lesneski and Carla Gallina. 2014. "Lighting Quality, Not Quantity," Library by Design, *Library Journal* (June 9, 2014). http://lj.libraryjournal.com/2014/06/buildings/lbd/lighting-quality-not-quantity-library-by-design/.

11

Integrating Technology

Edward M. Corrado

Technology is ubiquitous, and all library renovations, except possibly the most minor ones, will have various technological components to them. This is especially true of newly renovated spaces in academic libraries. This chapter is not meant to be a comprehensive how-to, a laundry list, or a case study. Instead it aims to provide some practical advice as well as some examples about different topics to consider when integrating technology into a library renovation. While not everything mentioned here will apply to all projects, especially smaller renovations, and there will likely be additional factors to consider based on local circumstances, the suggestions contained here should help frame the appropriate questions to ask and issues to investigate about when planning a library renovation.

PLANNING

Planning for the technological aspects of a library renovation is important. However, librarians and information technologists cannot stop at planning; they also need to be intimately involved with the ongoing management of the technology portions of the project. During a major renovation, mistakes can happen if someone who is familiar with the planned use of the space is not there. There are many stories of blueprints that were incorrect; for example, a room that did not have a door where you would expect or an elevator button that was placed too far away from the elevator to actually board the elevator before the door closed.

Simone L. Yearwood (2015) of Queens College, City University of New York, believes that "The most important thing to remember when planning your renovations is to insist that a practicing librarian serve on the planning and implementation team" (364). This is sound advice. It is also wise to include someone on your planning and implementation team who is familiar with the information technology used in libraries, in general, and how technology is planned to be used in the renovated space, in particular. The roles of librarian and information technology expert are important because they can bring a modern perspective on libraries and librarianship to the planning process. While building project planners will have the library's best interests in mind, if they haven't been involved in a recent library-related project, they may not have a current perspective on what a modern academic library is and "University libraries cannot afford to be seen as warehouses for printed materials" (Villa 2012, 310).

Shawna Sadler (2015), director of Digital Library and Innovation at Deakin University Library in Geelong, Victoria, Australia, offers some useful advice in her column that appeared in the *Journal of Library Administration* in 2015. Sadler outlines various items that a technology project manager should expect throughout a major renovation or addition to a library. She covers items and challenges from the beginning of the planning to the completion to the project. She discusses strategic planning, budgeting, conducting an environmental completion, understanding the construction process, soliciting feedback, investigating what technologies are available on the market, training, formal planning, considering accessibility and green technologies, construction infrastructure, working with blueprints, timelines, working with consultants and contracts on installation, and working with project managers. Sadler based her items and challenges on what she learned while working on the technological aspects of a major $200 million project with a $13 million technology budget. Obviously, the size and scope of Sadler's project are much greater than what most librarians will be involved with, and on smaller projects, all of the things Sadler outlines might not apply. Still, it is a valuable resource for librarians and information technologists to consult when embarking on a renovation with a major technology component.

There are many impressive new technologies available to libraries. However, when planning to integrate technology into a library renovation, it is important to keep the library's mission in mind. The mission should be leading the technological aspects of the renovation and not the other way around.

The planning process for technology should involve representatives from various stakeholder groups. Stakeholders may include students, librarians, other campus units, faculty, administrators, funders, information technology experts, and others. A highly participatory process is often desired in order to have the best input. Each renovation and each library has different needs. Therefore the "first step is to recognize the individuality in each institution and its library. There is not a one-size-fits-all library design" (Bostick and Irwin 2014, 4).

Julie Villa of Bond Architects recommends the following basic steps for planning a student-centered learning commons. The first step is to examine the student body by researching its habits and demographics. Different habits and demographics may require different spaces and thus require different types of technology. While examining the student body, library renovation planners should document the different "types of areas, equipment, and amenities that are most used in the current facility and those that are lacking" (Villa 2012, 314).

The second basic step that Villa recommends is to become familiar with the institutional goals of the university in order to understand the broader context of the project. Knowing what types of research and offerings the university is planning to offer will help plan the space. For instance, if there will be an increased focus on digital humanities at the university in the future, the library may want to consider adding a digital humanities lab that includes both specialized software and hardware. Another possibility, which Villa mentions, is that the university may have decided to focus on sustainability. If that is the case, it might be wise to incorporate low-power computers and other energy-efficient technology in the design.

Talking to users is the third step. Student groups, faculty, and librarians should be consulted. What do they want from the renovated space in terms of technology? Also, at this stage, it can be useful to talk to librarians and information technologists at other institutions that have recently been through a library renovation.

The fourth step is to identify needs. This may involve creating a list that includes various needs, including the needs of various stakeholders such as students, faculty, librarians, and staff.

Developing recommendations is the fifth step that Villa identified. Priorities for both short-term and long-term goals and objectives should be identified. In this first stage, the planners may make recommendations with the expectation that additional stages will be added in the future. This can help present the case to university administration for ongoing support. This is extremely important when dealing with technology because even the best technology today may be obsolete in five to ten years (in some circumstances, it might be even sooner than that).

The sixth step Villa recommends is to implement and test. Any new technology should be tested before widely implemented if possible. This may involve getting some demonstration units from the vendor or other libraries or institutions that use the same or similar technology. It is important to give any technology or technology-related service a trial period and then evaluate its effectiveness.

It is important to keep in mind purchasing requirements and the lead times necessary to order and deliver the technology components of your renovation. Obviously this applies to furniture and other aspects as well but it is very important with technology, especially with cutting-edge technology that may not already be on state contract if you are in a public institution.

FLEXIBILITY

Libraries in the past have had relatively fixed purposes. Bookshelves were in fixed locations and immovable with the overall library's "design that was often simple and static" (Bostick and Irwin 2014, 2). This type of design does not meet the needs of the modern or future library. Technology is changing at a rapid rate. It is difficult to predict what types of technology will be ubiquitous 5 years from now, let alone in the next 20 or 30 years, which may very well be the amount of time that will elapse before the next major library renovation. Because of this, it is important to design flexible spaces that can be reconfigured at little or no expense when adjustments are desired in the future. This is true of all aspects of a renovation, but flexibility may be particularly important for the technological portions of a renovation project. Librarians, information technologists, and others should "take into consideration future technologies, and plan for the rapid speed at which technology is evolving" (Yearwood 2015, 365).

A post-occupancy study of library building renovations conducted by Steven Carrico and Ann Lindell concluded that, among other things, "Libraries will need to continually reinvent their places and roles on academic campuses" and that "Easy access to computing equipment is still a need on academic campuses" (2012, 59). Changing technology and evolving user behavior requires that library spaces be designed to be able to continually adapt "to accommodate changing technologies and user behaviors" (59). Additionally Carrico and Lindell advise that "Flexibility is a virtue. Adaptable interior spaces and movable, modular furnishing allow users to self-configure spaces to serve different needs" (60).

Another way to accommodate the need for technological flexibility is to install a raised floor system that allows electrical outlets, Ethernet connectors, and other wiring to be easily moved when necessary. During renovations, raised floor systems can often be placed on top of an existing floor, which would be less expensive than it would be to install less-flexible wiring into the floor. Of course, the expense will vary on the construction of the building and the overall scope of the project. Even when installing a raised floor is more expensive in the short term, it may still be worthwhile because it can increase the multitude of ways the space can be utilized now and in the future.

Flexibility also includes providing different types of spaces to help "cultivate different courses of study. [. . .] Increasingly, students are requiring a variety of collaborative spaces" (Bostick and Irwin, 2014, 3). An example that provided different types of spaces for technology is the University of Central Florida's 2010 renovation of the Main Library's Knowledge Commons. This library renovation included areas that featured "modular, movable furnishings to accommodate both the solitary researcher and groups working together on projects" (Carrico and Lindell, 2012, 42–43). In a flexible environment such as this, a student or a group of students can organize the space for their particular needs.

VARIETY OF SPACES

Different types of spaces are needed in a modern library. More and more student work is done in a group setting, so it is important to have collaborative space. In many situations it is also extremely desirable to include state-of-the-art media spaces and maker spaces in a library renovation plan.

COLLABORATIVE SPACE

Because academic libraries are, by their very nature, interdisciplinary and neutral places on the campus, "Academic libraries are in the unique position of being able to provide the interdisciplinary collaborative spaces on campus that foster these new styles of learning" (Villa 2012, 311). These new styles of learning opportunities can be enhanced with the proper technology. Different types of collaboration can take place, and when planning a library renovation, it is wise to keep all of them in mind even though, depending on the scope of the project, they may not all apply in every situation. For example, Sharon Bostick and Bryan Irwin (2014) identified the following five different types of collaborations that might take place in the library: student to student, student to staff, staff to staff, faculty to faculty, and partner to partner. Undoubtedly there are additional possibilities for collaboration that can be identified in any given library as well. Different types of collaborations may require different types of technology. Solutions such as "group work tables that allow students to cluster around monitor screens and share information stored on individual laptops" (Villa 2012, 312) can provide a technological platform to enhance collaboration. However, a computer attached to a smart board may be better suited for staff-to-staff collaborations. Therefore it is important to consider the different types of collaboration that might take place in the renovated area of the library and then determine what technology might best support it.

MEDIA SPACES

Rich media spaces are becoming more and more important on college campuses and other types of environments. Many modern library renovations are including this type of technology. During the recent renovation of the Benjamin S. Rosenthal Library of the Queens College of the City University of New York, "A state-of-the-art seminar room with video conferencing and webcasting technologies was created along with the installation of three mediascape rooms" (Yearwood 2015, 363). A mediascape room is described as a glass-enclosed study room that integrates furniture and technology, including a large-screen television monitor that students can connect their own devices to, in order to enhance collaboration in a connected world (Yearwood 2014, 2).

In 2014, Texas Christian University announced that extensive renovations to the Mary Couts Burnett Library would include two new innovative study spaces. The spaces were to be called the Visualization Lab and the Sandbox. The Visualization Lab "will allow people to project information, such as data or virtual environments, onto the walls" and "The Sandbox will be similar in layout to an Apple Store and will be equipped with new technology and software for student and faculty use" according to Tony Hartin, an architect working on the project (McReynolds 2014). The dean of libraries, June Koeker, said that "media editing suites for projects that require multimedia elements will also be added" (McReynolds 2014).

Pennsylvania State University (Penn State) has developed a One Button Studio for the Media Commons in the university libraries. This project won a 2014 award from the American Library Association as a "Cutting-Edge Technology in Library Services." The One Button Studio is a simple, easy-to-use video recording studio that can be utilized by someone without any previous experience with video production. http://onebutton .psu.edu/. It is an excellent example of a rich multimedia creation space that can be incorporated into a library renovation.

MAKER SPACES

A popular addition in many libraries is a maker space. Maker spaces, which may also be referred to as hackerspaces or fablabs, are creative do-it-yourself spaces that allow people to come together to create and learn. While different maker spaces have different technology, "In libraries they often have 3D printers, software, electronics, craft and hardware supplies and tools, and more" (Kroski 2013). In addition to determining what technology to acquire for a maker space, there are other considerations. Some of the equipment installed in a maker space may have specialized requirements. For example, some types of 3D printers may produce fumes that may require additional ventilation. Other technological equipment may have specific electrical requirements. Staffing of a maker space is another important consideration. New staff may need to be hired or existing staff may need to be trained and have their job duties adjusted.

In some ways similar to maker spaces, data research labs and digital humanities centers, such as the Alabama Digital Humanities Center (ADHC) located in the Amelia Gayle Gorgas Library at the University of Alabama, require specialized software and staffing. The ADHC has two full-time employees, high-end Apple computers, a 65-inch multitouch monitor, high-end video projectors, and specialized software including Auto Desk AutoCAD 2011, ESRI ArcGIS, SPSS, and the <oXygen/>xml editor. When planning such a space during a library renovation, this type of technology as well as staffing needs must be considered.

TECHNOLOGICAL INFRASTRUCTURE

Students and other library patrons are often bringing and using their own devices in the library. This phenomenon is known as bring your own device or BYOD. IBM MobileFirst (2015) describes BYOD for businesses as "an IT policy where employees are allowed or encouraged to use their personal mobile devices—and, increasingly, notebook PCs—to access enterprise data and systems." In academic environments, the BYOD movement also encompasses students bringing their own technology to the classroom and the library to use during their scholarly pursuits. When library patrons bring their own devices, it can be more convenient for them and can save the library from having to purchase, install, and maintain as many computers as they would otherwise need to. However, BYOD does have implications for libraries, including the need for additional electricity and Internet bandwidth.

Although many of today's mobile devices have significantly longer battery life than in the past, having proper electrical capability in a technology-rich environment is important. A recent unpublished survey conducted by the student association at the University of Alabama identified the lack of electrical outlets as one of the most pressing concerns that undergraduate students have when it comes to the libraries on campus. A survey of University of Wisconsin students conducted in December 2013 showed that "67% [of students] need to charge at least one device every day during their time on campus" (Lockncharge 2014).

Installing additional electricity can be costly, especially in an old building where wiring and other electrical components may have not been updated. However, when integrating technology into a library renovation plan, it is important to consider and it has the potential to increase library usage. Strong antidotal evidence has shown that students of the University of Alabama use the library more often and for longer periods of time in areas where the library has recently added more electrical outlets.

"With the extraordinary preponderance of electronic devices in the library, there is now the need for charging capacity. Many libraries are not equipped to handle such a load. In addition, the locations of electrical outlets or sockets must be flexible as well" (Bostick and Irwin 2014, 3). As mentioned previously, one way to increase flexibility and to allow for electrical outlets in the middle of a large room is to install a raised floor. Georgia Tech's East Commons took another approach during its 2005 renovation. The renovated space features "movable extension outlets suspended from the ceiling, a feature that allows users to sit with a laptop anywhere in the room while having easy access to a power outlet" (Carrico and Lindell 2012, 45).

Electricity, of course, is important not only for BYOD. There needs to be enough electricity to support the library's computers, large-screen monitors, and various other technological offerings. While some universities have made the news by decreasing the number of computer labs and other computers available for student use, libraries cannot rely on BYOD for all of the library patrons' computing needs. Therefore, librarians and information technologists need to incorporate library-supplied computing into the environment. Although most students have personal computers, they don't always like to bring their computers with them because they might not be laptops, they may be too heavy or clunky to carry with all of their text books, or the owners may have a fear of damaging them or fear of theft. Additionally some students, especially economically disadvantaged ones, may not have their own computer, let alone a state-of-the-art laptop. Faculty might not have laptops that they can bring onto campus or into the library. For example, St. Louis Community College–Florissant Valley "is a commuter college, and the many students who depend on public transportation to attend must often carry their belongings with them throughout the day. While some students may own a personal laptop, many do not bring it to campus for that reason" (Villa 2012, 317).

Another reason to include computers in a library renovation instead of relying on BYOD is because there are many specialty applications that require high-end or very specific hardware or software. If a researcher is working with big data, he or she may need a high-end computer with a significant amount of memory and processing power. If students are working on a computer-aided design project, they may need expensive specialty software that they are not able to install on their computer because of licensing restrictions.

In today's day and age with online databases, eBooks, and the proliferation of other electronic resources, it is hard to imagine a modern library without significant Internet bandwidth. Internet connectivity can be delivered to devices in multiple ways. The two most common methods that a library would use to install Internet connectivity to devices during a renovation is wired Ethernet connections or a wireless local area network system (better known as Wi-Fi). While most BYOD technology will be better equipped for wireless connections, a library should also include wired Ethernet connections since wired connections offer some advantages over Wi-Fi. Wired Ethernet connections to the Internet are still considered more reliable and faster. Reliability leads to less time spent troubleshooting problems by library staff and less-frustrated users. The increased speed can offer significant advantages when students and other researchers are working with big data or are streaming high-definition video. Despite its limitations, Wi-Fi is still important in a renovated library space as well. In fact, Wi-Fi is a necessity in a BYOD environment. Many devices such as mobile phones, tablets, and some lightweight computers such as the Apple MacBook Air do not come with Ethernet connectors.

Sufficient bandwidth and wireless capability is important. People have more Internet-connected devices than ever before and that trend is still going up. At the end of 2014, it was estimated that there was 12 billion Internet-connected devices in use. That is an average of 1.7 devices for every person on the planet (Waring 2014). The number of Internet-connected devices in the United States (2.9 per person), Canada (3.0), and European countries such as the Netherlands (3.6), United Kingdom (3.1), and Germany (2.4) is even higher (Statista 2015). Strategic Analytics has forecasted that by 2020 that number of devices worldwide will be a staggering 33 billion, or 4.3 Internet-connected devices per person (Waring 2014). It is likely that most library patrons in the future will be carrying multiple mobile devices with them (if they aren't already). And students are not just using the mobile devices such as tablets or smartphones to play games, check social networking sites, or send text messages to friends. A study conducted by McGraw-Hill Education and Hanover Research reported that in 2014 over 80 percent of college students use tablets or smartphones to help them study (Hennick 2015).

Librarians and information technologists will need to make sure to include a wireless network that is capable and has enough bandwidth to handle multiple devices per patron in their library renovation plans. When preparing for a renovation, it is important to consider future usage as it is usually easier and cheaper to install technological infrastructure during a renovation than it is to go back later and ask university administrators for additional infrastructure. When planning for electricity and networking in any renovation, it is wise to put in more than you think you will need.

SPACES FOR LIBRARIANS AND STAFF

When integrating technology into a library renovation, it is important to keep in mind the technology needs of librarians and other library staff. As with technology-rich public spaces designed for library patrons, flexibility is an important aspect of design. Consulting librarians and staff who will work in the renovated space can assist in ensuring that the space meets current and future needs. As with public spaces, sufficient electrical and Internet capabilities are paramount. It is important to keep ergonomics and accessibility in mind as well.

ACCESSIBILITY REQUIREMENTS

It should be understood that when renovating any physical space, accessibility for people with disabilities must be considered. Unfortunately, sometimes technological accessibility is overlooked in the process. For example, touch screen–enabled digital signage, multimedia production studies, 3D printers, instructor podiums, or other technology need to be installed at the appropriate height and with the proper clearances for someone in a wheelchair. Most universities will have a department or person responsible for ensuring compliance with applicable laws and regulations; it is highly recommended that they be involved in any library renovation planning. In some cases, the ADA or other local laws might not require the most convenient mode of access for those with disabilities. It is recommended that, regardless of the minimum legal requirements, when renovating a space is made as accessible as possible given any limitations. Accessibility should not be just about compliance and what is required by law; rather, accessibility should be about expanding possibilities.

CONCLUSION

Libraries are valuable institutions that can be seen as the intellectual center of the university. Libraries offer information resources and services not only to current faculty students and staff. Research has shown that libraries are the second highest ranked facility on campus when prospective students are considering where to go for their degree (Oakleaf 2010). In order to continue to have this well-deserved reputation and impact, libraries need to meet current and future expectations. Including major technological offerings in newly renovated spaces is one that will help meet this challenge.

Integrating technology into an academic library renovation requires careful planning. The planning process needs to involve appropriate stakeholders including, among others, librarians, information technologists, students, faculty, and administration. When planning a renovation, it is important to consider current and future technological needs. This includes ensuring that the renovated space has enough electricity and networking to meet future demands. Also because learning styles and scholarly projects vary, it is wise to have multiple technology-rich environments in the library.

The rate of technological change is constantly increasing; in order to keep up with this change in the future with limited budgets, it is important to incorporate as much flexibility into the design as practical. Making sure that the space is accessible to all can help further the democratization of information that libraries are known for.

Additionally, planners need to remember not to forget the impact of renovated space on existing librarians and library staff. Is there a need for additional skillsets in the library? Is it necessary to offer training in the use of equipment? Will some librarians' roles change? It depends on the technology and services offered. However, by keeping these questions in mind as well as the library's and university's missions, a renovated space that is highly integrated with technology can successfully serve students and faculty for years to come.

BIBLIOGRAPHY

American Library Association. 2015. "ADA and Libraries." Accessed November 7, 2015. http://www.ala
.org/tools/ada-and-libraries.

Bostick, Sharon, and Bryan Irwin. 2014. "Library Design in the Age of Technology Planning for a Changing Environment." Paper presented at the International Association of University Libraries (IATUL) Conference, Nanyang Technological University, Singapore, June 4–7, 2014. http://docs.lib
.purdue.edu/iatul/2014/plenaries/3/.

Carrico, Steven, and Ann Lindell. 2012. "A Post-Occupancy Look at Library Building Renovations: Meeting the Needs of the Twenty-First Century Users." In *Meeting the Needs of Student Users in Academic Libraries*, edited by Michele Crump and LeiLani Freund, 37–68. Oxford: Chandos Publishing.

Hennick, Calvin. 2015. "How Colleges Are Rethinking Network Infrastructure to Support Student Demand." *EdTech Magazine*. Published October 27. http://www.edtechmagazine.com/higher/
article/2015/10/higher-ed-readies-next-network-upgrades.

IBM MobileFirst. 2015. "BYOD: Bring Your Own Device." Accessed December 17, 2015. http://www
.ibm.com/mobilefirst/us/en/bring-your-own-device/byod.html.

Kroski, Ellyssa. 2013. "A Librarian's Guide to Maker spaces: 16 Resources." *iLibrarian Blog*, March 12. http://oedb.org/ilibrarian/a-librarians-guide-to-makerspaces/.

Lockncharge. 2014. "Mobile Device Survey at the University of Wisconsin." Lockncharge. Published October 10. http://www.lockncharge.com/my/mobile-device-survey-at-the-university-of-wisconsin/.

McReynolds, Joey. "Extensive Library Renovations Will Include Cafe, Technology Labs and Media Editing Suites." TCU 360 (Fort Worth, TX), April 8, 2014. https://www.tcu360.com/story/32114
extensive-library-renovations-will-include-cafe-technology-labs-and-media/.

Oakleaf, Megan. 2010. *Value of Academic Libraries: A Comprehensive Research Review and Report*. Chicago: Association of College & Research Libraries.

Sadler, Shawna. 2015. "Building a Digital Library: What to Expect as a Technology Project Manager on a Library Construction Project." *Journal of Library Administration* 55 (3): 221–234. doi: 10.1080/01930826.2015.1034048.

Statista. 2015. "Average Number of Connected Devices Used per Person in Selected Countries in 2014." Accessed December 9, 2015. http://www.statista.com/statistics/333861/connected-devices-per-person-in-selected-countries/.

Villa, Julie. 2012. Positioning Collegiate Libraries for the Future: Creating a Distinctive Learning Commons to Meet Student Population Needs. *Planning for Higher Education* 41 (1): 310–325.

Waring, Joseph. 2014. "Number of Devices to Hit 4.3 per Person by 2020—Report." Published October 16. Mobile World Live. http://www.mobileworldlive.com/featured-content/home-banner/connected-devices-to-hit-4-3-per-person-by-2020-report/.

Yearwood, Simone L. 2015. "Catching Up with Time: Tips, Tricks, and Best Practices for Library Renovations." *College & Research Libraries News* 76 (7): 362–398. http://crln.acrl.org/content/76/
7/362.short.

Yearwood, Simone L. 2014. "Rosenthal Transformations: 2012–2014." *PageDown: The Newsletter of the Queens College Library* 16 (1): 2. http://library.qc.cuny.edu/information/newsletter/PD_1_1_
Fall14.pdf.

12

Protecting Your Collections

Steve Keller

This chapter is divided into two parts. The first discusses library security, particularly concerning special collections, and the second focuses on how a library can maximize the opportunities presented by a renovation or expansion project to improve security. The second part also will address technology and trends in library security and how one can best work with an architect and security consultant to achieve the goal of improved security.

The motivation to steal from a library's general collection is low. After all, the books are there for your free use any time you ask. I have found that the primary source of loss from the general collection is simply convenience. Of course, there are those who want a specific book for their personal library, but over the years, I have found that the failure to return a book is often attributed to laziness, not basic dishonesty. The desire to steal a book is often motivated by a desire to use the book longer than library rules allow. In one major museum's noncirculating library, an average year saw 600 expensive art books unaccounted for. But when security staff searched museum office bookshelves, they generally accounted for nearly all of them, "stolen" by curators who felt that their jobs would be easier if they had these books in their private offices and didn't have to endure the short walk to the library.

Special collections, however, are different. Special collections libraries might include, but would not be limited to, rare books, manuscripts, law books, and medical or scientific books. They are housed separately and have different security and user services and privileges. Some libraries include other formats in their special collections, such as maps or architectural drawings, and there are thematic collections, such as miniature books, as well.

The motivations to steal books from a special collections library are many. Books can be rare and valuable. And in the case of active collections like law libraries, the need to retain a copy of a book for the duration of a case is common. In one special collections library with sports memorabilia, family members of deceased professional sports stars often tried to steal the original newspaper articles for their genealogical records, thinking that they had a greater entitlement than the library did to retain these documents. It wasn't until the library staff started to ask visitors if they were there to research a family member that they reduced the number of thefts. This library gave family of sports legends a VIP pass to identify them "so that staff can make sure that you get the best quality photocopies with all materials you need on acid free paper to assure that your records last longer than the constantly deteriorating newspapers they are to be copied from." We will discuss special collections later.

RISKS LIBRARY COLLECTIONS FACE

This chapter does not address the problems of fire and water, two very significant threats to collections. Fire, of course, is the most devastating threat because even the best conservation methods can't turn ashes back into a book. From a security perspective, theft and mutilation are the most common threats. Mutilation involves cutting pages, often plates or other valuable and easily sold materials, out of the book or damaging the book in some intentional way. The risks to special collections differ with the nature of the collection but still center around theft and damage with the emphasis primarily on theft. What varies is exactly what is targeted for theft. In a library containing only books, the books or their pages are the targets but in collections with manuscripts, for example, the target could be a single sheet containing an autograph within a hundred or so sheets of less valuable materials.

I also don't address the problem of homelessness and how it affects libraries. I'm aware of the potential threat posed by some percentage of the homeless who use the library as their base of operation during certain hours of the day or weather conditions. The American Library Association has already addressed this well in its publication, "Extending Our Reach: Reducing Homelessness through Library Engagement." Similarly, information has been published on the program created by the Los Angeles Public Library that addresses teenage gang use of libraries.

Libraries should maintain a database of contact information for local rare book dealers, booksellers, and others in law enforcement to whom bulletins of thefts can be made quickly. While the intent is to reduce losses, losses are inevitable and recovery then becomes your primary goal. In many cases, you will need to actively pursue thefts of valuable items. If you fail to do so, you may lose your right of ownership years later when the items are finally recovered.

PROTECTING THE GENERAL COLLECTION

The state of the art in book protection today in libraries is the electronic article surveillance system in which a small tag is placed in the spine of the book. When the book passes through a "doorway" device, an alarm alerts the attendant. This protects the book from theft but not vandalism and is suitable for the general collection but not necessarily for rare and valuable special collections.

Libraries generally separate their most valuable or vulnerable books and manuscripts into special collections where the level of day-to-day security is greater than in the general reading stacks. Some larger institutions occasionally use closed stacks to reduce damage and loss, but this is done as much to ensure items are properly shelved as to control theft and mutilation.

In general, most libraries, except the very largest and those with valuable special collections, require a minimal building alarm system that detects the presence of an intruder or a stay-behind at night when the library is closed. This requires door position switches on exterior doors and strategically placed volumetric motion detection throughout the building. It also might involve detection on each floor outside elevators and fire stairs to detect movement from floor to floor, and trap detection at logical locations where an intruder or stay-behind might pass through.

During the day, the alarm system provides little value to the general collection except perhaps to alert attendants to someone opening an exterior door not normally available to the public or forcing a door open, or a break in through a wall or duct of a high-security storage area. We will address alarms in special collections and other high-security spaces later.

The issue of vandalism and mutilation of books is complex. Even if reading tables are located in the open where readers can be observed, readers are free to move around the building and commit vandalism in more remote locations out of view. The assumption is that books with valuable plates that could be removed and sold on places like eBay will be in special collections and that some of the vandalism to books involves acts like removing a page or chart to avoid having to take detailed notes or to avoid retyping it. Hopefully, with the liberal placement of digital cameras throughout the building, this problem will be alleviated, but making copiers available or allowing readers to bring with them small scanners can help, too.

Parcel control can also help control library losses. It may be impractical to station an attendant at the door to examine the books being carried in and out, but in some libraries, often those on college campuses, this is necessary. As a minimum, limiting access and egress points and requiring readers to pass an attended desk or even a security checkpoint is useful. Architects need to keep this in mind when designing or renovating a building. The fewer access points, the lower the operating costs of the building, if every access point has to be staffed with an attendant or security officer.

I'm often asked about the use of CCTV systems in libraries. Cameras serve a purpose in libraries but are not very effective in protecting the general collection. In most libraries, you simply can't provide surveillance for the entire area at risk. The value of cameras is generally limited to protecting special collections and reading rooms and keeping an eye on potential troublemakers. Cameras also play a role in securing exterior exits. Without a camera viewing an alarmed exterior door, someone can step outside for a smoke—or to remove something they want to steal—and by the time an employee responds to check out the alarm, that person is long gone. With a camera, you can identify the person responsible.

Nearly every library selects some date before which a book can be declared rare but age alone will not determine this. Condition, imprint scarcity, and collector value all are considered in declaring a book to be rare. One problem is that some libraries are rich in books that are sufficiently important and scarce to be declared rare but the library has little space to move the book into to assure that it is secure. A key to keeping rare books safe is to make sure that they remain isolated from the general collection. During the design of a new library or a renovation, this is an important programmatic issue to be considered. It is a valid reason to build a building larger than is currently needed. New books become old books and then become rare books over time and must be moved to the rare books collection. This is an ongoing process that never ends.

One principle of security is that disorder leads to more disorder, so sometimes the best course of action is to call the police when criminal or potentially criminal activity is noticed. Threats, assaults, vandalism, inappropriate sexual behavior, and so on, all merit a call to the authorities. If the rules of decorum are not observed, then disorder will ensure.

PROCESSING AND BACK-OF-THE-HOUSE FUNCTIONS

I once did a project for the Library of Congress and discovered numerous thefts, involving removal of valuable plates from books by employees. We discovered this by finding books in back areas stuffed under shelves. A careful examination revealed that they all had one thing in common: pages had been cut out. At another major library I found a similar theft. Staff must always be alert to this type of activity and investigate each instance.

Items in processing are especially at risk, and the more valuable these items are, the more vulnerable they are. Here is one of the places where an architect's design may solve a problem—or create one—for the life of the library building. More important, this is one of the places where we in security can do little to secure the collection from internal theft using conventional security methods. The only good solution is in the building's design. Let's look at the desirable characteristics for processing spaces.

When there is an arrearage in processing new materials, the sheer volume of items yet to be processed can be problematic. One solution is to provide a secure space for storage of this arrearage. Think of security from this perspective: If you don't yet know that you own it and it hasn't been officially accessioned into your collection and cataloged, what better place is there to steal something than from the yet-to-be-processed arrearage carts?

This becomes a serious problem when the library includes special collections, and an even greater problem when an archive is involved. If new accessions will not be immediately processed, there needs to be a secure space of sufficient size to store the more valuable materials waiting to be processed. This can be a working space with desks for the employees doing the processing. This space must be secure, meaning that it can be locked up at night, and is not on a traffic path where people need to pass through while materials are being processed.

In the case of valuable archives, this is more complex because archival materials often take longer to process than books. What often happens is that an archivist assembles an entire collection or group of like materials from the boxes of items received for processing. Let's say the state prison sends its old records including disciplinary files, fingerprint cards, and other data from prisoners in the past to the archive for archiving. Most of these records are from people like everyone's Uncle John who fell to temptation just that one time and found himself making license plates for the state for a couple of years. But some of these prisoners are famous, actually infamous, and their prison records might fetch a nice sum on eBay.

Cataloging and preparing finding aids for this much material is time consuming, not to mention boring. Archivists are notorious for working on several projects at one time to break up the day and relieve boredom. The result is that at each processing cubicle, we can easily find boxes of potentially valuable materials lying about for the months it takes to complete the project.

The solution here is to provide a cubicle with ample work surfaces for each archivist or library processor. Immediately next to the workstation sits a mini "garage" for parking the cartload of materials that the archivist or processor removed from more secure storage. As items are processed, they are returned to the cart and at the end of the day, or even at lunch time, the cart is placed into the mini garage and the overhead door closed and locked.

Libraries and their architects must recognize that materials in processing are at their most vulnerable. Depending upon the institution, items waiting to be processed can be considerable or may be minimal. Efforts must be made to learn how the processing staff works with materials during the processing phase. Every effort must be made to avoid what we see most commonly, and that is piles of materials sitting on desks or even lying in boxes on floors in hallways waiting to be processed.

SPECIAL COLLECTIONS

Special collections often have isolated stacks that are secured. If they aren't, they should be. Special collections should reside in spaces protected by an electronic card access system that requires a computer log-in, even for staff, and stacks should be closed to the public. In the case of exceptionally valuable collections, employees should be subject to a background check to qualify for access to the space.

Special collections, like all collections, are subject to theft by library users or readers as well as by employees. Let's concentrate here on keeping readers from stealing the materials. The key to protecting special collections is how the special collections library and its reading room function. This requires an architect who fully appreciates and understands the importance of providing for every one of the rules and regulations imposed on readers and paying attention to detail in the design process.

The elements of special collections operations are as follows:

- Access to the collection must be controlled.
- Readers in the reading room should not have access to the stacks.
- Materials in the collection should be divided into two categories: high vulnerability and standard vulnerability.
- Certain high-vulnerability items should have limited access and should be made available in a way that protects them. For example, a high school student can use copies of rare materials while a visiting scholar may need access to the actual item.
- Everyone must sign in and present ID. This access should be logged into a computer database and retained for a decade. Only certain IDs should be accepted. While a university ID might suffice for normal use in a university library, "real ID," that is, identification approved for use for government purposes such as boarding an airplane should be required in addition. Most state driver's licenses and nondriving personal IDs as well as passports meet the requirements of the real ID provision of U.S. law. "Lobby management" software is readily available that can scan most forms of ID and include this into the database instantly.
- During the sign-in process, readers should be asked to sign a form, stating that they have read the list of reading room rules. These rules should clearly state that video recordings are being made of activity within the room.
- The library should maintain an electronic list of individuals who have been banned from the library due to previous issues such as thefts, vandalism, or disruptive behavior. Individuals convicted of theft from other institutions should appear on this watch list. In institutions like universities with multiple reading rooms or special collections, this list should be available to all access-controlled areas and checked every time someone tries to sign in to use the space.
- What is carried into the reading room must be limited. A writing instrument, a laptop, a small camera, and similar items are usually permitted but not briefcases or bags. Large purses should also be restricted. This necessitates a secure way of storing the items that are not permitted into the reading room. Lockers are generally used.
- Readers should be assigned to a reading space at a table and the sight lines in the reading room must be clear from all angles so staff can see the table area from anywhere in the room, especially librarian workstations.

- Several tables immediately in front of the librarians' workstations and in clear view of library staff should be reserved for items in the collection predetermined to be high risk.
- Furniture and carts should be carefully selected and if necessary custom designed so that they don't block the view of cameras. Carts should not be piled high and parked immediately between the camera and a suspect.

The necessity of a security officer in a library special collections reading room is a question I am often asked. The answer is that, of course, having a security officer is important, but few libraries have the funds for one. Ideally, the security officer will not perform any of the sign-in procedures and will dedicate full time to viewing activity in the room, especially activity at the worktables.

CCTV is an important tool in a special collections library and the guard station provided must be designed to include sufficient space to house viewing monitors for the cameras. PC-based CCTV systems allow the security officer to view many camera images at one time in small format on a monitor and the number of cameras dictates the size of the monitor. This must be decided upon early so that the architect can provide for a suitable monitoring location where the officer not only can personally see all worktables but can also view worktables on the CCTV system.

Most cameras should be high-definition and multi-megapixel, which allow for digital zooming and close-up views. Some cameras should be conventional zoom, tilt, and pan units that provide views from multiple angles and allow the officer to zoom in on details. More than one manuscript has been stolen from a manuscript folder by sleight of hand. While this may seem counterintuitive, it is better to have more dedicated cameras than zoom, tilt, and pan cameras. Cameras that allow the security officer to pan around the room are always looking in the wrong direction when the theft occurs. Every portion of the room should be viewed by a camera and recorded digitally. One or two panning cameras are to allow close-up viewing of suspicious activity.

While CCTV coverage is required for all tables, the tables designated as high security should be viewed by multiple cameras and multiple angles at all times. Every camera in the system should be on continuous record mode for later retrieval should you discover a loss days later.

Recordings in general collections and low-security areas are often retained for just 30 days, then the system erases the data and starts over. But high-security tables and special collections reading room recordings should be retained for much longer, even up to the statute of limitations, and this can be very expensive and could require substantial hard drive space. The architect must know this in advance so that space in the IT closets can be provided for and the security system budget reflects this technology.

As a reader calls for a specific rare and valuable item, the information on that item should be logged digitally onto the database call slip for that specific reader showing the date and time he received the item, and then the time he returned that specific item. This allows you to track activity in your library by reader and by the items in the collection. Did John Smith handle the manuscript folder with the Lincoln signature? Who also handled the manuscript folder containing the Lincoln signature item? This information should be time-stamped so that the matching video can be located and played back much later if necessary.

Earlier I said that I prefer having a security officer in the reading room viewing activity. But what about using a library staff member? Most libraries I have worked with have opted to ask for a new position for a nonsecurity employee and have made the decision to use that person in a regular library administration role at the desk where the guard should be sitting and viewing the reading room readers. This has always been a big mistake. I understand and appreciate that libraries are shorthanded and that getting a new librarian is important. But it simply doesn't work to call that person a security attendant and give him or her library duties to perform. If you think that you can successfully watch readers as they handle rare and valuable materials while giving the person who is supposed to be watching them other duties to perform, you are kidding yourself.

With that said, I feel that if you can dedicate one person full time to a security function in the reading room, a librarian will do a better job than a security guard. Why? Because a security guard almost certainly has never been to grad school and doesn't understand how a scholar works with materials. Things that are suspicious won't be recognized by a guard and things that are not suspicions might be. A librarian has more experience in recognizing improper behavior in the reading room. So if you use a security officer, train her on what to look for. If you use a library professional, don't give her other duties to perform.

Sight lines are critical in a reading room, so thought should be given to where the security officer and the library staff sit in relation to the reader desks. Think in the design process about how sight lines can be blocked by banners, signs, and portable items like carts piled high with books. Some libraries use carts with a low profile or even transparent components or carts that sit lower than normal so more books can be stacked on them without rising to the height that they block a view of a reader with valuable materials.

ALARM SYSTEMS FOR SPECIAL COLLECTIONS

After the library closes and materials are safely back on their shelves in the special collections rooms, the risk changes. If the items are valuable enough, you might experience a break-in but it is more likely someone will just stay behind after closing. For this reason, libraries like other facilities need trap detection strategically located around the building to detect movement. Libraries are just too big to saturate every area with motion detection, but it is possible to easily identify certain traffic areas where a stay-behind might pass through at night. These include hallways near stairwells, outside of elevators, and so on. For those thieves who choose to break in, this trap protection will be effective as well. But your first line of defense is to detect anyone coming through a door or window. Detection in the general portions of the library is more basic and it gets more intense within the special collections library storage areas where more valuable items are stored.

Thought must be given by the architect and your security consultant as to how alarms will be turned off and on each morning and night, and by whom. Simple keypad systems in smaller facilities are not a problem but more complex PC-based systems can be a challenge for a staff member. Also to be considered is how and when the building will be cleaned and who will be doing the cleaning. Will the local jail guard use his key to open the library and let in the inmates from the city jail to sweep the floors and take out the trash? It happens! Giving them the password to the alarm system defeats the purpose of an alarm system.

Even if your cleaning contractor uses non-prison labor, many of them may be immigrants, making it nearly impossible to do any type of background check. If you find yourself in such a situation—and many campus libraries do—at least require that special collections storage areas only be cleaned under the supervision of one of your staff members and then only during the day.

MANUSCRIPTS

Manuscripts are especially vulnerable in a special collections. Each folder may contain a large number of items and among them might be items of extraordinary value or importance. It is rarely ever practical to inventory each document in a folder before returning it to the shelves, and at best if every item is inventoried, it is generally inventoried later in the day just before the folder is re-shelved. I recommend that you mark folders with unusually vulnerable items with a sticker that indicates the presence of items needing special attention, and then list these items inside the folder's cover. Before returning the folder to the shelf, check for these special items to be sure they are present, accounted for, and in good condition. If you don't do this, you won't know when the item was stolen let alone whom to look at as a suspect. Of course, people calling for folders with high-risk items should be moved to the high-security table to view the material directly in front of a librarian and under added video surveillance.

WHO IS IN CHARGE OF SECURITY?

Every library should appoint a library security officer who oversees the security program for the library and works with the police or parent organization. This person should be given the authority to take action when a theft or other type of criminal incident is reported.

GETTING YOUR STOLEN ITEMS BACK

Few librarians will disagree that each book in the general collection should be marked with a unique ownership mark. But unless there is a way of marking a book in a similar way as having been deaccessioned, the unique ownership mark will not do you much good in prosecuting the thief. When you deaccession books with an ownership mark, you defeat the purpose of that mark in the first place. So consider also marking deaccessioned items in an indelible way.

But what about marking rare materials? I advocate marking rare materials with a very few exceptions and so does the Association of College and Research Libraries and others. But just as paintings in a museum have unique features in addition to the image itself, such as flaws in the canvas visible from the back, so does each unique copy of a book, and these, too, should be recorded photographically or otherwise to aid in proving in court that the book in the possession of the thief is yours. Making the arrest is only half the battle. Recovery is often the hard part.

STAFF EXPECTATIONS

If you expect library users to follow the rules, you must make them aware of the rules. This same principle applies to the procedures to be followed and the deportment of readers in special collections areas. You have a right to expect honesty from your employees, too, but it is first necessary to tell them of your expectations. Don't make assumptions that everyone uses the same commonsense that you do.

EXPANDING OR RENOVATING YOUR LIBRARY

Every expansion program should be approached as an opportunity to fix as many problems as possible and this includes security problems. I recommend that you employ a security consultant who is experienced in library projects to conduct a security study of your facility prior to engaging an architect. Once an architect is engaged, his recommendations can be addressed during the programming phase of the design process. The more time that passes before you bring a security consultant on board, the less likely it will be that a solution can be found to fix any inherent problems. Too often the architect or programmer simply accommodates the existing security program in his or her design and fails to take the opportunity to use the programming process to anticipate the problems you can reasonably be expected to have in your new facility.

Let me give you an example. If your special collections processing area for, say, a rare book library resembles Grand Central Station with few, if any, access controls to keep unauthorized people out, the architect is likely to assess only whether the amount of space devoted to this function is adequate and then provide a similar amount of space in the new building. Unless someone specifically asks for access controls, you aren't likely to see them recommended in the program document. Earlier, I introduced the concept of providing secure "cart garages" for securing storage of materials being processed as a solution for the risks processing areas face. Without knowing that something like this has been recommended, an architect is almost certainly not going to provide for this added space in his or her program documents. So, the first step in improving your security is knowing what needs improvement and communicating those needs to the program architect. This can best be done by someone who knows library security as well as the architectural process, but this is not necessarily something that an architect who specializes in programming library project is good at. I've seen some big firms that specialize in cultural property projects fall on their face when preparing library programs. Your security consultant will not know the architectural programming process and your program architect will know very little about security. This work calls for a team.

Because architects cannot fully understand every engineering requirement in the building, they employ a range of engineers and advisers such as electrical engineers, mechanical engineers, and structural engineers. Every major library expansion or renovation project should also have a library security consultant on board from the beginning of the programming phase until the commissioning of the building's systems. I can't stress the importance of including the security specialist before programming begins, so input on security can be included in the program upon which the design is based. And I can't express enough the need for selecting a security consultant with library experience.

I'm often asked how much good security in a library should cost per square foot. While I might be able to provide figures like this for many types of facilities, I have never been able to accurately predict the cost per square foot for security in a library because the cost depends on so many factors. The cost per square foot for general stacks is virtually nothing, while the cost of card readers, electric locks, door contacts, cameras, and motion detectors in a small special collections storage space is higher. Another factor driving the cost of security is the appearance of the space itself. Buildings with historic fabric or highly decorative ceilings cost more to protect than buildings with less decorative decor, so reading rooms sometimes cost more as a result. And if the library has an area where collections are displayed in a museum-like setting, the cost can be even higher due to the cost of designing the systems so that the librarian or curator has maximum display flexibility. For example, if a separate infrastructure is provided for painting alarms, freestanding exhibit case alarms that can't be prewired during construction, or similar special collections, the cost will be higher.

As frustrating as it is, there is no way to predict the cost of the security system with some "rule of thumb" dollar per square foot number. During the programming phase, the architect may want to focus on a preliminary budget for security and may ask the building's cost consultant to provide an estimate. I have been involved in several projects of this type and have yet to see a professional cost consultant come up with even a remotely accurate budget. The reason is that they generally follow a flawed industry formula that fails to account for the higher security requirements in some spaces, and they never take into account the need to design flexibility into security in exhibit areas. Because this early estimate may lock you into a security budget that is unrealistically low, I recommend that you double the cost estimator's highest number until that number can be verified from an early design or by the security consultant.

Projects in academic libraries differ only slightly with regard to security when compared to traditional nonacademic libraries. But in renovation and construction projects, there are generally higher costs related to the campus-wide security standards that may force you into using products you might not otherwise select yourself. If the campus uses a standard student ID card that also serves as the dorm room key, the food service ID, and the library card, then you will be required to integrate your building's access control system with the campus system. In nearly every campus, this means that you must use the campus server and software, connect to it over the campus-wide computer network, and meet all of the campus requirements. While you won't have to pay for your own dedicated server and software, most campus libraries are assessed an annual fee as part of the campus system. So the annual operating costs of an electronic security system in an academic library are generally higher than in other environments.

Another cost included in academic libraries' security budgets involves added locations where card readers and security detectors are needed. In most nonacademic settings, there is no requirement to provide card readers on doors that might not exist solely to protect the collection. Doors to IT closets where computer racks are located, tactical response exterior doors that campus public safety use to enter the building, and doors needed for entry by campus building engineers who often do maintenance to heating, ventilation, and air-conditioning systems at night will add to your costs in an academic library project.

Requirements like these make it absolutely essential that in an academic library the security consultant be on board at the very beginning of the project, so you know who is buying the server and software, who will maintain it into the future, and what ongoing and escalating costs of ownership you might face. On most campuses, the library is charged an annual service fee by the administration. Often it is $500 per year per card reader door, and $500 per year for each camera on the system. In some, this covers service costs, but in others, it covers only the right to tap into the campus system and any software licensing.

Another difference between a traditional library and an academic library is that in most traditional libraries you get to choose the system you want and configure it how you want. Earlier I described a CCTV system and how it can be used to protect high-security areas of reading rooms in special collections libraries. Far too often the campus has selected a single product to be the campus-wide standard system used in all facilities. Standardization saves money so there are merits to selecting a system and requiring that it be used in most parts of the campus. But certain parts of the campus have higher risks than other parts, so exceptions must be made so that facilities like special collections libraries can buy a system with unique features that meet their unique needs. No one questions the high security on the campus nuclear reactor or the university's hospital pharmacy, but when the campus museum or library wants a system with unique features, and in spite of the high value in these collections, there is often resistance. This is something a security consultant can help you navigate through.

When an entirely new library is built, the institution has the opportunity to design a space with no built-in security pitfalls. But we rarely get such an opportunity and more often existing libraries undergo renovations or expansions. When this happens it is important to evaluate the building's infrastructure to ascertain if the security systems already in place can be adequately expanded to meet the needs of the larger facility. Many times they cannot, so unless you want the existing security system to remain in place in the older portions and a different system in the newer portion, you will have decisions to make about upgrading the security systems even in parts of the building not being renovated. Another question to ask is whether the existing system should be expanded even if it can be. It has likely been replaced several times over by new generations of components and software. How reliable is it? What is its expected life? Will it eventually not be supported by the manufacturer creating for you an expensive problem down the road?

Let me give you an example. Motion detectors and other security detectors that detect a break-in are electronically monitored. Each device is supposed to have a component called an end-of-line resistor at the detector that senses the electrical resistance on the wire that connects it to the monitoring computer or panel. That line constitutes a circuit. If that circuit is broken as it would be if someone tried to remove the detector during hours that the alarm system is off, the controller would detect a drop in electrical resistance and sound the tamper alarm. Every alarm system is supposed to work this way.

You decide that you will upgrade your alarm system into the new wing by replacing the old control panel with a new modern system, but you decide that you will continue to reuse the old detectors that are doing just fine in the older parts of the existing building.

Each system uses a slightly different resistance value, meaning that now you need to go around to each and every detection device in the existing portion of the building and replace the twenty-five-cent resistor with a new one with the proper resistance value. If you don't, all of the detectors in the existing building will think they have been tampered with. Your contractor will charge you around $75 in labor to go around to each location and replace those resistors. For $25 more you can probably replace the old 10-year-old detector that is approaching its end of life with a new model that is more reliable, is cheaper to own, and extends the life of your system in the older parts of your building by 20 more years. So before you make decisions on whether to expand or replace your existing security systems, your security consultant needs to explore your options in detail.

One thing you should never do when studying your security needs is to use the services of someone who has some security product to sell as your security consultant. The alarm company sales engineer will gladly sell you his solution but that may not be the solution you need.

NEW TECHNOLOGY

As we all know, the world is changing quickly. There are products for everything. Be very careful in selecting products that claim to be able to solve your problem. Before you adopt a piece of technology, ask to see it in operation in other libraries or in a facility such as a museum that has similar issues as yours. There is a small handful of companies that have proven products that work reliably in your environment. Seek them out and ignore the background noise from the others who want you to beta test their products at your expense. I have found that when it comes to specialty products for cultural property environments, you rarely find "big names" on their labels. Leading brands we are all familiar with didn't get big by selling to a market as limited as libraries. There are a lot of libraries but few have the millions of dollars to spare to buy the latest security technology. So the leading brands make products directed toward a general market or a market like the defense industry with money to spend.

CONCLUSION

Many problems libraries face can only be solved when the library renovates or expands or when a new building is built. This is your chance to fix problems that exist in the existing building and at the same time you need to prevent building in problems in your new facility. It will take a team to assist your architect in getting this right but it can reduce operating costs in the future for the life of the building, and, more important, you can devote resources toward doing what the library does, instead of on excessive security costs.

13

Storage Options: Making Decisions about Print Materials

Frank R. Allen

Shelving for print materials typically occupies the largest space component of an academic library, thus a consideration of shelving methods is an uppermost factor with any design planning. Several recent developments are adding urgency to the conversation about how much space to dedicate to print materials. Principally, students are coming to academic libraries in increasing numbers, putting pressure on administrators to create more seating within a given building envelope, and as a result reducing the amount of space allotted to books. The median weekly gate count for U.S. research-extensive libraries grew 46 percent from 24,082 in 2000 to 35,113 in 2012, an annual 3.2 percent increase, considerably outpacing growth in full time equivalent (FTE) enrollment.[1] Second, the growing sophistication of online public access catalog (OPAC) discovery software is making virtual browsing more palatable, reinforcing the justification for moving materials offsite or into closed stacks. Third, as digital content grows in relationship to content on shelf, library holdings may approach a logical tipping point where virtual browsing simply makes more sense than traditional physical browsing.

This chapter contains a brief history of collection access and retrieval in academic libraries, a summation of factors influencing storage decisions, and various options for housing print collections. The goal is to enable readers to make a decision about the best allocation of space in their library.

"COLLECTION PUSH" ERA

Throughout the 20th century, collection growth was a key driver of academic library building planning. Many larger academic libraries labeled themselves as "holders of record" for monographs, bound periodicals, and indexing/finding aids. In addition to serving the needs of their institutional constituents, many felt they had an obligation to serve as repositories of published scholarly content for future generations. One could label this period as the "collection push" growth era for American academic libraries. The larger a library's print holdings, the more prestige it lent the institution. This growth in print collections was accompanied by a shift toward the self-service open stack model of collection access.

Whereas closed stack had served as a common shelving method in the 19th century, the open stack emerged in the early to mid-20th century as the predominant access method, for understandable reasons:

- It paralleled a movement in retail toward self-service merchandising, by putting inventory immediately into the hands of the user and eliminating the storekeeper model of bringing out inventory from behind a counter.
- Self-service open stack reduced labor costs.
- The advent of security systems and a drop in book prices reduced concerns over theft.
- Simpler and more intuitive OPAC systems made it easier for patrons to find books on their own.

Closed stacks became the exception to the rule for academic library circulating collections by the middle part of the 20th century. A few notable research and public libraries with large closed stack collections today include the New York Public Library and the Library of Congress.

"SEATING PUSH" AND BIRTH OF THE INFORMATION COMMONS

As library collections continued to grow into the latter half of the 20th century, their size became a challenge for many academic libraries. Space for collections was increasingly competing with the need to provide more seating for students. As campuses grew, many of which becoming increasingly urbanized, the value of the real estate beneath library buildings increased. By the 1980s, the model of the library as a warehouse for books began to be questioned, and space-starved libraries started in earnest seeking alternative methods for housing their book collections. An excellent treatment of the history of collection storage and this turning point can be found in the Council on Library Resources.[2]

By the 1990s and certainly by the turn of the 21st century, academic libraries were increasingly self-conscious of the size of their on-campus collections, the footprint required to house these collections, and the underlying cost to store them on campus. A multitude of factors was influencing library building planning and print collection management:

- The growth of digital content
- The emergence of web scale discovery systems and virtual browsing
- The growth of team-based and collaborative classroom projects, which increased the need for group study areas
- A steady decline in the circulation of print materials—median annual circulations for libraries at U.S. Research Extensive Universities dropped from 330,314 in 2002, to 220,349 in 2012, a 33 percent decrease[3]
- Pressure to justify "book warehouses" in prime location campus property
- An increase in library gate counts and the recognition of "library as place"

The need for more space in libraries is now being driven toward increasing people space, interlaced with technology capability. This realization first manifested itself in the birth of the information commons circa mid- to late 1990s. With the advent of the commons concept, emphasis was now being placed on collaboration, synthesis of knowledge, and learning spaces, not just information storage and retrieval. At about the same time, the previous ironclad distinction between library and classroom buildings on campus began to blur. Hybrid buildings containing study/seating space, group study rooms, classroom space, and student support services—sometimes overseen by library management or jointly managed—began appearing in universities around the country under such names as "academic resource centers," or "academic commons." Examples are facilities at Clemson University, Georgia Institute of Technology, and the University of Denver. Increasingly, the library was no longer the overriding purveyor of study spaces on campus. This blurring of roles may be encouraging librarians to consider even closer the optimal use of public space in their buildings.

WHAT TO DO WITH THE PRINT?

As the model of an information commons takes deeper hold in academic libraries, and circulation of print materials declines, the obvious question for a library embarking on a renovation project is, what to do with the print? This is the elephant in the room with discussions of repurposing library space. What is a library without visible books? Is it even a library? What distinguishes a library with few books from an "academic learning center"? How do faculty respond to a library with 50 percent, 70 percent, or 80 percent of its print collection moved from open stacks to closed stacks (on-site or off-site)? How important is traditional browsing to faculty? To students?

Interestingly, even as circulation figures in academic libraries decline, libraries are still acquiring print materials in significant numbers, as illustrated in Table 13.1.

Thus the question to consider is not in what format to buy, but where to house it. In making this decision, libraries need to consider the following factors when contemplating wholesale transfer of print collections to closed stack:

- The personality, research, and library-use habits of the faculty
- Subject orientation of the institution and the library. Is it more STEM (science, technology, engineering and mathematics) focused or humanities/liberal arts focused?
- Students' desires in a physical library
- The university's perception of the appropriate physical manifestation of a library
- The image that the university attempts to convey to the community, prospective students, and parents
- How significant and robust is the library's print collection? Is it a strong, well-developed assortment, or just an ill-mannered bunch of books haphazardly and thoughtlessly acquired over the decades?
- What are the circulation trends? How well utilized is this collection? Is it worth dedicating valuable real estate to it, often in the heart of campus, or is the collection perfectly suited for another facility?
- How easily can patrons virtually browse the library's collection through its public access catalog?
- How many holdings of bound print serials, indexing, and abstracting aids make up the collection, and to what extent are these materials available in digital format? Serial sets often make up the "low hanging fruit" that can be moved off-site or in closed stack without a lot of controversy or hand-wringing.

Table 13.1   Median Books, Serial Backfiles and Other Paper Materials Added

U.S. Doctoral/Research Universities—Extensive and Intensive						
Year	2000	2002	2004	2008	2010	2012
Volume Additions	42,806	36,744	32,287	30,546	25,027	25,602

Source: NCES, http://nces.ed.gov/surveys/libraries/compare/default.aspx.

Because of the multitude of considerations, academic libraries are transitioning physical space at various rates. Some still look a lot like they did in the 1980s. A few new or renovated libraries have limited publicly accessible print materials. Many are in the process of slowly shifting the percentage of usable space toward more seating and less stack space. It is an expensive and disruptive undertaking, and the pace of this shift is uneven.

PRINT STORAGE OPTIONS—SPACE CONSIDERATIONS

An excellent detailed treatment of alternative collection storage systems can be found at Online Computer Library Center.[4] For a general overview, four common options are described here.

Conventional Open Stacks with Fixed Cantilevered Shelving

These are typically constructed seven shelves high and are double-sided with an aisle width of 36"–42". This is the predominant style used in academic libraries for decades and is included here to provide a baseline for comparison. Employing seven 12" deep shelves back to back creates a 25" deep row. Using aisle width of 42" produces a total "row" depth of 67". A section is defined as the area encompassing 14 three-foot wide double-sided shelves. The building block includes the section plus the aisle, which in this example totals 42" + 25" or 67" × 3', or 16.75 sq. ft. of floor space. Each section holds 42 linear of material (3 linear feet per shelf × 14 shelves). This arrangement creates a multiple of 2.51 linear feet per square foot of floor space (42 ÷ 16.75). One can further define this by volumes per square foot of floor space. Assuming an average volume width of 1.25", which is fairly standard for academic libraries, this arrangement allows for 24 volumes per square foot of floor space. (2.51 linear feet × 12" ÷ 1.25). Note this figure of 24 V/SF factors only the racking and aisle space immediately in front of the shelf. It does not include peripheral aisles, circulation space exterior to the internal stack area, or empty space on the shelf for growth.

Open stack collections are not easily shifted, thus is it advisable to leave several inches empty at the end of each 36" shelf, a common rule of thumb of which is 15 percent or 5" to 6". Also, some methods of calculating volume/square foot will factor in the perimeter aisle space surrounding each array of stacks. Incorporating these various additional factors can reduce the calculated density to as little as 10 volumes per square foot for smaller collections, and 15 V/SF for large research collections. Because of the wide range of assumptions, *fixed formulas should be viewed cautiously.*

Advantages:
- Facilitates self-service
- Does not require special equipment or labor
- Flexibility of use—shelving can be assembled and disassembled easily and quickly with hand tools requiring limited expertise

Disadvantages:
- Lowest density
- Necessitates highest floor plate of building space relative to yield
- Long-term costs after factoring building, land, and annual operating costs (utilities, lighting, building maintenance) are high relative to yield

Compact Movable Shelving

Shelves are on rollers (manually or electronically powered) to create compression of aisle space. Systems can be mounted on top of existing cantilevered stacks. Shelves are compressed against each other and opened up by the user to search in a row. The ratio of open to closed aisles varies from a low of 1:5 to 1:10, depending upon the amount of patron traffic. High user traffic necessitates more open aisles to accommodate simultaneous use. In the 1:10 scenario, the effective aisle space is 4.2" (versus 42") or one-tenth of open stack. The arithmetic formula produces a building block unit of 7.3 sq. ft. (4.2" + 25" × 36" ÷ 144" = 7.3 sq. ft.). Assuming 42 linear feet per section, this example yields 5.75 linear foot per square foot or 55.2 volumes per square foot (5.75 × 12" ÷ 1.25" = 55.2), or a little over double the density of conventional open stack. Note that compact shelving requires greater floor load strength to accommodate the additional weight of material; thus when installed in existing buildings, it is often located on ground floors. It is also possible to reinforce a structure to allow installation on upper floors, though this is a complex process. Any investigation of compact shelving must be accompanied by an engineering study to assess possible need for remedial floor strengthening.

Advantages:
- Combines flexibility and self-service of open stack with higher density
- Suitable for lower-use materials that still benefit from self-service
- Can be a relatively easy solution to implement

Disadvantages:
- Requires higher floor load and reduces the number of simultaneous users
- More expensive and requires more mechanical/electrical maintenance than open stack
- Some users express unease standing between movable shelves, despite safety systems

High Density (Static or Mobile)

Often referred to as the "Harvard Model," where it was first put in use in 1986, this method has grown in popularity the past 25 years.[5] This approach employs shelving 10 to 30 + levels high in a closed stack environment more akin to a warehouse. For lower-height systems 10 to 15 shelves high, human operators or "pickers" retrieve materials via non-motorized laddered platforms. Heights exceeding 15–20 shelves necessitate electric scissor lifts to boost operators to the required height. Materials of like-height are shelved in trays. High-density systems can employ static or mobile shelving. An example of a static system with 20 levels produces the following yield: double-sided shelving is 78" deep (contrasted with 25" deep for open stack) by 53.5" wide, with 40" wide aisles. The larger racks and trays allow materials to be stored two, three, and four books deep. This produces a building block, including aisle, of 118" deep × 53.5" wide or 43.8 sq. ft. Each shelf or tray has a capacity of up to 180 volumes. In a 20-shelf high configuration with 2 shelves per level back to back, this yields 7,200 (20 × 2 × 180) volumes per section or 164 (7200 ÷ 43.8) volumes per square foot of floor space. Greater vertical levels produce greater floor density.

Advantages:
- Densities three times or more that of compact shelving
- Represents a low-technology investment compared with automated storage and retrieval system
- Can utilize conventional air-conditioned high ceilinged warehousing

Disadvantages:
- Typically set up off-site, which necessitates 2+ or more hour delivery to patron
- Requires staff intermediation to retrieve materials, introducing a labor and delivery cost component

Automated Storage and Retrieval System (ASRS)

ASRS technology has been used in manufacturing and distribution applications for decades, and was first introduced in libraries at California State University, Northridge, in 1991. Materials are stored in a high-bay arrangement similar in appearance to the "Harvard" style, but retrieved robotically by a crane device with arms that pluck and deliver bins to a ground-level docking station. The typical library ASRS will be 40 or more levels high, and contain 3 to 7 aisles between double-faced racks. A robotic crane operates up and down the length of an aisle, dispatched by computer command to retrieve a bin weighing up to 800 pounds, and containing up to 100 bound volumes. Materials are stored by height, not by subject, so that all volumes in a bin and level are of similar height to minimize air space between vertical levels or tiers. The metal bins are typically 24" wide × 48" deep, retrieved by the robot's two "arms" and delivered to a docking station where a staff person removes the requested item from the bin with the aid of an overhead monitor highlighting the location of the volume. The system software is tied to the library's OPAC, so that a user request automatically dispatches the appropriate robot to retrieve the item and deliver to the dock in seconds. The staff person pulling the volume from the dockside bin transports it to a public pickup point in the library to be held for the patron. The whole process from patron request to patron pickup can be as little as five minutes. Speed is the chief advantage of the system, as it can be faster than if the patron were looking for the book on an open shelf. Density of a typical ASRS is as follows: A bin measuring 2' wide × 4' deep will hold approximately 100 bound volumes. Aisles are 4'-6" wide. A section of back-to-back bins will be 9' deep including steel supports. The building block is thus 13.5' deep (4.5' aisle + 9') × 29" wide including the racking, or 32.6 sq. ft. With each double-sided section containing 200 volumes (2 × 100), this produces a density of 6.14 volumes per square foot per "tier" or level. A 36-tier ASRS will yield 220 volumes/SF. A 50-tier ASRS can yield 300 volumes/SF.

Advantages:
- Very high density
- Can provide items in about the same time it would take a user to find on open shelves
- Friendly for patrons with mobility limitations
- Minimal staff mediation required compared with high bay "Harvard style"

Disadvantages:
- Expensive installation cost per volume
- Typically requires a specially built on-site facility, though there are a few examples of building retrofits

COST CONSIDERATIONS

Cost is often the second factor to be considered. Cost studies are complex, however. Is one costing only the initial equipment outlay? Does the cost of the building get factored into cost per volume? What about the value of the underlying land? Does one take into consideration annual costs such as building maintenance, utilities, and labor for shelving and reshelving? A complete discussion of unit cost goes beyond the scope of this report, so this chapter will focus only on the cost of initial equipment, hardware, and software to operate the system. Building and land cost are not included.

Table 13.2 illustrates typical densities and unit costs for four common storage and retrieval systems. Per-volume cost for cantilevered shelving runs a wide range due to economies of scale with larger footprints. The cost shown for mobile shelving is based upon an actual quote for approximately 900,000 linear inches of shelving, a very big installation. Cost per volume will increase for smaller jobs. The per-volume cost for high bay is quite low, but requires specialized high-ceilinged air-conditioned space as compared with the first two options. Moving into high bay and ASRS involves a large stepped-up initial investment. The range for ASRS covers a lower-density installation of 36 levels or tiers at

Table 13.2   Comparison of Storage and Retrieval Options

	Cantilevered Open Stack	Mobile Electronic Compact Shelving	High-Bay Static/Mobile	ASRS
Vertical tiers/ levels	7	7	10–30+	36–50
Immediate density/SF*	24 volumes	48–55 volumes	59–176 volumes; up to 286 volumes for mobile	175–300 volumes/SF
Equipment cost per volume**	$1.02–$1.81	$1.99–$2.29	As low as $1.00 static and $.69 mobile	$2.25 to $3.80
Per volume cost includes	Racking	Mobile racking, software, end-of-aisle hardware, safety sweeps	Racking, shelving software, end-of-aisle hardware, safety sweeps (does not includetrays or scissorlifts)	Racking, bins, robotic cranes, hardware software, docking stations
Typical facility requirement	Interspersed in body of library	Interspersed in body of library; requires extra floor load capacity	Off-site; conventional high-ceilinged warehouse	Typically requires specially built on-site facility
Retrieval method	Patron self-service	Patron self-service	Staff-mediated	Mechanical
Delivery to patron	Immediate	Immediate to several minutes	Typically 2+ hours	5–10 minutes

*Assumes 1.25" volume width. No provision for growth space on shelf. Includes interior servicing aisle only; does not include peripheral aisles, run-out space for equipment, or patron circulation space. NOTE: Volume densities should not be used for space planning, only for relative comparison.

**Equipment only. Does not include building or land. Does not include ongoing annual costs.

$3.80 per volume, down to approximately $2.25 for a higher-density installation. The mechanical cranes or robots are expensive and serve only one aisle; thus it is advantageous to create aisles as long and tall as possible to spread the cost of the cranes over more volumes.

TRADE-OFFS: "PERSON TO GOODS" VERSUS "GOODS TO PERSON"

Density reflects a predictable trade-off, with the self-service options offering lowest density. Compact storage is popular for slower-moving materials that still lend themselves to physical browsing. It offers roughly double the density of conventional open stack but at up to double the cost per volume. The cost advantage of compact shelving comes into play by allowing a smaller building and land footprint. Other considerations when comparing conventional versus compact shelving include maintenance and repair costs of the electronics of a compact system, possible patron unease with going into a compact shelf system, and wait times while someone else is in an aisle. Open stack compact systems are becoming less popular with the increasing acceptance of high-bay systems, which offer densities many times that of either conventional or compact storage.

"Harvard" style and ASRS lend themselves to comparisons with each other. Both closed stack solutions offer super high density. Both require high ceilinged space for optimal efficiency, so are most often placed in facilities that were not originally library space. The prime distinguishing factor between the two is speed of delivery. If delivery time is not a factor, "Harvard" style is clearly superior, as it is cheaper and less technologically complex. A library will find ASRS attractive if it has land adjacent to the central library, possesses the financial resources, and sees benefit in supplanting a large percentage of its open stack collection into a denser environment. The "Harvard" solution will be best for lower-circulating materials, while the ASRS is ideal for medium- to higher-circulation materials. A more complete discussion of high bay and ASRS follows later in the chapter.

Ultimately, traditional open stack and compact storage systems can be described as "person-to-goods" approaches. "Harvard style" and ASRS systems are more described as "goods-to-person" solutions. This drives to the heart of where the library wants to take itself, and how much it desires to dovetail print access with digital content, which is more of a "goods-to-person" approach.

OTHER CONSIDERATIONS: ACQUISITIONS, DEACCESSIONING AND EBOOKS

A library's print collection is not static. The idea of "making decisions about print materials" is not simply about shuffling finite numbers of books from one location to another. New materials are coming in, and older materials may be weeded if deemed irrelevant or detrimental. The future growth trajectory of the print collection should be an early consideration when considering investments in storage and retrieval systems. This trajectory is influenced by acquisition/deacquisition strategies, including the following:

- Patron-driven acquisition (PDA)[6]. PDA is the practice of buying titles on request versus buying on anticipated usage. The mode of acquisition tends to be e-format. In the typical arrangement, a library will lease an e-title, and after a certain number of user downloads, the library buys the title, essentially a rent-to-own concept.
- "Print-on-demand" systems, where the library has high-speed printing and binding capability on-site to produce a bound book on demand. The library may load catalog records for thousands

of titles in its OPAC, but not physically own any of them. This is the print "just in time" complement to PDA. A good example of an application can be found at the University of Michigan.[7]

- Substitution. Libraries have for years been deaccessioning print journal content for which the library secures online access. Back volumes are transferred to shared consortial repositories or may be destroyed if redundant.
- Greater reliance on e-acquisitions. The greater the number of e-resources as a percentage of the library's information resources budget, the more logical becomes the virtual browse process. Why browse in the physical stacks if a significant body of the library's "collection" is digital? At some moment in a library a tipping point may occur, much as has happened with many retail bookstore customers. With book shopping, the switch is from traveling to a store to purchasing online (for both print and eBooks). The principle is the same in a library moving from physical to virtual discovery. Consumers are moving from a "person-to-goods" shopping habit to a "goods-to-person" habit. Where the library sees itself in this spectrum will partly shape the manner in which it provides access to collection material.

VIRTUAL BROWSE ENABLES CLOSED STACK

Open stacks, uninviting to a certain percentage of users, were designed more out of necessity than efficiency. As collections and student enrollment grew in the mid-20th century, staff simply could not retrieve materials affordably or fast enough for thousands of users. The OPAC record, until very recently, revealed precious little about a title's content, so the best way to judge a publication was to hold it in one's hand. Open stacks have practical drawbacks however, namely misshelving, theft, challenges for persons with mobility impairments, and the lack of flexibility with growth. Open stack collections are constantly in need of shifting as subject areas grow and shrink, a major limitation to any sequential (versus random access) arrangement. Economic and technological factors are now rapidly pointing to the advantage of storage and retrieval of print materials in a closed stack arrangement, coupled with a strong virtual browse capability to "see the book." What began as a trickle in the 1980s and 1990s may soon become an avalanche. Libraries cannot give away used cantilevered shelving anymore; there is so much being retired. Today's 21st-century library patron is increasingly comfortable with the whole concept of virtual browsing, and is less enamored with having to navigate row after row of shelves to find materials.

In June 2013, Library Leadership and Management Association (LLAMA) (a division of the American Library Association) and the University of Chicago sponsored an ALA preconference and tour of the university's then recently completed Joe and Rika Mansueto Library, which features an ASRS with capacity for 3.5 million volumes. When fully loaded, the Mansueto collection will be one of the largest closed stack arrangements in the United States, made feasible through technology. Comments at the conference revolved around the synergy between the ASRS and virtual browse including the following:

- Virtual browse weaves print and digital holdings seamlessly together on a "virtual book shelf."
- The ASRS allows valuable but lesser-used print materials to be retained in the heart of campus.
- A growing percentage of academic library collections are in digital format; thus a patron browsing in the stacks may overlook digital content. The traditional browsing experience may be compromised without the patron's knowledge.
- Navigation and way-finding in open stacks are an increasingly foreign practice for a new generation of students accustomed to clicking their way into information resources.

- A patron who uses an automated retrieval system can call a book to a service counter faster than most would find the book on the shelf.
- Closed stack storage of materials eliminates misshelving, reduces the likelihood of theft, and creates a superior atmospheric preservation environment.
- Closed random access collections do not have to be periodically shifted.

Increasingly the "highest and best use" of the 21st-century library building, typically located in the heart of campus, is primarily a people's space, often achievable by compressing space for materials. Print materials are compressible; people are not compressible.

A CLOSER LOOK AT ASRS

Historically, the chief weakness of closed stack systems was speed of delivery. Open stacks are set up for quick self-service navigation and retrieval. Don't like this title? Put it back and pull another next to it off the shelf. The patron can review and research titles as fast as she or he can navigate the stacks. Closed stack systems historically promised turnaround times measured in hours or days. Some libraries promise quicker turnaround. The libraries at Emory University and Georgia Institute of Technology are partnering in building a (nonrobotic) joint storage and retrieval system located between the two campuses, scheduled for opening in January 2016, which will deliver materials to service points in two hours.[8] Even two hours, however, can slow down research if the researcher is not quite sure of what she/he is needing. An interactive "hunt and peck" browse process interrupted by two-hour gaps can stretch into days.

The chief selling point of the ASRS system is super-rapid delivery in less than 10 minutes, often half of that. The patron sees a title of interest online and clicks the "get it" button and an automated crane in the ASRS immediately engages to retrieve a bin containing up to 100 volumes. The crane delivers the entire bin to a docking station at the end of an aisle. A library staff member searches the appropriate quadrant of the bin, with assistance from a computer screen, and pulls the volume from the bin. The book is then delivered to a public pickup station. This process works best if the library and ASRS are adjacent to each other, so it is not just the ASRS technology that creates the fast turnaround, but the adjacency of the ASRS collection to the user.

To illustrate the ASRS concept in more detail, a diagram of a typical configuration is shown in Figure 13.1.

This is a five-aisle system, with five cranes and five docking stations. Each tiny rectangle depicts a 24" × 48" bin. This is an overhead view, so in actuality the ASRS contains a stack of these bins located on top of each other in racks. Each vertical stack is called a bay. The horizontal layers are called tiers. This configuration has 36 tiers (horizontal layers) and 355 bays (stacked rectangles), which yield 12,768 bins. The bins in this example hold on average 97 volume equivalent items, so this ASRS has a capacity for 1,238,496 volume equivalents. While bin width and depth are fixed, bin height can vary, typically either 8", 10", 12", or 15". Books of similar height are stored in the same bin standing up—for example, a 10" bin is designed to hold books of height 8" to 9¾". A tier or layer will have all the same height bins, which creates minimum air space in the racks. The ASRS creates density by both being very tall, some as high as 50' or more, and also by having similar height books shelved horizontally on the same tier. The crane's response time is one minute or less, so the total elapsed delivery is more a function of how quickly the staff person

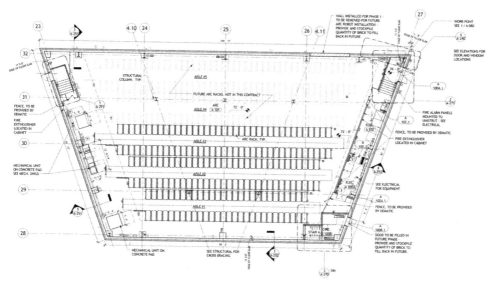

Figure 13.1 "Birds eye view." Typical ASRS arrangement. Courtesy Holzman Moss Bottino Architecture.

pulls the book from the bin and delivers it to the pickup spot. Upon retrieval, an item remains in "building use" status until the patron elects to discharge the book.

One of the earliest documented discussions of an ASRS application to academic libraries was by California State University Northridge at the ACRL Fourth National Conference, April 9–12, 1986. Oviatt Library at Cal State went on to open the first library ASRS in 1991. Since then roughly two dozen academic libraries around the world have opened or are planning ASRS facilities. The decision to build an ASRS rests on several factors. The first is having the land to build one. The ASRS depicted in the illustration resides in a building of 9,600 sq. ft. of floor space. The total site to accommodate the structure will be larger. Second, the ASRS will ideally be physically contiguous to the library, allowing materials to be shuttled immediately from the docking station to a public space inside the library for patron pick up. Third, the technology is expensive. As illustrated earlier, this ASRS cost out at approximately $4.00 per volume capacity, including racking, cranes, and software, but not including building or land.

THE HIGH-BAY ADVANTAGE

The ASRS solution is going to be attractive to only a niche number of libraries looking for storage solutions. It is expensive and optimally requires land right next door to the existing library, or is built into a newly constructed library. As of 2014, there were an estimated 20 known ASRS library facilities in operation, with several more in development. In contrast there are approximately 75 North American high-density library facilities, at least 15 of which are shared by multiple libraries. The high-bay solution is more populous for several reasons:

1. Capital investment can be less than $1.00 per volume, versus up to $4.00 for ASRS.
2. It is possible to utilize existing warehouse facilities that are air-conditioned and sufficiently high-ceilinged.

3. Human-operated scissor lifts are far less expensive and complex than the robotic crane technology in an ASRS, so maintenance and servicing costs are less.
4. Retrieval rates for high-bay installations are typically low, so the labor premium to manually retrieve material (versus robotic) may be immaterial.
5. High-bay racking systems can be mounted on mobile tracks to achieve even more density. Mobile racking is not possible with ASRS systems.

A "Harvard style" high-bay system could conceivably be located immediately adjacent to the public space of the library, which would greatly shorten delivery time. This is typically not the case, however, as the high-bay solution is usually arrived at on the basis of economics or lack of adjacent space next to the library; hence most high-bay "Harvard style" facilities are situated off the main campus or in a separate facility on campus.

The final decision between high-bay "Harvard Style" and ASRS is usually not arduous. They are very different solutions predicated upon differing goals and objectives. Assuming the university has the means and the land, the ASRS will typically be attractive if it wishes to move a large percentage of its circulating collection into a high-density environment. The high-bay approach will be more attractive for lesser-used materials. Ultimately it comes down to economics. Newer, higher-demand materials will justify a higher per volume cost solution. A library with an ASRS will typically retain in open stack its newest materials using the same decision logic.

Figure 13.2 Stationary XTend static high-bay shelving. Courtesy Spacesaver Corporation.

Figure 13.3 XTend mobile high-bay shelving at UW Madison. Courtesy Spacesaver Corporation.

WHERE OPEN STACK SHINES

The discussion comes full circle. As academic libraries travel deeper into the digital age, the question increasingly being asked by librarians and university officials is no longer "Do we need print books?" but "Which ones need to be in a traditional open setting?" The answer depends on many factors, including subject material, currency of publication, and format. By culling or relocating material that is better accessioned electronically, libraries can accentuate boutique open stack collections that lend themselves to a print "hands-on" experience. Examples are map collections (in concert with GIS centers), children's and young adult literature, art and book-art materials, "new and notable" titles, local interest materials, and titles displayed as parts of exhibits. All are ideally suited for open display and can be prominently featured to create corners of browsing and research interest. Essentially, the strategy borrows from the playbook of public libraries that have adopted a more retail approach in marketing the library as a cultural and informational department store.

CONCLUSION

Multiple factors, including a reappreciation by students of library as place, virtual discovery technology, the undeniable if uneven growth of eBooks, and the inherent value of the real estate under our libraries, are accelerating a rethinking of library space utilization as the 21st century continues to unfold. Every institution will approach the calculus in their own way, but the model of dedicating 40%–60% of usable space in academic libraries to shelving is rapidly fading. This is an exciting development especially for renovations as it can unharness thousands of square feet of library space for reimagining. Students will continue to use the physical library as long as it is relevant to their needs. The academic library can maintain and even heighten its place as the "intellectual heart of campus" through thoughtful building design that leverages information resources and their gateways, learning spaces, and knowledge creation labs into a dynamic hub of intellectual activity that maximizes the library building's utility to the university community.

NOTES

URLs last accessed December 14, 2015.
1. Data gathered through the National Center for Education Statistics' Academic Libraries Survey, which is administered biennially to 3,900 U.S. academic libraries. http://nces.ed.gov/surveys/librar ies/compare/default.aspx.
2. Willis E. Bridegam, *A Collaborative Approach to Collection Storage: The Five-College Library Depository* (Washington D.C.: Council on Library Resources, June 2001).
3. NCES, http://nces.ed.gov/surveys/libraries/compare/default.aspx.
4. Lizanne Payne, *Library Storage Facilities and the Future of Print Collections in North America* (Dublin Ohio: OCLC Online Computer Library Center, Inc., October 2007), http://www.oclc.org/content/ dam/research/publications/library/2007/2007–01.pdf.
5. Ibid.
6. http://www.ala.org/acrl/publications/keeping_up_with/pda.
7. http://www.lib.umich.edu/espresso-book-machine.
8. "Emory, Georgia Tech to open joint Library Service Center," http://news.emory.edu/stories/2014/11/ upress_library_service_center/.

FURTHER READING

Barclay, Donald. "Turning a Page: Downsizing the Campus Book Collections." *The Conversation*, August 19, 2015. https://theconversation.com/turning-a-page-downsizing-the-campus-book-collec tions-45808.

Heinrich, Helen, and Willis, Eric. "Automated Storage and Retrieval System: A Time-Tested Innova- tion." *Library Management* 35 (6–7) (2014): pp. 444–453. http://conference.ifla.org/past-wlic/2012/ 102heinrich-en.pdf.

Payne, Lizanne. "Winning the Space Race: Expanding Collections and Services with Shared Deposito- ries." *American Libraries Magazine*, September 23, 2014. http://americanlibrariesmagazine.org/2014/ 09/23/winning-the-space-race/.

Teper, Thomas H. "Shared Storage: Financial Models & Possibilities for Collaboration in Collection Development." From Symposium on Sustainable Models for Print Storage in the 21st Century, Harvard University, Cambridge, MA, October 1–2, 2014. https://www.ideals.illinois.edu/handle/ 2142/55235.

Ward, Suzanne M. *Rightsizing the Academic Library Collection*. Chicago: American Library Association, 2015.

Index

About the Editor and Contributors

MARTA MESTROVIC DEYRUP, PhD, is head of technical services at Seton Hall University Libraries. She is a freelance acquisitions editor for ABC-CLIO/Libraries Unlimited and acquisitions editor for the Library Information Technology Association guide series. She is the author of several books and numerous articles.

FRANK R. ALLEN is a senior associate director for administrative services, University of Central Florida Libraries. Prior to joining UCF Libraries in 1998, Frank served as head, administrative services, at Virginia Commonwealth University Libraries from 1993 to 1998. Frank holds a MLS from University Tennessee, Knoxville; MBA from University of Texas at Austin; and BSBA in Finance from the University of Florida. Frank's research interests include the economics of information and library facilities and renovations.

JANETTE BLACKBURN, AIA, is an architect and principal at Shepley Bulfinch, one of the country's top library and academic design firms, where she is a leader of the education practice. Her work is informed by a deep understanding of library research and learning environments and the variety of programs supporting community life within colleges and universities. Blackburn presents and publishes regularly, and her paper, "Breaking down Barriers to Working and Learning" was included in the book *A Field Guide to the Information Commons*. She is an active member of the American Library Association (ALA) and the Society for College and University Planning. She received her Bachelor of Architecture degree from Ball State University and was a Fulbright Scholar at the Helsinki Institute of Technology in Finland.

MARY M. CARR's career as a librarian and teacher spans 43 years. She recently retired as the executive director of Library Services, Community Colleges of Spokane. Prior to that, she held library positions at North Idaho College, Gonzaga University, and Gonzaga Preparatory School, where she also taught Latin. Besides a master's in librarianship, Carr holds a MS in Human Resources Management and is certified as a Sustainable Building Advisor and a LEED-accredited professional (AP), specializing in Building, Design and Construction (BD+C). She is the author of several articles and books including *The Green Library Planner: What Every Librarian Needs to Know before Starting to Build or Renovate*.

EDWARD M. CORRADO is associate dean, library technology planning and policy, at the University of Alabama, where he is responsible for information technology operations and planning, and executing a strategic vision for library technology. Before coming to Alabama, he was director of library technology and associate librarian at Binghamton University (NY) where he provided leadership for information technologies and digital initiatives and overall direction, administration, and management of information technology in the libraries. Corrado has published and presented nationally and internationally on various topics including digital preservation, cloud computing, open source software, emerging technologies in libraries, and the role of libraries in democracy 2.0. Corrado earned his MLS from Rutgers University and has a BA in mathematics from Caldwell University.

PATRICIA KOSCO COSSARD is art librarian, University of Maryland Libraries. Prior to joining the University of Maryland, she was the director of reader services at the Historical Society of Pennsylvania, where she worked as a member of senior leadership with Venturi Scott Brown on the historic renovation of its building and library http://www.vsba.com/projects/historical-society-of-pennsylvania/. She has held academic appointments at St. Joseph's University Library and Princeton University Library. She has also served as a research consultant to Meyer, Sherer & Rockcastle Architects, Maryland office. She received her BA from Douglass College, Rutgers; her MA from the University of Toronto; and her MLS from Rutgers.

JODY LEE DRAFTA is the assistant to the dean of Seton Hall University Libraries. Drafta joined Seton Hall in 2013. Prior to her work at Seton Hall, Jody was the assistant to the university librarian at Columbia University for seven years. She is a visual artist in sculpture and works on paper and writes exhibition reviews on contemporary art. She earned a BA in German literature and humanities from Reed College (Phi Beta Kappa), a bachelor's in fine art from the University of Washington, and an MFA from Southern Methodist University.

UCHE ENWESI is the director of user and system support for the University of Maryland Libraries. He received a BA in criminal justice from the University of Maryland, College Park, and a MS in information technology management from the University of Maryland, University College. Enwesi is responsible for IT support of all the UMD Libraries, both computer and server support.

CARLA GALLINA is the design principal of the architectural consulting firm, Gallina Design LLC. Gallina has a master of architecture degree from the University of Illinois at Urbana–Champaign and is currently on the Illuminating Engineering Society of North America (IESNA) Library Lighting Committee. She has over 25 years of experience as lighting professional.

STEVE KELLER is president and managing partner with Architect's Security Group, Inc., a security consulting and engineering firm that works exclusively on projects involving museums, libraries, and other cultural properties. His firm is located in Ormond Beach, Florida. He is a graduate of American University in Washington, D.C.

TRACI ENGEL LESNESKI, CID, IIDA, LEED-AP BD+C, is a principal at Meyer, Scherer & Rockcastle (MSR). She joined MSR in 1996 and has 22 years' experience, mainly in designing learning spaces. As head of interiors, Traci promotes an integrated design approach, believing that projects are most successful when multiple disciplines have a role in shaping them. Designing spaces that can positively impact a person's life motivates and inspires her—whether for a public library, an arts building, a university community center, or a workspace. She holds a bachelor of fine arts in interior design from the University of Wisconsin–Stout and regularly gives presentations and workshops on library design for ALA, IFLA, PLA, and other national and international audiences.

GILI MEEROVITCH, CID, IIDA, LEED-AP, NCIDQ-certified, is an award-winning interior designer whose work focuses on planning for behaviors and creating architecturally integrated spaces. Meerovitch has emerged as a nationally recognized voice in the design of interiors for educational facilities and cultural projects. A principal at Pfeiffer Partners Architects, she leads the firm's library planning and brings to her projects current and comprehensive knowledge of trends and planning issues.

PIXEY ANNE MOSLEY received her MLS from Louisiana State University. After serving in a series of managerial and leadership roles at Texas A&M University Libraries, she is currently associate dean for administrative and faculty services and holds the rank of tenured professor. She has written three books and numerous articles about library leadership and career development and was coeditor of *Library Leadership & Management*, the official journal of ALA–LLAMA. Prior to her career in libraries, she obtained two aerospace engineering degrees.

HENRY MYERBERG, FAIA, is the founder of HMA2, an architectural firm launched in 1986. Myerberg's notable education projects include work for American University of Central Asia, Amherst College, University of Virginia, Hampshire College, Bryn Mawr College, and Wofford College. He had also served as the volunteer design director for the Robin Hood Foundation's L!BRARY Initiative, which is committed to reinventing libraries for New York City's 650 public elementary schools. His extensively published projects have won numerous awards, including the 2001 National Award from the American Institute of Architects and the American Institute of Architects and the American Library Association award for Bryn Mawr College's Rhys Carpenter Library.

DARIA PIZZETTA is an architect with many years of experience in the design of libraries. She is a partner with H3 Hardy Collaboration Architecture, a New York City–based firm. Pizzetta holds a bachelor of architecture degree from Mississippi State University. She particularly enjoys the programming and planning stages of a project, where the goals and aspirations of the project are initially documented.

JACK POLING is senior principal and managing partner of MSR. He has 26 years of professional experience and joined the firm in 1991. Poling has received AIA Minnesota Honor Awards for the renovation and expansion of the Ramsey County Roseville Library and the new Dallas Public Library Lochwood Branch, and the adaptive reuse of a former grocery store into Denton Public Library's new North Branch. The Denton project served as a case study for a presentation Poling gave at the 2008 Public Library Association conference entitled "Rethinking the Big Box: Restocking the Shelves with Books." He has led workshops at *Library Journal*'s Design Institute seminars and at conferences for the Minnesota Library Association and Wisconsin Association of Academic Librarians. Poling holds a master of architecture from the University of Minnesota and a bachelor of science in environmental design from Texas A&M University.

CYNTHIA SORRELL has 10 years of collection development experience in public and special libraries. Previous to her current position as assistant head of collection development at the University of Maryland, she was gifts coordinator for the flagship's seven campus libraries. She has worked as head librarian at a special library in Howard County, Maryland. Sorrell earned her MLS from the University of Maryland.

CPSIA information can be obtained
at www.ICGtesting.com
Printed in the USA
LVOW04s0055300817
546899LV00003B/30/P